Crisis Information Management

CHANDOS
INFORMATION PROFESSIONAL SERIES

Series Editor: Ruth Rikowski
(e-mail: Rikowskigr@aol.com)

Chandos' new series of books is aimed at the busy information professional. They have been specially commissioned to provide the reader with an authoritative view of current thinking. They are designed to provide easy-to-read and (most importantly) practical coverage of topics that are of interest to librarians and other information professionals. If you would like a full listing of current and forthcoming titles, please visit www.chandospublishing.com or e-mail wp@woodheadpublishing.com or telephone +44(0) 1223 499140.

New authors: we are always pleased to receive ideas for new titles; if you would like to write a book for Chandos, please contact Dr Glyn Jones on e-mail gjones@chandospublishing.com or telephone number +44(0) 1993 848726.

Bulk orders: some organisations buy a number of copies of our books. If you are interested in doing this, we would be pleased to discuss a discount. Please contact us on e-mail wp@woodheadpublishing.com or telephone +44(0) 1223 499140.

Crisis Information Management

Communication and technologies

EDITED BY
CHRISTINE HAGAR

CHANDOS
PUBLISHING

Oxford Cambridge New Delhi

Chandos Publishing
Hexagon House
Avenue 4
Station Lane
Witney
Oxford OX28 4BN
UK
Tel: +44 (0) 1993 848726
E-mail: info@chandospublishing.com
www.chandospublishing.com

Chandos Publishing is an imprint of Woodhead Publishing Limited

Woodhead Publishing Limited
80 High Street
Sawston
Cambridge CB22 3HJ
UK
Tel: +44 (0) 1223 499140
Fax: +44 (0) 1223 832819
www.woodheadpublishing.com

First published in 2012

ISBN: 978 1 84334 647 0

British Library Cataloguing-in-Publication Data.
A catalogue record for this book is available from the British Library.

The publisher makes no representation, express or implied, with regard to the accuracy of the information contained in this publication and cannot accept any legal responsibility or liability for any errors or omissions.

The material contained in this publication constitutes general guidelines only and does not represent to be advice on any particular matter. No reader or purchaser should act on the basis of material contained in this publication without first taking professional advice appropriate to their particular circumstances. All screenshots in this publication are the copyright of the website owner(s), unless indicated otherwise.

Typeset by RefineCatch Limited, Bungay, Suffolk
Printed in the UK and USA.

For my dearest mother Ella Hagar and her four adorable great granddaughters, Ella, Evie, Ruby, and Isabelle

Contents

List of figures and tables

Figures

Tables

Acknowledgments

I would particularly like to acknowledge the contributions of the following:

- The authors of the chapters. Many thanks for your excellent examples from research and practice and for your collegiality during the process of completing the book.

- Graduate students at the Graduate School of Library and Information Science, Dominican University, River Forest in my Crisis Informatics class for their engaging discussions and interest.

- All at Chandos Publishing who made this publication possible.

- Barbara Nesbit and Elizabeth Smith for reading parts of the manuscript.

- My friends for their never failing encouragement – Barbara, Diane, Nina, Olwen, and Sharon.

About the contributors

Ban Al-Ani is a Research Scientist at the Donald Bren School of Information and Computer Sciences University of California, Irvine (UCI). She was a tenured lecturer at the University of Technology, Sydney Australia (prior to joining UCI), where she also received her PhD in Computer Systems. Her dissertation research was in the area of analysis of early informal requirements. Her current work spans three main research areas within the general domain of software engineering, namely requirements engineering, distributed collaboration, and human–computer interaction. She is currently investigating trust in distributed teams, interviewing developers in Fortune 500 organizations in addition to research into use of technologies by non-profit organizations and marginalized groups. Ban has been invited to contribute to several communities including the International Conference on Global Software Engineering (ICGSE – PC member) 2010–12, ICSE education workshop (PC member) 2008, IEEE Special Issue Journal Software Process: Improvement and Practice 2009, Special Issues of IEEE software 2009–10, International Community on Information Systems on Crisis Response and Management (ISCRAM 2009), and *Journal of the Brazilian Computer Society* 2010, and was an invited speaker to the KNOWing workshop held in conjunction with ICGSE 2010. Her most recent contribution has been to accept an invitation to be a panel member of the Requirements Engineering workshop held in conjunction with the Ground System Architectures Workshop in 2011.

Kenneth Mark Anderson is an Associate Professor of the Department of Computer Science at the University of Colorado at Boulder, and Co-director of Project EPIC. He is the Associate Chair and Director of Undergraduate Studies of his Department and a fellow of CU's ATLAS Institute. His research interests include hypermedia, software and web engineering, software architecture, and the design of large-scale software infrastructure. His current research supports the design and implementation of a large-scale data collection and analytics infrastructure for crisis informatics and how such software supports the analysis and understanding of the behaviors of members of the public in mass emergency events. His past research has examined the utility of applying hypermedia techniques to various aspects of software development. He was fortunate to spend a sabbatical at the University of Aarhus in Aarhus, Denmark in 2005–6 designing infrastructure for contextual hypermedia systems; that work received the Engelbart Best Paper award at the 2006 ACM Hypertext conference. Professor Anderson earned his BS (1990), MS (1992) and PhD (1997) degrees in Information and Computer Science from the University of California, Irvine.

Mossaab Bagdouri is an MS candidate in Computer Science at the University of Colorado at Boulder. He received the Fulbright Foreign Student Scholarship Grantee award in 2009 after getting his State Engineer degree in Computer Science from Ecole Nationale Supérieure d'Informatique et d'Analyse des Systèmes (ENSIAS) and working as a Project Engineer in Information Systems at Maroc Telecom, both in Morocco. Mr Bagdouri is interested in the Information Retrieval and Natural Language Processing fields. He is currently working under the supervision of Professor Leysia Palen in Project EPIC (Empowering the Public in Crisis). With an interest in the use of social media during political crises, he is examining the usage of topic modeling as an unsupervised analysis approach to understand the impact of the Iraq war on the Iraqi blogosphere.

Fredrik Bergstrand is a PhD student at the department of Applied Information Technology at the University of Gothenburg, Sweden. In his PhD project he studies the use and design of information technology in emergency response and crisis management.

Mario Antonius Birowo completed his PhD in the School of Media and Information at Curtin University of Technology, Perth, Australia in 2010, sponsored by an Endeavour International Postgraduate Research Scholarship (EIPRS); thesis title 'Community radio and grass-roots democracy: a case study of three villages in Yogyakarta Special Region, Indonesia'. He completed a Masters degree in Communication Science at Ateneo de Manila University, Philippines in 1998; thesis title 'Re-examining participatory communication: a study of four NGOs in Indonesia'. He has been a lecturer in the Communication Department, Atma Jaya Yogyakarta University, Indonesia since 1993, with research interests that include participatory communication, public health communication, and intercultural communication. He contributed a chapter titled 'Community radio and the empowerment of local culture in Indonesia' in *Politics and the Media in Twenty-First Century Indonesia*, edited by Krishna Sen and David Hill (Routledge, 2010).

Stephanie Ganic Braunstein is Head Government Documents and Microforms Librarian at Louisiana State University (LSU) Libraries in Baton Rouge. As the head of the Government Documents Department, she also serves as the Regional Coordinator for Federal Depository Libraries (FDLs) in southern Louisiana, having direct oversight of fifteen selective FDLs and shared oversight of eleven more who report to the other Louisiana Regional Coordinator for the northern and western part of the state. Of the first fifteen mentioned above, all but four are located in New Orleans; and several of those were affected by the hurricanes of 2005. Braunstein is also a library liaison to the Political Science faculty and graduate students at LSU, teaches as an adjunct for the LSU graduate program in Library and Information Science (the Government Information course), and is one of two faculty senators. She has presented at many conferences and published in several scholarly/professional publications, including *Collaborative Librarianship, Codex: the Journal of the Louisiana Chapter of the ACRL* and a new reference work entitled *Great Lives from History: African Americans*, to be published in fall 2011 by Salem Press. Most recently, Braunstein has been appointed for a three-year term, beginning in June 2011, to the Depository Library Council by the Public Printer of the United States, William J. Boarman. In addition to her MLIS from San Jose State University, she holds an MA in English from California State University Sacramento, where she taught English Composition as a Lecturer for several years.

John L. Brobst is a PhD candidate at the Florida State University College of Communication and Information, and Research Associate at the Information Use Management and Policy Institute (*http://www.ii.fsu.edu*). His research interests include federal information policy, website usability and accessibility, and emergent trends in library management. Mr Brobst has extensive professional experience in the field of information technology management, with over 20 years of experience in the areas of systems development and project management. This experience includes leading such innovative technology management initiatives as international website developments, federal policy formulation, and simulation-based acquisition programs for improved systems development. Mr Brobst holds the following degrees: MS (Information Management; Syracuse University), MBA (Finance; Kent State University) and BS (Mathematics; Kent State University).

Sarah Gannon is a Product/System Manager with Ericsson AB. She developed a solution with the United Nations (UN) to solve the local technical communication problems that are involved in a humanitarian response to a disaster situation. She has worked in the field with UN information and communication technology field engineers supporting operations in Banda Aceh, Indonesia after the 2004 tsunami, as well as after the 2005 Pakistan earthquake and the 2010 Haiti earthquake. She has been a volunteer in Ericsson's philanthropy program, Ericsson Response, since 2003; via this program she has contributed to technical forums such as WGET (Working Group for Emergency Telecommunications).

Elisa Giaccardi is an Associate Professor in the Department of Computer Science and Institute of Culture and Technology at Universidad Carlos III de Madrid, Spain. Prior to this position, she was Senior Research Scientist at the University of Colorado at Boulder, where she was the recipient of a National Science Foundation grant investigating the use of social technologies in outdoor recreation and natural heritage practice. She has combined academic and professional activities in digital media, interaction design, and community informatics since 1996, and graduated in 2003 from the Science Technology and Art Research program at the University of Plymouth in the UK with an interdisciplinary PhD in metadesign. Her work currently focuses on issues of public authoring, collective storytelling, and place-making with an active interest in the area of 'new heritage'. She has lectured and published her work on several occasions, including journals and venues such as *International Journal of Heritage Studies, International Journal of Human–Computer Interaction, International Journal of Human-Computer Studies, Design Issues, Digital Creativity, Communications of the ACM, Museums & the Web,* ACM Conference on Human Factors in Computing Systems (CHI), and ACM Designing Interactive Systems Conference. Giaccardi is currently editing a book for Routledge on heritage and cultures of participation, and is editor of the On Heritage forum for ACM Interactions.

Christine Hagar is an Associate Professor at the Graduate School of Library and Information Science, Dominican University River Forest, USA where she teaches courses in community informatics, crisis informatics, and research methods. She holds a PhD in Library and

Information Science from the University of Illinois at Urbana-Champaign (UIUC), USA. Dr. Hagar's research explores how communities manage, organize, and disseminate information in crisis and emergency situations. Prior to working at Dominican University, she was Director of Library Development for an international NGO, INASP, where she managed a UNESCO information literacy project in the South Caucasus and facilitated a library and information science curriculum review project at the University of Dar es Salaam, Tanzania. Dr. Hagar worked as a lecturer at the School of Library and Information Science, San Jose State University, California, USA; the International Centre for Information Management Systems and Services, University of Nicholas Copernicus, Torun, Poland; and at the Department of Information Studies, Northumbria University, UK. She worked in the USA and UK as an academic librarian and as a consultant with the British Council and the UK Department for International Development. She was a Visiting Fellow at the Mortenson Center for International Library Programs, UIUC.

Thomas Heverin is a PhD student in Information Studies at the iSchool at Drexel, Philadelphia, USA. His research interests include investigating the use of information communication technologies by the public and public safety agencies during times of crisis. Mr. Heverin has published papers on the public's use of microblogging in response to a violent crisis and on city police departments' use of microblogging for communicating with the public. He also teaches an iSchool online course on informatics for registered nurses in the RN-BSN completion program. While completing the PhD program at Drexel, Mr. Heverin serves as an academic science librarian meeting the information and research needs of undergraduate students, graduate students, and faculty members in the sciences. Prior to working in higher education, Mr. Heverin served several years as a ship officer in the US Navy. Thomas holds a Master of Science in Library and Information Science from Syracuse University and a BS in Meteorology from the Pennsylvania State University – University Park.

Will Hires is the engineering and scholarly communication librarian at Louisiana State University. As a native Floridian, he is familiar with natural disasters associated with tropical storms and hurricanes and has developed a healthy respect for nature. Knowing that it is not always possible to anticipate the impact of natural phenomena, Hires understands their sometimes disruptive and destructive potential. He most recently closely followed the circumstances associated with the BP Gulf oil spill and knows the importance of planning and preparedness. He is enthusiastic about being involved in writing about how libraries are affected by disasters and about how management in times of crisis provides important implications for information handling and communication technologies. He is a US Marine Corps veteran and during his military service career he held specialties in electronics, maintenance management, nuclear ordnance, and signals intelligence/ electronic warfare. His undergraduate education is in electrical engineering, and he holds additional graduate degrees in systems management, library and information science, and organization and management, the latter with a specialization in information technology management. Since graduating from the LSU School of Library and Information Science in 1995, Hires has worked as a librarian at Ohio State University, Vanderbilt University, and the Johns Hopkins Applied Physics Laboratory. His research interests include a focus on the system of scholarly communication and on the importance of open access for the sharing of information, for collaboration on research, and for the general advancement of knowledge.

Amanda Hughes is a PhD student at the University of Colorado at Boulder in the Computer Science Department. She is interested in designing and building technologies that support emergency management in times of crises. Her perspective is unique as she is able to incorporate social observations and data gathered during times of crises in the design and implementation of technology. Ms Hughes has a BS in Computer Science from Brigham Young University and an ME in Computer Science from the University of Colorado, and is additionally trained in social methods and disaster studies. Prior to her current position, she worked for six years at Avaya as a software developer. In her spare time she enjoys music, sewing, gardening, and spending time with her family.

Jonas Landgren, PhD, is Assistant Professor at the department of Applied Information Technology at Chalmers University of Technology, Gothenburg, Sweden. His current research topics include documentation practices, use and design of information technology, and collaboration in complex response networks.

Sophia B. Liu is a PhD candidate at University of Colorado at Boulder (CU) in the Technology, Media and Society interdisciplinary program at the Alliance for Technology, Learning and Society (ATLAS) Institute. She is also a National Science Foundation (NSF) Graduate Research Fellow.

Ms Liu is currently a graduate research assistant at Professor Leysia Palen's Connectivity Lab and a member of Professor Palen's Project EPIC (Empowering the Public in Crisis) research team conducting research in the area of crisis informatics. She studies sociotechnical phenomena at the intersection of information science, crisis informatics, and digital heritage studies. She uses ethnographic and computational methods to study the social media landscape and has experience conducting quick response research in the crisis domain. Her dissertation research focuses on how social media are being used to sustain the living heritage of historic crises through an emerging sociotechnical practice she calls *socially-distributed curation*. Ms Liu has published her work in venues across multiple disciplines, such as the ACM Conference on Human Factors in Computing Systems (CHI), *Social Science Computer Review*, the Information Systems for Crisis Response and Management (ISCRAM) conference, *Cartography and Geographic Information Science Journal*, and *The Routledge Handbook of Participatory Cultures*. Prior to her current position, she was a graduate research assistant at the University of Colorado's Natural Hazards Center and also earned her Bachelor's degree from University of California at Irvine in Social Science specializing in Research and Analytical Methods with a minors in Computer Science and Digital Arts.

Charles R. McClure is Francis Eppes Professor of Information Studies and Director of the Information Use Management and Policy Institute at the College of Communication and Information, Florida State University. Under his direction since 1999, the Information Institute has completed over $5 million of funded research. From 1986 to 1999 he was at Syracuse University School of Information Studies – the last five as a Distinguished Professor. He teaches courses in planning/evaluation of information services, US government information policies, evaluation of networked services, library/information center management, and research methods. He completed his PhD in Library and Information Services at Rutgers University, New Jersey. He has published extensively on topics related to planning and evaluation of library services, including some 45 monographs. His most recent co-authored book is *Public Libraries and Internet Service Roles: Measuring and Maximizing Internet Services* (American Library Association, 2009). With John Carlo Bertot, McClure has conducted the national survey 'Public Libraries and the Internet' since 1994; the most recent report is *Libraries Connect Communities 3: Public Library Funding & Technology Access Study* (American Library Association, 2009).

Casey McTaggart is a Masters student at the University of Colorado in the Computer Science department, working in the Project EPIC lab with Leysia Palen and Ken Anderson. She studies the design and implementation of software during disasters. Since 2010, Ms McTaggart has developed the Tweak the Tweet (TtT) web client in collaboration with Kate Starbird. The client allows users to sign on to Twitter and either create new tweets or modify existing tweets in the specified TtT format. Prior to her current position, Ms McTaggart received an MS in Environmental Engineering from University of California, Berkeley (2009) and a BS in Computer Science from Princeton University (2001). In between her two existing degrees, she worked at Pixar Animation Studios doing computer animation infrastructure work for feature films. She likes rock climbing, skiing, hiking, yoga, and hanging out with her dog.

Lauren H. Mandel is a doctoral candidate at Florida State University's College of Communication and Information and Research Coordinator at the Information Use Management and Policy Institute. Her research interests include Public Library Facility Design, Wayfinding, and Geographic Information Studies. She holds a BA from Vassar College and an MS in Library and Information Science from Simmons College. Recent co-authored publications include 'Assessing Florida Public Library Broadband for E-Government and Emergency/Disaster Management Services' *in Public Libraries and the Internet: Roles, Perspectives, and Implications* (Libraries Unlimited, 2011) and 'Utilizing Geographic Information Systems (GIS) in library research' (*Library Hi Tech*, 2010).

Gloria Mark is a Professor in the Department of Informatics, University of California, Irvine. Her principle research areas are in human–computer interaction and computer-supported cooperative work. Her research focuses on the design and evaluation of collaborative systems. Her current projects include studying multi-tasking of information workers, IT use for resilience and adaptation in disrupted environments, and mobile platforms for telemedicine. She received her PhD in Psychology from Columbia University. Prior to joining UCI in 2000, she worked at the German National Research Center for Information Technology (GMD) in Bonn, Germany (now the Fraunhofer Institute). In 2006 she received a Fulbright scholarship and worked at Humboldt University in Berlin, Germany. She has been the technical program chair for ACM CSCW'06 and ACM GROUP'05 conferences, is the technical program chair for ACM CSCW'12, and is on the editorial board of ACM

TOCHI, CSCW: *The Journal of Collaborative Computing*, and *e-Service Qu@rterly*. Her work has appeared in the popular press such as *The New York Times*, *Time*, and *The Wall Street Journal*.

Leysia Palen is an Associate Professor of Computer Science at the University of Colorado, Boulder and a faculty fellow with the Institute for the Alliance of Technology, Learning and Society (ATLAS) and the Institute of Cognitive Science. She is the Director of the Connectivity Lab and principal investigator on the US National Science Foundation-funded *Project EPIC: Empowering the Public with Information in Crisis* and *Data in Disaster* research efforts. Her work focuses largely on ethnographic studies of coordination and practice that inform technology design, implementation, and policy. Her most recent work is in the area of crisis informatics, though she has also worked in areas of commercial aviation, digital privacy behavior, personal information management, mobile technology diffusion, domestic uses of ICT, health informatics, and heritage and ICT studies. Palen earned a PhD and MS from the University of California, Irvine in Information and Computer Science and a BS from the University of California, San Diego in Cognitive Science. From 2005 to 2006, she was a visiting professor at the University of Aarhus, Denmark. In 2006, she was awarded an NSF Early CAREER grant. She has worked at Xerox PARC, Microsoft, and The Boeing Company, in each case working on projects in the area of human-centered computing.

Jenna Ryan is a Reference and Instruction Librarian and the Virtual Reference Coordinator at Louisiana State University in Baton Rouge. Her areas of specialty include Biological Sciences, Coastal Sciences, and Environmental Science. She is a contributing member of the Louisiana Libraries Oil Spill Information Service (LLOSIS) and has done extensive work on the Oil Spill subject guide provided by the LSU Libraries. She earned her MLIS and MA in English from the University of South Carolina in Columbia in 2005 and has undergraduate degrees in English and Marine Science from the same institution. She has been published in the *Electronic Journal of Academic and Special Librarianship*, *The Handbook of Research on Computer Mediated Communication*, and the *Journal of Information Technology Education*. She has also published an annotated bibliography of popular literature on Hurricane Katrina in *Codex: the Journal of the Louisiana Chapter of the ACRL*. Her research interests include virtual reference, social networking in the classroom, emerging technologies, disaster librarianship, and bibliographic instruction.

Chris Schenk is a professional research assistant with Professor Aaron Clauset in the Department of Computer Science at the University of Colorado at Boulder. Mr Schenk currently works in the area of complex systems and dynamics in networks applied to a variety of areas, including disaster response and local influence of users on Twitter, as well as team dynamics in competitive multiplayer online video games. He holds an MS in Computer Science from the University of Colorado at Boulder.

Aaron Schram is currently a graduate research assistant at Professor Kenneth M. Anderson's Software Engineering Research Lab (SERL) in the Department of Computer Science at the University of Colorado at Boulder (CU). Prior to returning to CU to pursue his PhD in Software Engineering, Mr Schram held several senior software engineering positions at technology startups in the Boulder area, including Rally Software Development where his efforts aided in the Rally product winning four consecutive Jolt Awards. His primary research is in support of the NSF-funded Project EPIC (Empowering the Public in Crisis) where he currently focuses on the development of software infrastructure to enable real-time collection and analytics of social media data. Mr Schram has primarily published his work in the International Conference on Software Engineering (ICSE).

Bryan Semaan is a PhD candidate in the Department of Informatics, University of California, Irvine, where he is being advised by Dr Gloria Mark. He obtained his MS in Information and Computer Science (ICS) from UC Irvine in 2007, and graduated with a BS in ICS from UCI in 2005. His general research interests are Computer Supported Cooperative Work (CSCW) and Human–Computer Interaction (HCI). Mr Semaan is currently studying how people living through disaster (e.g. war) adopt, use, and re-appropriate technologies to maintain their routines, and his goal is to develop technologies that can help people in such situations live as normally as possible. He has been invited to contribute to several communities such as Computer–Human Interaction (CHI), Transactions on Human–Computer Interaction (TOCHI), and the Information Systems for Crisis Response and Management Conference (ISCRAM). He was also invited to give a talk and serve as a panelist at the 2010 Borah Symposium – an event that attempts to understand the causes of war and the conditions for peace. He received an Outstanding TA Award in 2006, was a recipient of the Coalition Advocating Human Security Fellowship in 2007, and was awarded the Roberta Ellen Lamb Endowed Memorial Fellowship in 2009. He has consulted for Southern California

Edison's IT Department during the introduction of a new organizational technology. He is part of a small Iraqi minority group – the Assyrians and Chaldeans – and is a member of Chaldean-Middle Eastern Social Services, a San Diego-based NGO that provides refugees with psycho-social services.

Kate Starbird is a PhD student at the University of Colorado at Boulder at the Alliance for Technology, Learning and Society (ATLAS) Institute. She is also a National Science Foundation (NSF) Graduate Research Fellow. Ms Starbird is a member of Professor Leysia Palen's research group as well the NSF-funded Project EPIC (Empowering the Public in Crisis) research team. Her research focuses broadly on the use of social media during crises and mass emergencies, and specifically examines the self-organizing of volunteer groups during these events. She combines ethnographic methods with quantitative analysis of large datasets of microblogging (Twitter) communications to investigate patterns of human behavior that constitute the 'crowdsourcing' phenomenon during crises. Ms Starbird co-created the 'Tweak the Tweet' concept, an idea for leveraging Twitter as a crisis-data reporting platform, during a Random Hacks of Kindness (RHOK) barcamp event in 2009, and has since helped to deploy the idea during numerous events and significantly developed the software architecture to support it. She has also developed a software system for the qualitative analysis of large computer-mediated communication (CMC) data sets (E-DataViewer), utilized for several research efforts within Project EPIC. Ms Starbird has published work at the ACM Conference on Human Factors in Computing Systems (CHI), the ACM Conference on Computer Supported Cooperative Work (CSCW), and the Information Systems for Crisis Response and Management (ISCRAM) conference. She earned her Bachelor's degree from Stanford University in Computer Science.

Sarah Vieweg is a PhD candidate at University of Colorado at Boulder in the Technology, Media and Society program, which is part of the Alliance for Technology, Learning and Society Institute (ATLAS). Her dissertation research focuses on the use of social media sites and microblogging services to communicate timely, relevant information during mass emergency events. Ms Vieweg combines discourse analysis, ethnographic methods, and natural language processing methods in identifying communication patters and creating computational tools for the automatic extraction of critical information from microblog communications during crises. She has published research in the ACM

Conference on Human Factors in Computing Systems (CHI), the ACM Conference on Computer Supported Cooperative Work (CSCW), *The Information Society*, *Social Science Computer Review*, and the *IEEE Computer Magazine*. Prior to her position as a research assistant in Professor Leysia Palen's Connectivity Lab, Ms Vieweg earned her MA in Linguistics with a certificate in Human Language Technology (HLT) from the University of Colorado at Boulder, and her BA with a double major in Economics and French from the University of Illinois at Urbana-Champaign.

Joanne White is a PhD student at University of Colorado at Boulder (CU) in the Technology, Media and Society interdisciplinary program at the Alliance for Technology, Learning and Society (ATLAS) Institute. She is a graduate research assistant at Professor Leysia Palen's Connectivity Lab and a member of Professor Palen's Project EPIC (Empowering the Public in Crisis) research team conducting research in crisis informatics. Ms White's research interests lie in how online communities are formed and what effect crisis has on online relationships. She has presented her work in multiple venues, and her co-authored book chapter dealing with social media literacy and education was published by Emerald Publishing in the UK in 2011. Her Masters thesis, completed at CU in 2010, considered the online community of mom bloggers and their reaction to Nestlé's funding of a two-day trip for a small number of them. She is a strong proponent of expanding the presence of women and girls in technical fields, and her Mediamum blog focuses on topics related to social media, women, and parenting. Ms White has an undergraduate degree awarded through Griffith University in Queensland, Australia, and a postgraduate degree in adult education from Charles Sturt University, NSW, Australia.

Lisl Zach is an Assistant Professor at the iSchool at Drexel, Philadelphia, where she teaches in the area of competitive intelligence and knowledge management. Dr Zach's research interests include investigating the role of information professionals during natural and man-made disasters and developing ways of providing critical information to vulnerable populations in times of crisis. She is currently working on a project with the Drexel University's 11th Street Family Health Center to examine the use of mobile information and communications technology to deliver health information to the population being served by the Center. Dr Zach has published award-winning articles on the contributions of information services in hospitals and academic health science centers and on the ways in which administrators look for, evaluate, and use information. Before coming to Drexel, Dr Zach spent almost 20 years working in various areas of administration and financial management, as well as directing and conducting applied research projects to identify ways of satisfying the information needs of user groups as diverse as field artillery officers, nuclear power plant operators, and symphony orchestra managers, staff, and volunteers. Her professional career has focused on making critical information accessible to users by developing and improving presentation formats, information services, and training materials. She has carried out numerous user needs assessments, task analyzes, benchmarking studies, and program evaluations. Dr Zach holds a PhD in Information Studies from the University of Maryland – College Park, an MBA from New York University, and an MSLS from the University of North Carolina – Chapel Hill.

Introduction

Christine Hagar

A crisis defined as 'an interruption in the reproduction of economic, cultural, social and/or political life' encompasses a whole range of situations (Johnston, 2002). In the first quarter of 2011, the world has witnessed many natural and human-made crises on an unprecedented scale: the earthquake in Christchurch, New Zealand; political disruption in North Africa and the Middle East, and one of the worst natural disasters to hit Japan, a 9.0 magnitude earthquake, resultant tsunami, and the explosions occurring at the Fukushima Daiichi nuclear complex.

Crises precipitate an increase in communication and present complex information environments. The management of information before, during, and after a disaster can have a direct influence on how well the crisis is managed (Putnam, 2002). Over the past ten years, events such as the Haiti earthquake, Hurricane Katrina, and 9/11 have demonstrated that there is a great need to understand how individuals, government, and non-government agencies acquire, organize, access, share, coordinate, and disseminate information within communities during crisis situations. Information management and technology problems have been cited as significant factors in the failed responses to many crises. Post-crisis reports have devoted sections to information and communication lessons learned (Anderson, 2009; FEMA, 2011).

The information challenges in a crisis may include:

- information overload or conversely lack of information;
- the many diverse actors and agencies involved who increase the amount of information produced;
- integration and coordination of information by these actors and agencies;

- connecting informal and formal channels of information creation and dissemination;
- changing information needs at various stages of a crisis;
- information uncertainty;
- trustworthy sources of information;
- conflicting information; and
- getting the 'right' information to the 'right' person at the 'right' time.

Information and communication technologies (ICTs) have changed the face of managing information in crisis preparedness, warning, impact, and response. Existing and new ICTs increasingly enable the capture and preservation of information and experiences that result from disaster and mass emergency situations. With advances in ICTs vast amounts of information can be distributed easily to a large audience. As crises unfold, ICTs enable events to be communicated around the world within minutes or even seconds of the crisis occurring. Social media tools allow citizens to mobilize and spread their messages where governments have suppressed the free flow of information.

ICTs allow volunteers to work together to create platforms for information aggregation and processing – 'crowdsourcing' – to solve real-world crisis problems. These creative platforms provide powerful visualizations and interactive mapping of crises.[1] The recent *Libya Crisis Map* project[2] is a prime example of how technologies enable collaborations between a variety of organizations – the United Nations Office for Coordination of Humanitarian Affairs (UNOCHA), the United Nations Operational Satellite Applications Program (UNOSAT), the Google Crisis Response Team, Crisis Mappers, and several other ICT-oriented volunteer groups.

However, amid the accolades for innovative technologies, it is important to remember how human-centered approaches and person-to-person interactions support communities in crisis, particularly in contexts where technologies are unavailable or difficult to access. Technologies may be interrupted by natural causes and also by human interventions, as was the case in early 2011 when the Egyptian government cut off nearly all access points to the Internet and closed down cell phone services.

This book aims to give a snapshot of some of the ongoing research and practice by the many individuals and groups engaged in designing information infrastructures and systems to support crisis and emergency information management.

In Chapter 1, 'The effects of continual disruption: technological resources supporting resilience in regions of conflict', Bryan Semaan, Gloria Mark, and Ban Al-Ani report on an ongoing empirical study looking at how technology can enable resilience during war. The authors conducted interviews with Iraqi citizens who experienced the Gulf War (2003), and Israeli citizens who were living in Northern Israel during the Israel–Lebanon War (2006). Semaan, Mark, and Al-Ani describe how technology played a major role in enabling people to maintain work and social collaborations, continue education, travel, and obtain information in an otherwise chaotic environment.

As the first chapter highlights, social media have become an important platform to disseminate information locally and globally during crises. Social media tools create volumes of crisis data, including much 'noise', for crisis responders to filter and process. The use and exploration of Twitter in emergency and crisis scenarios is the focus of Chapters 2 and 3.

Thomas Heverin and Lisl Zach in 'Law enforcement agency adoption and use of Twitter as a crisis communication tool' (Chapter 2) describe the results of a study investigating the adoption and use of Twitter as a crisis communication tool by law enforcement agencies in large US cities. The results indicate that law enforcement agencies (LEAs) primarily use Twitter to disseminate crime- and incident-related information and that Twitter is a valuable tool for providing accurate, up-to-the-minute information that can be communicated directly to the public without going through the news media. The authors suggest that additional research is needed to identify the degree to which Twitter use by LEAs is valued by the public and whether the one-way model of LEA communication remains appropriate in an age of increased interactive use of social media.

Within Twitter a new language – 'tweet', 'retweet', 'tweak', 'Twitterverse' – has evolved describing features of information redistribution. In Chapter 3, 'Promoting structured data in citizen communications during disaster response: an account of strategies for diffusion of the "Tweak the Tweet" syntax', Kate Starbird, Leysia Palen, Sophia B. Liu, Sarah Vieweg, Amanda Hughes, Aaron Schram, Kenneth Mark Anderson, Mossaab Bagdouri, Joanne White, Casey McTaggart, and Chris Schenk discuss the idea of 'Tweak the Tweet' for enabling citizen reporting via microblogs during crisis events. This chapter describes efforts to deploy the 'Tweak the Tweet' syntax during several crisis events in 2010: the earthquakes in Haiti and Chile and the Fourmile Canyon Fire in Boulder, Colorado. The authors describe how syntax, instructions, and the nature of such a campaign evolved within and across events, and share the insights gained about the use of structured data reporting during mass emergencies and disasters.

As technologies of memory storage change, cultural understanding of crises may also change. In Chapter 4, 'Heritage matters in crisis informatics: how information and communication technology can support legacies of crisis events', Sophia B. Liu, Leysia Palen, and Elisa Giaccardi offer an agenda for how information science and human-centered computing communities might conceptualize digital heritage as an emergent research effort in the crisis domain. The authors discuss how the social and cultural value of such traces, when collectively generated and shared across people and over time, can enhance or even dramatically change how we remember crises. They draw from several disciplines concerned with digital heritage and discuss three historically significant disasters: the Bhopal gas leak, the September 11 attacks, and Hurricane Katrina.

Animal and human viral diseases, in the form of SARS, H1N1 (swine flu), and Avian influenza caused great disruption to societies worldwide. This type of viral disease crisis may create a 'crisis of isolation'. In Chapter 5, 'Information needs and seeking during the UK 2001 foot-and-mouth disease crisis', Christine Hagar explores the multiple information needs that faced a farming community who became physically isolated and confined to their farms. The crisis unfolded in a series of information and communication problems, primarily from government to farmers, with consequences for action in a time of crisis.

In Chapter 6, Sarah Gannon discusses the role of Ericsson, a global provider of telecommunications equipment and services, who have been engaged in supporting disaster and emergency response initiatives in partnership with the United Nations (UN) and other aid agencies for over ten years. In her chapter 'In the light of experience: the Ericsson Response – a ten-year perspective', Gannon draws some conclusions about the information and communication needs which emerge and evolve in the different stages of a humanitarian emergency or crisis, and about the factors which inhibit full effectiveness of the aid agencies' response. Gannon includes a critique of the role played by the Ericsson Response and by commercial organizations generally in providing communications infrastructure and support at times of humanitarian crisis. The chapter speculates as to the potential for engaging some leading-edge and experimental technologies in transforming the effectiveness of disaster response.

The role of technology in crisis and emergency response organizations has drastically changed in the last ten years. Many of the challenges faced today are the results of organizational changes involving a move to more sophisticated technological platforms intended to improve existing work practices. In Chapter 7, 'Information systems in crisis', Fredrik Bergstrand and Jonas Landgren present and discuss possibilities for current and future information environments, and how these could be designed to better support ongoing work activities, organization, and situation awareness. The chapter presents insights into how key information sources such as verbal and visual information can be captured, stored, and used.

It is important to recognize the cultural contexts in which crises occur. From a 'traditional' technology perspective, Mario Antonius Birowo in 'Community media and civic action in response to volcanic hazards' (Chapter 8) discusses the various roles of community radio in disseminating and coordinating information in natural disaster management in Indonesia. Community radio stations played key roles in sharing information between NGOs, distributing information about health and safety, and connecting missing people. The Indonesian community radio response to the natural disasters was unique, in that the broadcast information came directly from victims of the crises, who were interviewed by the radio reporters.

Libraries and information centers can play multiple roles in crises. One particularly important role for libraries is to direct the many stakeholders in crises to trustworthy sources of information. In this new role, libraries have responded to disasters by taking steps to better prepare for the information needs of their communities arising from emergency situations.

The hurricane damage that the United States Gulf Coast has sustained over the past decade was a catalyst for a study by John L. Brobst, Lauren H. Mandel, and Charles R. McClure. In Chapter 9, 'Public libraries and crisis management: roles of public libraries in hurricane/disaster preparedness and response', the authors explore the service roles public libraries provide in preparedness for and response to disasters such as hurricanes. Libraries have taken major steps to better meet community needs arising from these emergency situations. This chapter identifies new public library service roles, and discusses successful technology solutions and communications programs that public libraries can employ to assist local communities prepare for, and recover from, hurricanes and other disasters.

Finally, in Chapter 10, from an academic library perspective, Stephanie Ganic Braunstein, Jenna Ryan, and Will Hires in 'Academic libraries in crisis situations: roles, responses, and lessons learned in providing crisis-related information and services' highlight the roles that academic libraries can play during a crisis. The authors present academic library responses to three crises: the Deepwater Horizon rig explosion and consequent oil spewage into the Gulf of Mexico; and flooding at Tulane University's Howard-Tilton Memorial Library and at the University of Hawaii at Manoa's Hamilton Library.

I hope that this book will be of interest to a variety of researchers, practitioners, and policy-makers in the areas of library and information science, information management, information systems, knowledge management, emergency management and planning, non-governmental organizations, risk management, communications, computer science, community planners, public health, and more.

This book is required reading for the *Crisis Informatics* course which is taught at the Graduate School of Library and Information Science, Dominican University, River Forest, Illinois, USA. I hope that it will also be of interest to other graduate and undergraduate programs.

I wish to express my sincere thanks to each contributing author for sharing their research, experiences, and expertise. Our thoughts are with those who have lived through and are recovering from major crises. One thing is for sure: the world will face more disasters and we need to be prepared for a variety of scenarios, the expected and unexpected.

Christine Hagar, Editor
April 2011

Notes

1. Crisis Commons: *http://crisiscommons.org*; Random Hacks of Kindness: *www.rhok.org*; Ushahidi: *www.ushahidi.com*.
2. *Libya Crisis Map*. Retrieved April 18, 2011 from *http://libyacrisismap.net/page/index/5*.

References

Anderson, I. (2009). *Government's response to the Foot-and-Mouth Disease 2007 Review*. Cm. 7514. Section on 'Lessons Learned: Communication and local knowledge', p. 15. Retrieved April 20, 2011 from *http://archive.defra.gov.uk/foodfarm/farmanimal/diseases/atoz/fmd/documents/anderson-090203.pdf*.

Federal Emergency Management Agency (FEMA). (2011) Lessons Learned Information Sharing (LLIS.gov). Retrieved April 20, 2011 from *https://www.llis.dhs.gov/index.do*.

Johnston, R.J. (2002). *Dictionary of human geography* (pp.123–5). 4th ed. Oxford, UK: Blackwell.

Putnam, L. (2002). By choice or by chance: how the internet is used to prepare for, manage, and share information about emergencies. *First Monday,* 7 (11), Retrieved April 7, 2011 from *http://firstmonday.org/htbin/cgiwrap/bin/ojs/index.php/fm/article/view/1007/928.*

1

The effects of continual disruption: technological resources supporting resilience in regions of conflict

Bryan Semaan, Gloria Mark, and Ban Al-Ani

Abstract: This chapter reports on an ongoing empirical study looking at how technology can enable resilience during continual disruption. We conducted 125 interviews with civilians from two countries who were living through war: (1) Iraqi citizens who experienced the current Gulf War beginning in March 2003; and (2) Israeli citizens who were living in Northern Israel during the Israel–Lebanon War that took place in August 2006. We describe how technology played a major role in enabling people to maintain work and social collaborations, continue education, travel, and obtain information in an otherwise chaotic environment.

Key words: disrupted environments, resilience, collaboration, routines, empirical study.

Introduction

Information and Communication Technologies (ICTs) are changing the way that citizens are responding to environmental disruptions. In conflict zones it can be dangerous for people to travel and maintain their normal activities. However, with ubiquitous technologies such as the mobile phone and Internet applications, people can coordinate and communicate to help restore activities through negotiating travel, increasing situational awareness, and conducting online social interaction.

In this chapter, we will describe research from an ongoing study where we are trying to better understand how technology can enable resilience when used by civilians experiencing war (Mark and Semaan, 2008; Mark, Al-Ani, and Semaan, 2009; Semaan and Mark, 2011).

Researchers have been studying the social effects of disasters for many years. Studies of disaster events have looked at how affected populations deal with being socially disrupted, and how individuals, groups, and organizations modify their behaviors in order to continue acting in this new context (e.g. Mileti, Drabek, and Haas, 1975). This perspective is highly applicable to war situations – when people are living in a war zone, normal life is disrupted and people must modify their behaviors accordingly.

While the term *disaster* has received various definitions (Quarantelli, 1998), disasters have generally been viewed as non-routine events causing social disruption and physical harm with the following key properties: (1) length of forewarning, (2) magnitude of impact, (3) scope of impact, and (4) duration of impact (Kreps, 1998). Disruptions caused by violent conflict are also non-routine events that cause social disruption and physical harm. Civilians living in a conflict zone may need to halt routine activities, such as going to work, due to the constant exposure to bombs, militias, and other disruptive, life-threatening elements. However, there is one key defining characteristic that differentiates a violent conflict from a disaster. Disasters are generally single events in time and space that disrupt a society (Dynes, 1970). Unlike disasters, when individuals live in a conflict zone they must deal with constant risk and uncertainty in their environment. It is difficult to predict when or where a bomb will fall or a militia may strike. As such, civilians living in a war zone deal with random events on a daily basis for a prolonged period of time and must make themselves continuously aware of what is taking place around them in order to act.

The focus of the majority of disaster studies has been on the short periods before, during, and after a disaster takes place (Quarantelli, 1996). By studying disruption as caused by war we can better understand how individuals maintain routine life on a daily basis during long-term disruption that may last for years. In a normal environment, we often engage in various practices for work, social life, education, travel, and obtaining information. By studying life in war environments, we can understand how people who are living through prolonged disruption maintain these practices in light of their situation.

Technologies to aid resilient behavior

During disruptive events, where the environment is unstable and activities are greatly unpredictable, civilians in the impacted area may be forced to change the way in which they live. Thus, when people face the unexpected on a daily basis, expectations for routine life may change. On the one hand, when people live through extreme situations they may no longer be able to travel to and from work or university. On the other hand, people may find ways to be resilient to maintain these routines. Resilience has been defined in various ways, but the most common definition centers around people's reactive abilities – how people 'bounce back' and persevere despite the situation (Kendra and Wachtendorf, 2003b).

Researchers have identified various ways in which individuals, groups, and organizations are resilient in maintaining aspects of their daily lives during disaster (e.g. Buenza and Stark, 2003; Kendra and Wachtendorf, 2003b), where one of the major sources of resilience is improvisation (Weick, 1993). When people are unable to act in traditional ways during disruption, they often engage in new behavior in order to cope (Rodriguez et al., 2006).

During various types of disasters ranging from hurricanes to tornadoes, people have improvised by altering their work locations (Webb, 2004) or developing ad hoc facilities to maintain organizational function (Buenza and Stark, 2003) when workplaces were damaged or inaccessible. For example, Buenza and Stark (2003) reported how a Wall Street trading organization moved to a temporary site following the September 11th attacks on the World Trade Center and resumed operations six days after the event. Additionally, people improvise by modifying their work hours in order to accommodate growing needs (Quarantelli, 1996). For example, it may be necessary for individuals to work for longer periods of time to maintain proper organizational functions. In other cases, resilience has been observed according to people's ability to improvise by assuming various organizational roles, or developing new roles – where roles are defined as expected tasks associated with specific individual occupations. Role improvisation may ensure group and organizational stability during a disruptive event (Weick, 1993; Webb, 2004). A web developer assuming a clerical position when co-workers are unable to travel to work is an example of this type of resilience.

Other properties of resilience, in addition to the improvisational aspects covered thus far, enable an effective response to situations that are ambiguous with rapidly changing conditions. The properties identified are communication, creativity, wisdom, and respectful interaction

(Weick, 1993; Kendra and Wachtendorf, 2003a). Resilience has also been discussed as a series of properties for maintaining organizational function during disruptive events, namely, robustness, resourcefulness, redundancy, and rapidity (Kendra, 2001; Bruneau et al., 2002).

Resources also play a critical role in enabling resilient behavior. When disruption occurs, people often improvise the tools or equipment used to perform tasks (Weick, 1993). One theory of social practice, structuration theory, explores the relationship between human agency and social structure (Giddens, 1984). In this view, Giddens realized that social structure and people's agency (their ability to act) form a recursive relationship – one where human agency can shape social structures, and where agency is mediated by social structures. Here, social structure is composed of rules and resources, both of which are important elements in guiding people's actions. Resources have received special attention from researchers in psychology (Hobfoll, 1989, 1998) and the organizational sciences (Feldman, 2004), as they enable people to act in various contexts. Feldman (2004), in looking at resources from an organizational perspective, showed how when people's practices change, so do the ways in which they use resources. To this effect, the use of resources (e.g. materials and information) is contextual: their meaning and use changes depending on the situation. This is important for the study of disasters, because when the environment in which people live is no longer normal, the meaning and use of resources can change accordingly.

Tool and equipment improvisations have been well documented. For example, wooden doors have been used as makeshift stretchers to transport injured civilians when normal stretchers were not available (Webb, 2004). More recently, the role technological resources play during emergency situations has emerged as an active research topic in the Computer Supported Coooperative Work (CSCW) and Human-Computer Interaction (CHI) communities (e.g. Hagar and Haythornthwaite, 2005; Palen and Liu, 2007; Torrey et al., 2007; Vieweg et al., 2008). These studies have mostly focused on the use of technology in the short period following a specific disaster event. Here, however, we are interested in how technological resources can enable resilience during continual disruption as caused by war.

Research setting

The findings of our investigation into technology use during conflict need to be considered within the context of the conflicts themselves; here we present a description of each setting. We interviewed civilians living in two regions that were undergoing severe conflict.

We interviewed people living in Israel during the Israel–Lebanon war that took place in the North of Israel (Haifa) from July 12, 2005 to August 14, 2006. Although a war was taking place in the country for 34 days, the infrastructure remained robust. Citizens in the conflict zone continued to have uninterrupted access to landline telephone systems, cellular and broadband Internet networks, electricity, and clean water. Additionally, the majority of Israel's residents had adopted and integrated various technologies into their daily repertoire prior to the war. For example, 74 percent of all households have broadband Internet[1] (Internet World Stats) and there are currently more cellular phones in use than there are people.

Various disruptive elements, however, made it difficult for citizens of the country to maintain their routines. First, bombs, i.e. Katyusha rockets, were exploding randomly, thus making it difficult to travel within the country. Our informants were unable to easily travel to work, or to visit friends and family, or even the grocery store. Second, sirens notifying citizens of impending danger were also altering the way in which people were accustomed to managing their daily lives. When people heard a siren, they would often halt what they were doing and flee to the nearest bomb shelter. Lastly, many fled the impact area and sought refuge in other countries or safe zones within the south of Israel. In various cases, members of organizations were no longer working in collocated environments, as team members were traveling from place to place. As explained by our informants, the country had two completely different environments. For those not living in Northern Israel, it was as if a war was not taking place; people were conducting their daily lives as usual.

We also interviewed civilians who experienced conflict due to the current Gulf War in Iraq. The eight-year Iran–Iraq war (1980–88), the war with with Kuwait two years later, and the United Nations-imposed embargo lasting approximately 13 years, along with numerous attacks from the US throughout the years of embargo, all combined to weaken the infrastructure and limit the country's ability to recover from each of these conflicts. The UN embargo (1990–2003) meant that Iraq was cut off from all technological development during this time. Iraqis had very limited access to ICTs during these years and were almost completely isolated from the world outside as a result of the strong censorship and monitoring of information flow by the Ba'ath regime in power at that time.

The most recent war in Iraq was initiated in 2003 and led to the current ongoing conflict within the Iraqi borders. This conflict has led to an almost complete breakdown of normalcy experienced by Iraqis. Unlike Israel, the infrastructure has deteriorated to the extent where there is often no running water and no electricity from traditional providers. This has meant that most households within Iraq rely on private, expensive, and unreliable electrical generators. In addition, they often rely on water drawn from wells for everyday use and bottled water for drinking.

Fuel to power the privately owned generators is also in short supply because many of the refineries have been targeted by militias. Iraqis are forced to stand in long queues to buy such fuel (the demand has driven the prices to record-level highs), while being subjected to constant risk of death due to random bombs exploding in public places, sniper fire, and militia attacks.

Civilians within Iraq are also exposed to random acts of violence both in the privacy of their own homes and in public places. These attacks are often persistent and impose a heavy toll on civilian lives; the Iraqi government often imposes curfews that last several days in an attempt to limit civilian casualties during major battles between government-led forces and militias. Iraqis often find themselves unable to leave their homes for several days, with no guarantee of safety once the curfew has been lifted.

Militia forces belonging to one faction or another maintained control of certain suburbs within the capital at the peak of the conflict. This led to concrete walls being erected to keep 'undesirable' civilians from entering a suburb. Road blocks, controlled by militia forces, were also erected at random, which stopped people traveling along that route. These circumstances made routine trips a dangerous undertaking and many could not be completed.

Despite the challenges that many within Iraq face daily, there has been a widespread uptake of ICTs, especially cellular phones, since these technologies became available early in 2003. While there are no reliable reports of technology penetration, major cities are reported to have relatively widespread access to the Internet and cell phones have been adopted by most demographics. Unlike Israel, however, the Internet and cellular networks are unreliable – our informants have reported that their communications networks do not work all the time.

Technological resources supporting resilience

In this chapter we report results based on 125 semi-structured interviews in both English and Arabic with informants who lived in Israel and Iraq.

Informants were found using a snowball sampling approach (Biernacki, 1981). Our informants were diverse with respect to their age and education levels as well as their educational backgrounds and work roles. We were unable to travel to either war zone to conduct observations and interviews. We conducted interviews in two ways. First, we interviewed Israeli and Iraqi participants living in their respective war zones using several technologies (e.g. telephone, Skype, e-mail and Instant Messenger). Second, we conducted face-to-face interviews with recent Iraqi émigrés to San Diego and Los Angeles (both of which are cities in California). In order to gain insight into how technology could be used to make people resilient in maintaining their routines during extreme disruption, we asked our informants how they conducted their daily lives *before* and *during* their respective conflict situations. The main topic we covered centered on whether or not technology played a major role in their ability to maintain their routines when living through war. Through comparison we were able to highlight the ways in which technology can facilitate people's ability to conduct their daily lives in extreme environments. Further details of the methodology can be found in Mark and Semaan, 2008; Mark et al., 2009; and Semaan and Mark, 2011.

Our investigation revealed that civilians living in these war zones were highly innovative in their ability to maintain various aspects of their lives. We provide illustrations which show how technology can support resilient behavior, by enabling people to maintain practices for work, social life, education, travel, and obtaining relevant situational information (Mark and Semaan, 2008; Mark et al., 2009; Semaan and Mark, 2011).

Technology and work collaborations

During both the Israel–Lebanon war of 2006 and the Gulf War in Iraq, our informants have adopted and re-appropriated technologies, e.g. Internet and cellular phones, to conduct virtual work from safe locations, eliminating the need to travel to and from work in a dangerous environment. In fact, those informants whose work was the least disrupted had conducted virtual work before the war (Mark and Semaan, 2008). For example, one Israeli engineer, who worked for a large distributed multinational corporation in distributed teams, was able to take his laptop with him when he was called up as a reservist into the army. He continued to participate in his distributed international team, even while in intensive training.

Maintaining a social life amid 'social destruction'

In both countries before the wars, people had the freedom to safely travel throughout the country to visit friends and family, attend sporting events, or go to clubs. When the war began, however, people were unable to travel as they did before. One informant characterizes this situation:

> . . . when I get home I become a prisoner in my own home because of the security situation in Iraq. I cannot leave the house because it is not safe. I cannot go to plays, or clubs. No one drives and there is no public life, no café, no clubs, restaurants . . .

Despite their inability to socialize in collocated settings, through the adoption and use of technological resources (e.g. the mobile phone, Instant Messenger and Facebook) our informants have reported that communication frequency has actually increased because it is now easier to connect with others (Semaan and Mark, 2011). By using various technologies, Iraqi citizens now spend several hours a day perusing their Facebook network, reconnecting with people who had left the country, chatting with friends via Yahoo Messenger™, or talking to their friends and family via the mobile phone. Our informants reported relying on technological resources to communicate with friends and family who were outside of the country, as well as others who resided in areas that were difficult to access via conventional methods.

Our informants also reported that societal trust has declined. The decline of interpersonal trust (Abdul-Rahman and Hailes, 2000) has been described by those in our sample as the most devastating aspect of current-day Iraq that has emerged due to the war. Following the war, the Sunni–Shiite conflict forced people to move to Sunni- or Shiite-only neighborhoods within the country. Many people were constantly shifting to different neighborhoods, and people did not feel safe interacting with their neighbors. One of our informants describes this in greater detail:

> The thing changed after the war . . . the greatest destruction was not the infrastructure . . . as much as the social destruction. This distrust which was created. I think this was the . . . like, the big knock that left people feeling uncomfortable with each other. Even at the market, or even in your workplace. You would feel like unsafe. Sometimes . . . I won't say most of the time if I'm talking

about the college. But in the street. Even taxi drivers. The market. I can say this. You didn't know who is your friend and who is your enemy.

Not only were people unable to visit friends and family with whom interpersonal trust existed, they also found it difficult to trust people living in close proximity. In order to continue socializing, a new practice emerged where several of our informants began using technology to meet people online. The new friends they made were located in various countries ranging from the United States and China to other Middle Eastern countries. In the most extreme cases, four people in our sample initiated romantic relationships with people they met online, one of which led to marriage. This denotes a structural shift in Iraqi society, as traditionally people find suitable marriage partners through familial and friend-based connections.

Although the way in which finding life mates differed, people still followed traditional cultural practices (Mark et al., 2009). One of our informants, for example, met an American online who was working in the green zone in Baghdad (a safe area where most American operations take place). After eventually meeting in person, they decided they wanted to get married. In Iraq, traditionally the man's family must travel to the woman's family to engage in what is known as the 'promise' or 'word' – it is essentially an agreement between the families that their children will get married. After explaining to her boyfriend about this custom, our informant's father and her boyfriend's father (who could not travel to Iraq from America) scheduled to meet over the webcam, where the official promise was made between the families. Thus, technological resources enabled people to maintain relationships and develop new relationships in an untrustworthy physical environment, as well as develop romantic relationships online (which is not customary in Iraqi culture).

Continuing education with the aid of technology

We also observed people's use of technological resources for maintaining education during the current Gulf War (Mark et al., 2009). We interviewed several students – the majority attending one of the universities in Iraq – who discussed how difficult it was to continue their educational routine in their unstable environment. When the war started, new obstacles emerged (e.g. curfews, bombs, and militias) which made it difficult for Iraqi citizens to consistently travel to the university or study with their peers face-to-face. It was especially difficult from 2004 to the beginning of 2008 for students to attend lectures on a daily basis.

In some cases, when students were unable to attend a lecture they would not receive the materials for the day. In other instances, students would use their mobile phone to call friends from the university to obtain lecture materials, as well as course updates. Unlike other student groups in our sample, our medical school informants described how they proactively developed robust technology-enabled practices to maintain education – these practices have now become embedded institutional praxis (Mark and Semaan, 2008).

Using CDs, flash ROMs, and message boards, students began to archive course materials. First, students devised coordinated plans for note-taking; students who missed class could then go to copy centers to pick up what they missed. Additionally, lecture notes were distributed on CDs and students also shared notes via flash ROMs. If the Internet network was available, notes were also uploaded to a message board created by a medical student where students could provide updates on whether classes were to be held, as well as to discuss course material and share information.

When students could not attend anatomy or pathology laboratories, they could obtain pictures of slides or dissections taken by students with digital cameras. These pictures were available on CDs. In these cases, students were proactive in using technological resources to continue their education.

Restoring infrastructure for travel

Our informants adopted new ways in which to repair infrastructure and create new systems that enabled them to maintain the flow of essential services necessary for a normal life. We consider transportation, electricity, and emergency services, in addition to information and communication as essential services (Edwards, 2003). We first highlight how people developed new practices to maintain their ability to travel (e.g. Mark et al., 2009; Semaan and Mark, 2011).

In Israel, informants reported relying on cell phones to support their travel. One informant described a 'cell phone battle plan', where she would call her friends about 30 seconds before arriving to pick them up so that they could race into the car. Another informant described how every day he phoned his family (who lived in Germany) before making the 45-minute drive to his workplace.

In Iraq, transportation modes changed from government-instituted public transportation and taxis to private means of transportation. The cell phone is central in helping to organize the transportation, as well as figuring out the route to take. There were several reasons why Iraqi civilians no longer felt safe using old transportation methods. Mainly, our informants reported that while government-instituted travel was no longer reliable, they could not trust bus and taxi drivers as it was difficult to determine whether they were militia members or insurgents. Many people also feared being kidnapped or even murdered due to their religious and political affiliations or their job roles (the educational elite were often targeted during the war), as well as their ethnic identities. In order to maintain routines for travel, our informants reported a new practice of using cell phones to organize car pools with others in their community, place of study, or workplace. They developed trust-based travel arrangements where they would call friends from before the war and family members to seek trustworthy drivers who would not harm them.

One female informant, for example, who works in a bank, stated she organized a minibus to transport her and other employees to work. She was living in one of the unstable neighborhoods in Baghdad and did not feel safe driving herself, nor did she feel comfortable using random taxis with people whom she did not trust. In order to maintain her ability to travel to and from work, she used her cell phone to contact people she knew who could either act as a 'private bus' for herself and her colleagues from work, or recommend someone who would fulfill that role. After locating a trustworthy individual, she was able to continue traveling to and from work.

Furthermore, a new practice also emerged where our informants reported that they also relied on their social networks to determine which routes to take when attempting to reach their destinations. Parents relied on their social networks to find private drivers to transport their children when they could not. Females are particularly susceptible to attacks and parents of young girls went to great lengths to ensure their safety. The following experience is reported by a female informant who describes an instance in which communicating by cell phone helped them avoid the dangers her daughter and her daughter's friend would have encountered if they had taken the usual route home with the driver:

> . . . there was bombing and an exchange of fire, so she called me from just outside the blocked road, the bridge leading into the district, and told me that the driver suggested we have lunch with

him in a safer place, and this was at 3:00 in the afternoon because they have long working hours. And I told her not to go out with the driver, but to tell the driver to take her to her grandparents' house with her friend. And so she had lunch there with them. And then the driver called them and told them that he had phoned friends and friends told him that the roads were still blocked. But the driver told them that he could take them to the bridge that takes them to Al Razalia, and he can drop them off there and they can walk from there. So my daughter called me and told me what was happening and what the driver had told her, and I said yes, that's a good idea. Let him drop you off and you can walk home. And when the driver dropped them off near the closed bridge, their father was waiting for them on the other side to pick them up, so they walked a short distance and my husband picked up our daughter and her friend and took them home.

This example illustrates how people used communication technology extensively to support travel. Faced with a situation in which there were bombs exploding when her daughter was due home, the mother used her cell phone to notify her daughter of the danger ahead. Rather than relying on a public service or announcements through radio or TV, citizens became responsible for organizing their own travel routes.

Cross-checking information

We also investigated the ways in which technological resources can be used during war to seek reliable, trustworthy, accurate, and timely information (Mark et al., 2009). In Iraq, before the war, the majority of our informants were limited to television news networks, radio stations, and newspapers that were controlled by the Ba'athist regime. After the war, however, we found that Iraqis typically have access to a lot of information through a diverse set of information media such as numerous satellite channels, newspapers, radio stations, and websites.

While they often enjoyed the freedom these choices gave them, they also recognized the need to verify the accuracy of the information provided through these various media. We found that this verification process involved checking and cross-checking information deemed vital by individuals. Thus, news from one source would typically be checked against that reported by another source from the same medium, and often checked again against news reported by other sources and types of media. The number of checks and cross-checks performed by an individual usually depends on how important the information is and the impact it will have on the individual's everyday activities.

Information is also cross-checked against personal accounts of events by individuals within their personal social network. Several informants reported they would typically contact a friend or relative by cell phone, e-mail or Instant Messaging to verify a popular media report of events that occurred within Iraq, e.g. the number of victims of an explosion. The following statement made by a male informant is typical of such practices:

> . . . I rely on the news on the satellite, through the satellite TV. I don't trust all the news that's available, or that's broadcast on satellite. I don't trust every channel; it's different on every channel. The news is different. Some say there were that many killed, and others say there were this many killed, and neither of them match up . . . I rely on people. I rely on the people who were actually there, where the disturbance occurred. Like when a bomb goes off, I rely on people who were actually in the place, or on site when the bomb happened, when the bomb went off. I also rely on word of mouth, and the news that is transferred from one person to the other. I feel that's a reliable source. You just believe . . . you disbelieve the news from regular sources, or official sources, but you rely on people that you know, and the news that they're telling you.

This individual statement is typical of many who did not trust news channels and predominantly relied on news relayed to them by people they trusted in their social network. Here too, 'word of mouth' is possible only through the use of communication technologies like e-mail, Instant Messenger, and cell phones.

Concluding remarks

We have presented cases of how people living in regions of conflict have adopted and appropriated technologies to help them negotiate and navigate through their dangerous environments. We found that our informants used ICTs to reconstruct, to modify, and in some cases to develop completely new patterns of actions. In some cases, deep structural changes occurred, such as when the Iraqi medical students became collaborative in their studies to share information with those who could not travel to class.

The people whose routines changed the least were those who were already using ICTs intensively for their work or social life. Communicating and coordinating through technology enables people to be independent of their environment. When people are restricted by living in a dangerous environment, ICTs can expand people's reach, serving as a way to augment their life in these settings.

War is a particular type of crisis that is ongoing, producing continual disruption that can last for years. However, there is a lack of research focusing on how civilians experiencing violent conflict can use ICTs to maintain their daily lives. We believe that our research can especially benefit the disaster studies research community, which has predominantly focused on social behavior during disaster events, e.g. hurricanes and earthquakes. Already some researchers are beginning to examine how citizens use ICTs to cope with the effects of disasters (e.g. Palen and Liu, 2007). We hope that our research can spark further studies into deepening the understanding of how ICTs can support people in regions of conflict.

Note

1. Internet World Stats, Israel: Internet usage and marketing report. Retrieved June 13, 2011 from *http://www.internetworldstats.com/me/il.htm* (accessed June 13, 2011).

References

Abdul-Rahman, A., and Hailes, S. (2000). Supporting trust in virtual communities. *Proceedings of the Hawaii International Conference on System Science*, 34, 1–9.

Biernacki, P. (1981). Snowball sampling: problems and techniques of chain referral sampling.' *Sociological Methods and Research*, 10(2), 141–63.

Bruneau, M., Chang, S., Eguchi, R.T., Lee, G.C., O'Rourke, T.D., Reinhorn, A.M., Shinozuka, M., Tierney, K., Wallace, W.A., and von Winterfeldt, D. (2002). *A Framework to Quantitatively Assess and Enhance Seismic Resilience of Communities*. Multidisciplinary Center for Earthquake Engineering Research, Buffalo, NY: State University of New York at Buffalo.

Buenza, D. and Stark, D. (2003). The organization of responsiveness: innovation and recovery in the trading rooms of Lower Manhattan. *Socio-Economic Review*, 1(2), 135–64.

Dynes, R. (1970). *Organized Behavior in Disaster*. Lexington, MA: Heath Lexington.

Edwards, P.N. (2003) Infrastructure and modernity: force, time, and social organization in the history of sociotechnical systems. In Misa, T.J, Brey, P. and

Feenberg, A. (eds.), *Modernity and Technology*. Cambridge, MA: MIT Press, pp. 185–225.

Feldman, M.S. (2004). Resources in emerging structures and processes of change. *Organizational Science*, 15(3), 295–309.

Giddens, A. (1984). *The Constitution of Society*. Berkeley, CA: University of California Press.

Hagar, C. and Haythornthwaite, C. (2005). Crisis, farming and community. *Journal of Community Informatics*, 1(3), 41–52.

Hobfoll, S.E. (1989). Conservation of resources: a new attempt at conceptualizing stress. *American Psychologist*, 44, 513–24.

Hobfoll, S.E. (1998). *Stress, Culture, and Community: The Psychology and Philosophy of Stress*. New York: Plenum Press.

Kendra, J. (2001). Resilience. Internal working paper, Disaster Research Center, Newark, DE: University of Delaware.

Kendra, J. and Wachtendorf, T. (2003a). Creativity in emergency response to the World Trade Center disaster. In Monday, J.L. (ed.), *Beyond September 11th: An Account of Post-Disaster Research*. Boulder, CO: Natural Hazards Research and Applications Information Center, pp. 121–46.

Kendra, J. and Wachtendorf, T. (2003b). Elements of resilience after the World Trade Center disaster: reconstituting New York City's Emergency Operations Centre. *Disasters*, 203, 27(1), 37–53.

Kreps, G. (1998). Disaster as systemic event and social catalyst. In Quarantelli, E.L. (ed.), *What is a Disaster? Perspectives on the Question*. New York: Routledge.

Mark, G. and Semaan, B. (2008). Resilience in collaboration: technology as a resource for new patterns of action. *Proceedings of the ACM Conference on Computer Supported Cooperative Work*, 137–46.

Mark, G., Al-Ani, B., and Semaan, B. (2009). Resilience through technology adoption: merging the old and the new in Iraq. *Proceedings of the ACM Conference on Human Factors in Computing Systems*, 689–98.

Mileti, D.S., Drabek, T.E., and Haas, J.E. (1975). *Human Systems in Extreme Environments: A Sociological Perspective*. Boulder, CO: Institute of Behavioral Science, University of Colorado.

Palen, L. and Liu, S. (2007). Citizen communications in disaster: anticipating a future of ICT-supported public participation. *Proceedings of the ACM Conference on Human Factors in Computing Systems*, 727–36.

Quarantelli, E.L. (1996). Emergent behaviors and groups in the crisis times of disasters. In Kwan, K. (ed.), *Individuality and Social Control: Essays in Honor of Tamotsu Shibutani*. Greenwich, CT: JAI Press.

Quarantelli, E.L. (1998). *What is a Disaster? Perspectives on the Question*. New York: Routledge.

Rodriguez, H., Trainor, J., and Quarantelli, E.L. (2006). Rising to the challenges of a catastrophe: the emergent and prosocial behavior following Hurricane Katrina. *Annals of the American Academy of Political and Social Science*, 604, 82–101.

Semaan, B. and Mark, G. (2011). Creating a context of trust with ICTs: restoring a sense of normalcy in the environment. *Proceedings of the ACM Conference on Computer Supported Cooperative Work*, 255–64.

Torrey, C., Lee, M., Burke, M. Dey, A., Fussell, S., and Kiesler, S. (2007). Connected giving: ordinary people coordinating disaster relief on the Internet. *Proceedings of the Fortieth Annual Hawaii International Conference on System Science.*

Vieweg, S., Palen, L., Liu, S.B., Hughes, A.L. and Sutton, J. (2008). Collective intelligence in disaster: examination of the phenomenon in the aftermath of the 2007 Virginia Tech shooting. *Proceedings of the Information Systems for Crisis Response and Management Conference.*

Weick, K.E. (1993). The collapse of sensemaking in organizations: The Mann Gulch Disaster. *Administrative Science Quarterly*, 38(4), 628–52.

Webb, G.R. (2004). Role improvising during crisis situations. *International Journal of Emergency Management*, 2(1–2), 47–61.

2

Law enforcement agency adoption and use of Twitter as a crisis communication tool

Thomas Heverin and Lisl Zach

Abstract: This chapter describes the results of a research study investigating the adoption and use of Twitter as a crisis communication tool by law enforcement agencies from large US cities (cities with populations greater than 300,000). The study consisted of two parts – an analysis of Twitter use based on publicly available posts authored by 30 law enforcement agencies that have active Twitter accounts and an analysis of data collected through 17 semi-structured interviews with law enforcement public information officers and public media specialists.

Key words: crisis informatics, crisis communications, technology adoption.

Introduction

Traditionally law enforcement agencies (LEAs) have used a one-way communication model: sending information to the public either directly or through the news media and not receiving communications back from the public. Increasingly, LEAs are responding to calls to make such organizations more accessible and participatory by instituting communication and information programs aimed at changing the ways in which they interact with the public, especially in times of crisis. One approach that is being used is communicating through social media tools, including microblogging applications such as Twitter. This study is focused primarily on the adoption and use of Twitter because it is a social media tool that is ideally suited to the communication of short, timely messages to the general public. This makes it a natural choice for use as a communication tool by LEAs during crisis situations.

The Technology-Organization-Environment (TOE) framework identifies three contexts that influence adoption and use of technological innovations: organizational, technological, and environmental (Tornatzky and Fleischer, 1990). Using the TOE framework, the researchers investigated the adoption and use of Twitter as a crisis communication tool by LEAs in large US cities, both by analyzing publically available Twitter posts and by interviewing LEA public information officers (PIOs) and public media specialists. The results of this study provide a snapshot of current use of Twitter by police departments and a deeper understanding of what factors contribute to the adoption of Twitter in a sample of large US cities, as well as indications of why or why not such a tool may be adapted elsewhere.

The research questions addressed by this study were:

■ What types of information are shared by LEAs through the use of Twitter?

■ Why or why not do LEAs adopt and use social media tools such as Twitter to communicate routine or crisis-related information to the public?

■ What, if any, are the barriers to or challenges for LEAs in adopting social media tools such as Twitter to communicate routine or crisis-related information to the public?

Background

Adoption and use of new technology

Adoption of new technology at an organizational level, in this case LEAs, is subject to a variety of factors. Organizational adoption occurs in two stages: initiation and completion (Zaltman, Duncan, and Holbek, 1973). In the initiation stage, the organization becomes aware of the innovation, develops an attitude about the innovation, and evaluates the innovation. In the completion stage, the organization decides to acquire the innovation and use it. The innovation process is a success when the innovation is accepted and integrated into the organization (Rogers, 1995).

In the diffusion of innovations theory, Rogers identified five attributes that impact the rate of adoption: relative advantage, compatibility, complexity, trialability, and observability (Rogers, 1995). Relative advantage is the degree to which an innovation is perceived to be better than the idea, practice, or object that it supersedes. Compatibility focuses on how consistent the innovation is with the existing values, needs, and past experiences of members of the organization. Complexity centers on the difficulty in using, learning, and understanding the innovation. Trialability is the degree to which the innovation can be experimented with on a partial or step by step basis. Observability measures how the results of the innovation are made available to others.

The TOE framework states that three aspects of a firm's context influence technology adoption and implementation: technological, organizational, and environmental context (Tornatzky and Fleischer, 1990). Organizational context is defined as the characteristics of the organization including the firm's size, degree of centralization, degree of formalization, and managerial structure. The technological context includes the internal and external technologies that are relevant to the firm. The environment context includes the firm's competitors, market structure, macroeconomic context, and the regulatory environment. Later studies validated the view of the TOE framework and found that the technology adoption decision relies on both internal and external environments of the organization (Chau and Tam, 2000; Kim and Galliers, 2004; Kuan and Chau, 2001; Zhu, Kraemer, and Xu, 2002).

Law enforcement communication with the public

Police departments' communications with the public are generally conducted through designated channels within the LEAs. The personnel responsible for communications are either sworn police officers or civilian specialists; these personnel communicate with the public and news media, as well as involve the public in law enforcement activities (Motschall and Cao, 2002; Surette and Richard, 1995). Those that serve in these roles are typically called PIOs; however, they may also be called public relations specialists. This discussion will use the term *public information officer* to refer to all designated professionals who serve under these varying titles. The PIO function and role was established in response to the need for law enforcement to engage more effectively with the public. The primary roles of the PIO are to manage the flow of information sent to the news media, promote a positive image of the police department, and disseminate information during crises (Surette and Richard, 1995). The role of the PIO has become important as LEAs have attempted to change their communication methods from controlled, closed systems to more open systems of communication (Motschall and Cao, 2002).

Traditionally, PIOs have sent information to the news media to be disseminated to the public as well as using established alert and warning systems (Pechta, Brandenburg, and Seeger, 2010). The relationship between police departments and news media has been described as mutually beneficial: the media needs the police to provide them with accurate sources of crime information, while the police work with the news media to promote a positive public image (Dowler, 2003). Police departments often view working with the news media as a way of 'demonstrating transparency; reassuring people; achieving publicity for unsolved crimes; projecting positive stories; and projecting a positive police image' (Mawby, 2010). As the most visible members of the criminal justice system, police recognize the power of the media and attempt to use it to promote the image of the police (Chermak and Weiss, 2005).

As the public has become more technologically and media oriented, distributing information to the public through information communication technologies is viewed as integral to police operations (Motschall and Cao, 2002). Technological developments, including the development of social media tools, have created opportunities for police departments to bypass traditional media channels and communicate directly with the public (Mawby, 2010). Social media tools can contribute to new cultures of openness (Bertot, Jaeger, and Grimes, 2010) and provide an opportunity to develop more personal relationships with citizens (Edmiston, 2003). Social media tools now create possibilities for interpersonal, participatory, and interactive communications (Pascu, Osimo, Ulbrich, Turlea, and Burgelman, 2007). Tolbert and Mossberger (2006) suggest that using information communication technologies to communicate with the public can make the government more responsive, transparent, accessible, and participatory, all of which can increase the trust that citizens place in government agencies. If police departments actively seek contact with citizens they can improve public satisfaction with police (Bridenball and Jesilow, 2008).

Some LEAs that have decided not to adopt social media tools such as Twitter to communicate with the public may lack interest or time to invest in another communication tool. Other LEAs may face barriers common to e-government challenges such as organizational and managerial challenges (resistance to change), legal challenges (the questioning of the official communication status of social media messages), and city communication policies (Gil-García and Pardo, 2005).

The public has been receptive to government agency use of social media. A 2010 Pew Research Center report finds that '31% of online adults have used social tools such as blogs, social networking sites, and online video as well as e-mail and text alerts to keep informed about government activities' (Smith, 2010). Additionally, the study reports that new social media tools appeal to population groups that have historically used online government services to a lesser extent than other groups. More specifically, African Americans and Latinos were more likely to say that it is 'very important' for government agencies to distribute information on social networking sites including Twitter (Smith, 2010).

Twitter and its use as a crisis communication tool

Twitter is a popular form of microblogging that allows users to send brief updates (up to 140 characters in length) via the web, mobile devices, and other applications. Twitter membership has increased rapidly since its inception in 2006 to a current level of over 100 million users. According to a recent Pew Research Center report, the number of US adults online who use Twitter or a service like Twitter to share or see updates of others has jumped from 11 percent in December 2008 to 19 percent in October 2009 (Lehnhart and Fox, 2009). Twitter differs from other social media sites in that it offers an easy method for sending short, real-time updates to a large audience (Zhao and Rosson, 2009). There are numerous conventions Twitter users have developed over the past few years, including retweeting, replying to or mentioning other users, using hashtags, and creating lists that demonstrate interactive and conversational aspects of Twitter (Boyd, Golder, and Lotan, 2010; Honeycutt and Herring, 2009).

People and organizations use Twitter for a variety of reasons. Java, Song, Finin, and Tseng (2007) developed a taxonomy of user intentions in Twitter and found the main user intentions to be daily chatter, conversations, sharing information/URLs, and reporting news. Zhao and Rosson (2009) conducted semi-structured interviews with 11 participants and identified various reasons for using Twitter including keeping in touch with friends and colleagues, raising visibility, gathering useful information, seeking help and opinions, and releasing emotional stress. Companies can use Twitter to interact with customers, gauge customer sentiments, and gather market information (Jansen, Zhang, Sobel, and Chowdury, 2009).

At no time is communication more essential than during times of crisis. Through social media tools such as Twitter, citizens can now generate and disseminate their own crisis-related information and disseminate it rapidly to a wide audience. In times of crises and disasters Twitter has been used by citizens for information production, broadcasting, brokering, and organization (Hughes and Palen, 2009; Starbird, Palen, Hughes, and Vieweg, 2010). The citizen use of Twitter to generate crisis-related content has been analyzed during violent attacks (Heverin and Zach, 2010a; Oh, Agrawal, and Rao, 2010) and during natural disasters (Hughes and Palen, 2009; Longueville, Smith, and Luraschi, 2009; Starbird et al., 2010; Vieweg, Hughes, Starbird, and Palen, 2010). Researchers have found that the public uses social media as an additional channel outside of official communication channels to create, share, validate, and disseminate crisis information.

Research design

The research study investigates the adoption and use of social media tools by LEAs in US cities with populations greater than 300,000. The study focuses primarily on the adoption and use of Twitter because it is a social media tool that is ideally suited to the communication of short, timely messages to the general public. According to a 2009 US Census Bureau report (*Annual Estimates of the Resident Population for Incorporated Places Over 100,000, Ranked by July 1, 2008, Population: April 1, 2000 to July 1, 2008*) there are 60 US cities that have populations greater than 300,000. An analysis of publicly available Twitter posts during the spring of 2010 identified 30 LEAs that had active, publicly available Twitter accounts. These LEAs were in cities that ranged in size from 319,057 to 8.3 million and were distributed geographically across the country. A maximum of 300 tweets sent by each police department were collected. If a police department had authored more tweets, the researchers collected only the 300 most recent tweets. If a police department had authored fewer than 300 tweets, the researchers collected all tweets authored by that department. A total of 4,915 discrete tweets were identified and collected.

The researchers conducted a content analysis of the 4,915 tweets collected using an open coding approach (Strauss and Corbin, 1998). Non-exclusive categories of tweets were identified, revised, and described while reading the contents of the tweets. Ten major categories of tweets evolved from the coding including the following: crime/incident information, general department information, planned event information, traffic information, crime prevention tips, person identification requests, reply/mentioning other Twitter users, retweeting other Twitter authors' tweets, sharing data, and other.

In addition to the analysis of the publicly available Tweets, the researchers invited 41 law enforcement PIOs from the 60 largest US cities (both with and without an active Twitter presence) to participate in semi-structured telephone interviews during the summer of 2010. Eighteen PIOs accepted the request to participate in the study. Of the 30 LEAs with active Twitter accounts, 17 PIOs agreed to be interviewed; only one PIO from an LEA without an active Twitter account responded to the invitation. Eight telephone interviews were recorded and transcribed. Eight PIOs preferred not to be recorded; detailed notes were taken during these telephone interviews. One PIO requested to reply to the interview questions via e-mail. No identifying data regarding the location of the LEA were included in the interviews, and confidentiality of the responses has been maintained in accordance with university Institutional Review Board (IRB) policies. The responses (paraphrased in the case of those who requested not to be recorded) are attributed to individual interviewees in the text by number, i.e., T-1 through T-17. For the purpose of this discussion, only responses from the 17 PIOs interviewed who utilize Twitter for communicating with the public were included.

Interviews were sequenced using a modified replication strategy (Zach, 2006). Replication was carried out in two stages – a *literal* replication stage, in which participants were selected (as far as possible) to obtain similar results, and a *theoretical* replication stage, in which participants were selected to explore and confirm or disprove the patterns identified in the initial interviews. The initial departments contacted consisted of departments that use Twitter extensively (authored over 1,000 tweets), followed by departments that authored fewer than 1,000 tweets, and then departments that do not have a presence on Twitter.

Interview questions focused on the current use of social media tools, reasons for adopting social media, perceived benefits, challenges, and contribution of social media tools in communicating with the public in day-to-day operations and during crises. The interview protocol is found in the appendix to the chapter.

The interview data analysis involved a detailed content analysis of the interview transcripts and the notes taken during the non-recorded interviews. The analysis consisted of a series of iterative steps including reviewing initial interviews for themes, reviewing later interviews for new themes, and going back to the initial interviews to look for the new themes. Each interview was reviewed numerous times to look for both confirming and non-confirming evidence.

Findings

LEA use of Twitter to share information

From analyzing the public Twitter profiles of 30 LEAs in large US cities with active public Twitter accounts, the researchers found a total of 10,931 police authored tweets, 62,226 followers of the police Twitter accounts, and 3,991 lists with the police accounts named (as of May 1, 2010). The researchers found that LEAs with active public Twitter accounts come from larger cities (population mean of 845,433) compared with LEAs that do not have Twitter accounts (population mean of 560,080). The average LEA has had an account for 10 months, authored 364 tweets, has 2,074 followers, and is listed in 133 lists.[1]

The content analysis of the collected tweets showed that almost half (45.3 percent) of the tweets authored by LEAs contained crime or incident information about shootings, stabbings, accidents, arrests, robberies, murders, and abductions, as well as reports of police on scene at an incident, and investigations. Tweets that identify specific persons comprised 5.6 percent of the tweets analyzed. During violent crises, identification of suspects is an important part of information dissemination. These tweets consisted of descriptions and names of suspects or missing persons and requests for assistance in identifying suspects or missing persons. These tweets often contained URLs linking to photographs, sketches, descriptions, and videos of named suspects, unnamed suspects, and missing persons. Traffic tweets consisted of 8.1 percent of the tweets and described traffic-related events such as closures of roads, heavy congestion, and options for alternate routes. As shown below in Figure 2.1, crime/incident, person identification, and traffic tweets accounted for 59 percent of the tweets sent.

LEAs also used Twitter to provide the public with information about the department (14.0 percent), including individual officers, and about

Figure 2.1 Percent of law enforcement agency authored tweets by content type (5,117 total tweets)

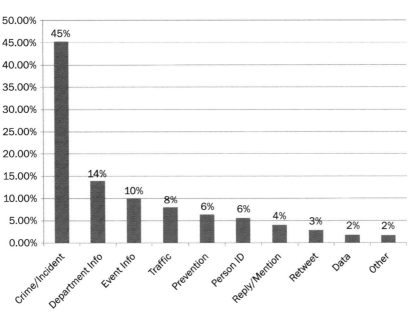

events (10 percent). These types of tweets can help let the public know that there is more to the department than just crime information. However, the overwhelming majority of tweets authored by LEAs consist of one-way communications to the public; only 4.1 percent of Tweets fell into the 'Reply/Mention' category in which a member of the LEA responded to other Twitter users publicly on Twitter or mentioned other Twitter users' usernames.

Interviews with PIOs from 17 major US cities confirmed the findings of the analysis of publicly available Tweets and provided insights into the issues surrounding adoption and use of social media tools to communicate with the public. Fifteen of the 17 PIOs interviewed responded that Twitter is one of several social media tools they use to increase the public's awareness of and access to information about police activities. Figure 2.2 summarizes the types of social media tools used by LEAs interviewed in this study.

As found in the analysis of publicly available tweets, the most frequent uses of Twitter identified by PIOs is to provide information about crimes, traffic and road conditions, and other types of breaking news that the LEA wants to provide quickly. Several PIOs commented on the efficiency of Twitter as a tool for getting the message out: 'It is very timely. You can

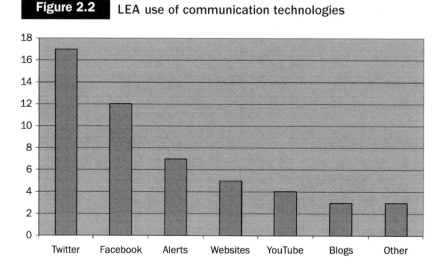

Figure 2.2 LEA use of communication technologies

update very quickly; if we have something, we can send it out immediately. We can get it out when we want it' (T-10). Four PIOs described how they use Twitter in conjunction with Nixle, a system for sending out safety alerts. 'By linking Nixle to Twitter, the department can send out real-time notifications about crime and traffic' (T-3); another PIO related how during a particularly high-profile case, 'the PD wanted to get information out first [ahead of the news media] – Nixle/Twitter helped the PD [police department] do that' (T-16).

Benefits of using Twitter for LEAs

Twelve out of 17 PIOs mentioned specifically the advantages of controlling the flow of information to the public: 'The main advantage to using social media is communicating with the community directly and with an unfiltered message' (T-6); 'It's something that we control. Through the news we can't always control our message' (T-10); 'So many people can now get the information first hand straight from the PD instead of getting information from the news media' (T-16). Other PIOs expressed the opinion that social media 'allows us to put out positive information about our department' (T-13), in a way that filtered messages through the news media do not. The overwhelming perception on the part of the PIOs interviewed was that the public used and appreciated the flow of information directly from the LEAs: 'We know the community values it. It helps us conduct outreach to the community . . . since so many people use cell phones, we have a way of sending information to them [as] quickly as possible' (T-4). 'Twitter [provides] the ability to send out information to the community and to people who want to receive the information' (T-7).

While Twitter is perceived by many LEAs as the quickest way to reach the public with a targeted message, it is not seen as a channel for two-way communication. As one PIO commented, 'I don't see the use of the police department in engaging back and forth. My job as PIO is to put the information – the facts – out there and let the public make their own decisions' (T-4). Another PIO confirmed this sentiment: 'We are not involved with conducting a conversation. We just use [Twitter] to push out information' (T-17). Only one PIO talked about two-way communication with the public; the example he used was that 'they can provide feedback on the [Facebook] posts that the police department puts out' (T-12). However, another PIO made the point that Twitter requires 'a lot less monitoring on our end. With Facebook a lot of people comment on their walls. That is not something we necessarily want' (T-10).

Adoption of Twitter and other social media tools

None of the PIOs interviewed identified any significant barriers to LEA adoption of Twitter as a communication tool. Several LEAs had already been using other forms of communication tools such as Facebook, so the step to Twitter was relatively easy. One PIO described how the idea received 'mixed reviews' the first time it was presented, but when it was positioned as a positive outlet for connecting with the public, the Chief's office had no issues with using it (T-3). Several PIOs mentioned the need for LEAs to 'keep up with the times' (T-1). Using social media tools such as Twitter and Facebook is perceived by LEAs to help their public image. One PIO compared the uses of Twitter and Facebook by saying that, while Twitter allows the LEA to send out real-time information, Facebook 'is relevant to community policing; the public can see the officers as people and not just as enforcers of the law' (T-3). A similar comment was made by another PIO: 'We use Twitter for breaking news, when people are missing, when looking for a suspect, a major road closed from a crash or something . . . We put all the positive stuff on

Facebook . . . pictures of our horses and dogs or cars that are run on natural gas . . .' (T-18).

The most common concerns voiced by the PIOs regarding the use of Twitter and other social media tools related to the amount of time or staff required to implement the services. 'They [the police department] need more staff to use more social media tools and to update them more consistently. If the police department had more staff to use social media they could send out more stuff and be more proactive' (T-16). Another PIO pointed out that social media use needs to be part of an integrated communication model – 'You can't just update it once a month. It really has to be staffed' (T-5). Other PIOs commented that 'higher ranking officers need to be trained on the benefits of Twitter' (T-3) and 'a lot of the senior administration . . . don't know a lot about social media so they are kind of indifferent' (T-13).

Implications for Twitter as a crisis communication tool

Nine PIOs stated that sending out the correct information in real time and being able to quickly correct misinformation are the main advantages of using Twitter in times of crisis. Some PIOs interviewed described specific examples of using Twitter to communicate with the public during crises. As one PIO stated, 'the importance though is you have to make sure the correct information is being put out there. We had a shooting at [a local] hospital and the information that was going out on social media not from the police but others wasn't accurate. So we have to make sure we are monitoring this so we can make sure the information put out is correct' (T-5). During one reported violent crisis, a PIO stated that some members of the public claimed there was a shooter on a local college campus. The news media picked up the story; however, there was no shooter on the campus and the PIO used Twitter to immediately correct the misinformation (T-12). Another PIO stated that, in times of crisis, although Twitter is a quick method for sending out crisis information, the LEA focuses on getting the right information out even if it takes extra time: 'That's why our office works so hard to be as quick as possible but sometimes there is a delay because we are checking our facts before we hit the forward and send button' (T-4).

Prior to the adoption of Twitter, one PIO reviewed the LEA's actions during a violent crisis by identifying how Twitter could have played a role in crisis communications – '. . . like critical incidents type things like a mall shooting back in 2007 and [we] discussed how Twitter could have played into that, what we would have done to help people . . . We had to go through the media to get out the information. We thought this [Twitter] would have been a great way to let people know what was happening, to stay away, that kind of stuff' (T-18).

Although not all PIOs described a specific use during a crisis, the implications for Twitter as a crisis communication tool could be seen from its general use. As described by the PIOs, some of the advantages of using Twitter for crisis communications are being able to communicate directly with the public, communicating in real time, and sending out an unfiltered message. Two PIOs stated that using Twitter provides an effective means for combating misinformation in daily communications (T-14, T-12). The public can receive regular updates either via their computers at work or at home, or through their mobile devices.

> Using the Nixle-Twitter set up, the PD can send out information specific to a local area with a quarter-mile radius. People can sign up and set up for what area they want to receive alerts in. It is a way for the PD to get what it thinks is the most relevant information out to a local community. (T-16)

This type of functionality has obvious applications in the event of natural or man-made crises. It is already being used in the case of specific crimes, such as bank robberies or carjackings, so applying the same technologies to communicating imminent threats would require little adaption. However, before Twitter or other social media can be used as reliable crisis communication tools, the issues related to adequate staffing and integration into the overall communications plan would need to be addressed.

Discussion

The adoption and use of Twitter at the organizational level among LEAs in major US cities is a relatively new phenomenon. Based on an analysis of publicly available Twitter profiles, only half of the 60 US cities with populations over 300,000 have an active presence on Twitter. As of spring 2010, the 30 LEAs in the sample have had accounts for an average of ten months. Interviews with PIOs from LEAs with an active Twitter presence confirm relatively short experience with using Twitter as a communication tool. One PIO reported that his department had launched their Twitter presence in October 2010. As is often the case with the adoption of new technology at an organizational level, several LEAs went through an initiation stage during which they had experience with other types of social media tool, the most frequent of which was Facebook. During this period, the LEAs developed a generally positive attitude towards the use of social media tools for communication with the public and began to understand the benefits of more direct and more timely communication available through such tools. Further factors, such as the technological and environmental context in which the LEAs operate, also contributed to the adoption and use of social media tools, specifically the desire to stay up to date with current technology and the need to find alternative ways of providing information as traditional news media have reduced or eliminated local coverage.

Further research needs to be done to identify factors that may contribute to non-adoption of Twitter and other social media tools by those LEAs who are not currently using Twitter. Based on the analysis of which of the 60 largest US cities do and do not have an active Twitter presence, it appears that population size (and by implication financial resources) may be a consideration. LEAs from large cities seemed to be more likely to have active Twitter accounts than LEAs from smaller cities. Availability of staff to implement new communication services using social media tools was identified as a concern by several PIOs. Other possible factors mentioned in the interviews that might have a bearing on adoption and use include senior administrators' lack of familiarity with social media tools and a possible reluctance to expose the organization to two-way communication from the public. However, the general trend of adoption of social media tools among the general US population would indicate a growing level of familiarity and acceptance.

Overall, the attitude towards the adoption and use of social media tools by the PIOs interviewed was positive. The key benefit identified by PIOs is the speed with which the LEA can provide its own message to the public without going through the editorial filter of the news media. In addition, the PIOs interviewed felt that using social media tools was popular with the public and provided a desired level of transparency about police activities. Some PIOs interviewed described how Twitter can be used for communication. Though other PIOs did not discuss the use of Twitter in times of crises, it is clear from their comments that the same characteristics that they find beneficial in day-to-day communications (speed of access and control of the message) would be important during natural or man-made crisis situations.

Conclusion

The outcome of this research furthers our understanding of the current and potential use of Twitter as a crisis communication tool by city LEAs. The analysis of 4,915 Tweets from 30 active Twitter profiles from US cities with populations larger than 300,000 indicates that these LEAs primarily use Twitter to disseminate crime- and incident-related information. Interviews with 17 PIOs from LEAs with active Twitter accounts confirm this finding. The PIOs also confirm that Twitter is a valuable tool for providing accurate, up-to-the-minute information that can be communicated directly to the public without going through the news media.

In the TOE framework, the main drivers of Twitter adoption for the LEAs fall in the environmental context (the increased use of social media by the public and the failure of news media to pick up LEA stories) and the organizational context (senior leadership acceptance of social media). The implications for Twitter use as a communication tool during times of crisis are that if LEAs have an active Twitter presence in place at the time of a natural or man-made crisis situation, the public will receive critical information through a channel with which they are already familiar. Additional research is needed to identify the degree to which Twitter use by LEAs is valued by the public and whether the one-way model of LEA communication remains appropriate in an age of increased interactive use of social media.

Note

1. A detailed description of the content analysis and results can be found in Heverin and Zach (2010b).

References

Bertot, J.C., Jaeger, P.T., and Grimes, J.M. (2010). Using ICTs to create a culture of transparency: e-government and social media as openness and anti-corruption tools for societies. *Government Information Quarterly*, 27(3), 264–71.

Boyd, D., Golder, S., and Lotan, G. (2010). Tweet, tweet, retweet: conversational aspects of retweeting on Twitter. Paper presented at the Hawaii International Conference on System Sciences-43, Kauai, HI.

Bridenball, B. and Jesilow, P. (2008). What matters: the formation of attitudes towards police. *Police Quarterly*, 11(2), 151–81.

Chau, P.Y.K. and Tam, K.Y. (2000). Organizational adoption of open systems: a 'technology-push, need-pull' perspective. *Information and Management*, 37(5), 229–39.

Chermak, S. and Weiss, A. (2005). Maintaining legitimacy using external communication strategies: an analysis of police-media relations. *Journal of Criminal Justice*, 33(5), 501–12.

Dowler, K. (2003). Media consumption and public attitudes toward crime and justice: the relationship between fear of crime, punitive attitudes, and perceived police effectiveness. *Journal of Criminal Justice and Popular Culture*, 10(2), 109–26.

Edmiston, K.D. (2003). State and local e-government: prospects and challenges. *The American Review of Public Administration*, 33(1), 20–45.

Gil-García, J.R. and Pardo, T.A. (2005). E-government success factors: mapping practical tools to theoretical foundations. *Government Information Quarterly*, 22(2), 187–216.

Heverin, T. and Zach, L. (2010a). Microblogging for crisis communication: examination of Twitter use in response to a 2009 violent crisis in the Seattle-Tacoma, Washington area. Paper presented at the 7th International ISCRAM Conference, Seattle, WA.

Heverin, T. and Zach, L. (2010b). Twitter for city police department information sharing. Paper presented at the 73rd American Society for Information Science and Technology Annual Conference, Pittsburgh, PA.

Honeycutt, C. and Herring, S.C. (2009). Beyond microblogging: conversation and collaboration via Twitter. Paper presented at the Hawaii International Conference on System Sciences-42, Kauai, HI.

Hughes, A.L. and Palen, L. (2009). Twitter adoption and use in mass convergence and emergency events. *International Journal of Emergency Management*, 6(3), 248–60.

Jansen, B.J., Zhang, M., Sobel, K., and Chowdury, A. (2009). Twitter power: tweets as electronic word of mouth. *Journal of the American Society for Information Science and Technology*, 60(11), 2169–88.

Java, A., Song, X., Finin, T., and Tseng, B. (2007). Why we twitter: understanding microblogging usage and communities. Paper presented at the 9th WebKDD and 1st SNA-KDD 2007 Workshop on Web Mining and Social Network Analysis, San Jose, CA.

Kim, C. and Galliers, R.D. (2004). Toward a diffusion model for Internet systems. *Internet Research*, 14(2), 155–66.

Kuan, K.K.Y. and Chau, P.Y.K. (2001). A perception-based model for EDI adoption in small businesses using a technology-organization-environment framework. *Information and Management*, 38(8), 507–21.

Lehnhart, A. and Fox, S. (2009). 'Twitter and status updating', Fall 2009: Pew Internet Project.

Longueville, B.D., Smith, R.S., and Luraschi, G. (2009). 'OMG, from here, I can see the flames!': a use case of mining location based social networks to acquire spatio-temporal data on forest fires. Paper presented at the 2009 International Workshop on Location Based Social Networks, Seattle, WA.

Mawby, R.C. (2010). Police corporate communications, crime reporting and the shaping of policing news. *Policing and Society*, 20(1), 124–39.

Motschall, M. and Cao, L. (2002). An analysis of the public relations role of the police public information officer. *Police Quarterly*, 5(2), 152–80.

Oh, O., Agrawal, M., and Rao, H. (2010). Information control and terrorism: tracking the Mumbai terrorist attack through Twitter. *Information Systems Frontiers*, 13(1), 33–43.

Pascu, C., Osimo, D., Ulbrich, M., Turlea, G., and Burgelman, J.C. (2007). The potential disruptive impact of Internet based technologies. *First Monday*, 12(3).

Pechta, L., Brandenburg, D., and Seeger, M. (2010). Understanding the dynamics of emergency communication: propositions for a four-channel model. *Journal of Homeland Security and Emergency Management*, 7(1).

Rogers, E. (1995). *Diffusion of innovations*. New York: Free Press.

Smith, A. (2010). *Government online*. Washington DC: Pew Research Center.

Starbird, K., Palen, L., Hughes, A.L., and Vieweg, S. (2010). Chatter on the red: what hazards threat reveals about the social life of microblogged information. Paper presented at the 2010 ACM Conference on Computer Supported Cooperative Work, Savannah, GA.

Strauss, A. and Corbin, J. (1998). *Basics of qualitative research: Techniques and procedures for developing grounded theory*, Thousand Oaks, CA: Sage Publications, Inc.

Surette, R. and Richard, A. (1995). Public information officers: a descriptive study of crime news gatekeepers. *Journal of Criminal Justice*, 23(4), 325–36.

Tolbert, C.J. and Mossberger, K. (2006). The effects of e-government on trust and confidence in government. *Public Administration Review*, 66(3), 354–69.

Tornatzky, L. and Fleischer, M. (1990). *The Process of technology innovation*. Lexington, MA: Lexington Books.

US Census Bureau (2009). *Annual estimates of the resident population for incorporated places over 100,000, Ranked by July 1, 2008, Population: April 1, 2000 to July 1, 2008* (2009). US Census Bureau.

Vieweg, S., Hughes, A.L., Starbird, K., and Palen, L. (2010). Microblogging during two natural hazards events: what twitter may contribute to situational awareness. Paper presented at the 28th International Conference on Human Factors in Computing Systems, Atlanta, GA.

Zach, L. (2006). Using a multiple-case studies design to investigate the information-seeking behavior of arts administrators. *Library Trends*, 55(1), 4(18).

Zaltman, G., Duncan, R., and Holbek, J. (1973). *Innovations and organizations*. New York: John Wiley and Sons.

Zhao, D. and Rosson, M.B. (2009). How and why people Twitter: the role that micro-blogging plays in informal communication at work. Paper presented at the ACM 2009 International Conference on Supporting Group Work, Sanibel Island, FL.

Zhu, K., Kraemer, K., and Xu, S. (2002). A cross-country study of electronic business adoption using the technology-organization-environment framework. Paper presented at the ICIS 2002, Barcelona, Spain.

Appendix: interview protocol

City Police Department adoption and use of Twitter as a crisis communication tool

1. Does your agency use social media technologies to communicate with the public?

2. What social media tools does your agency use? Who is responsible for putting content on them?

3. What contributed to the department's decision to use these social media tools? (Person, event, other . . .)

4. Were there any challenges in the decision-making process of adopting social media technologies?

5. What do you see as the benefits of using social media? (Note: interviewee may have stated benefits in question 3; if so, ask if there are others.)

6. What do you see as disadvantages or what problems have you experienced with using social media? (Note: person may have stated disadvantages in question 2; if so, ask if there are others.)

7. During an emergency, crisis, or disaster, what is your view on using citizen created social media content in the official response to the emergency, crisis, or disaster?

8. Does your agency have a policy in place stating how social media technologies should be used? If so, please describe the policy.

9. If you could, how would you change the social media policy or what do you think should be included in a social media policy?

10. Is there anything else that you can tell me that you think is important about the LEA's adoption and use of Twitter?

3

Promoting structured data in citizen communications during disaster response: an account of strategies for diffusion of the 'Tweak the Tweet' syntax

Kate Starbird, Leysia Palen, Sophia B. Liu, Sarah Vieweg, Amanda Hughes, Aaron Schram, Kenneth Mark Anderson, Mossaab Bagdouri, Joanne White, Casey McTaggart, and Chris Schenk

Abstract: 'Tweak the Tweet' is an idea for enabling citizen reporting via microblogs during crisis events. It instructs users of Twitter to tag and structure their messages to make them machine-readable using what is known as a microsyntax. This chapter describes efforts to deploy the Tweak the Tweet syntax during several crisis events in 2010. We describe how syntax, instructions, and the nature of such a campaign evolved within and across events, and share the insights gained about the use of structured data reporting during mass emergencies and disasters.

Key words: citizen reporting, crisis informatics, computer-mediated communication, Haiti earthquake, microblogs, social media, Twitter.

Introduction

On December 29, 2010, in the midst of a major snowstorm, the mayor of Newark, NJ, Cory Booker, used Twitter to identify and communicate with stranded residents, then set out to help them himself, digging residents out of the snow and even delivering diapers (Shear, 2010). An onslaught of media attention ensued, capping off a year of similar stories and growing enthusiasm regarding the use of social media, particularly Twitter, during crises. In August 2010, the American Red Cross hosted an event gathering practitioners and researchers from both the disaster and social media domains to discuss how to deal with 'crisis data,' the information distributed through social media about unfolding crisis events. An ongoing concern, addressed in that conference, is the great volume of crisis data, and the inability of crisis responders to filter, process, and respond to it all in real time (American Red Cross, 2010). This issue is compounded by social media communications (e.g. Facebook updates or tweets) that are typically 'unstructured' and currently require manual processing – human interpretation – of each message or tweet. Though Mayor Booker and his assistants were able to read and respond to several tweets during the Newark snowstorm, one could easily imagine a greater-impact event on a larger city where even teams of organized responders could not filter and process all of the data being shared, much less respond to it all.

'Tweak the Tweet' (TtT, Starbird and Stamberger, 2010) was conceived as a solution for the Twitter platform to this problem of filtering and processing disaster information, asking users to structure their tweets in such a way as to make them machine-readable, which would enable remote computers to filter and process the information in real time. This chapter describes the original TtT idea, how it was deployed during multiple crisis events in 2010, and how the concept and the tools to support it developed and evolved through those efforts.

Social media and disaster: the emergence of the citizen reporter

Sociologists of disaster have long recognized that members of the public will spontaneously converge on the site of a disaster event to offer assistance (Fritz and Mathewson, 1957; Dynes, 1970; Stallings and Quarantelli, 1985; Kendra and Wachtendorf, 2003). We now know that this social phenomenon extends to information communication technology (ICT), including social media. Social media are digital platforms that enable users to distribute and discuss information, often within the structure of a user-articulated social network. These online sites provide virtual places for people, even people quite remote from an event, to converge after a crisis to offer assistance to warning and response efforts (Vieweg et al., 2008;

Hughes and Palen, 2009; Starbird et al., 2010). Often, this activity takes the form of seeking and providing information (Palen and Liu, 2007).

Though the phenomenon of spontaneous convergence is not new, increasingly ubiquitous ICT that allows *members of the public* (or *citizens*)[1] to collect and transmit data is opening up new opportunities for seeking and providing information during disasters. One outgrowth of these new technologies is an emerging role for the *citizen reporter* or *citizen-as-sensor* (Shneiderman and Preece, 2007). The vision is that individuals on the ground during an event, armed with little more than the smart phone they already carry and the services they use for everyday communication, can contribute to their community's collective awareness by sharing their observations with others via personal text messages, Twitter, Facebook, and other tools. Aggregation of social media data can be an important resource for members of the public seeking information. The shared information is also a potential data source for emergency responders, who are beginning to attend to the emerging role of social media in disaster response (Palen et al., 2010).

Twitter and its potential for citizen reporting during crises

Twitter is a popular microblogging service that allows users to send messages of up to 140 characters, called *tweets*, to groups of listeners, termed *followers*. Reciprocally, users can read the tweets of other Twitter users, or *Twitterers*, that they elect to follow. Users of Twitter can access the platform and broadcast their tweets from the web or from a mobile device, including any cell phone with SMS functionality. They can also embed GPS location information into the metadata of their tweets, and add photos or links to other websites. Though users broadcast and receive information within their networks of followers, most tweets and their associated metadata are public to all, and available for search through Twitter's front-end search box feature and their three programmer's APIs, as well as a vast number of third party search applications.

Twitter's short lifespan has been marked by a rapid succession of user-driven adaptations of the environment, specifically in the form of new linguistic conventions introduced to make the platform more usable and more useful. The hashtag (#), one of these emergent norms, is a way to mark up tweets with topical keywords. Originally promoted by Messina (2007) for use during the 2007 California Wildfires to assist in tweet searchability, recent research shows that 10.1 percent of all tweets and

20.8 percent of retweets contain at least one hashtagged term (Suh et al., 2010).

Though Twitter's potential as a channel for crisis communications has been recognized by many, some substantial obstacles need to be overcome before it can be effectively leveraged for citizen reporting. One of the concerns of formal responders, as well as citizens trying to monitor Twitter for relevant information during disaster, is that there is too much data (American Red Cross, 2010). In the case of a large-scale crisis event in a connected population, citizen reporting via social media opens the door to potentially millions of tweets per day. Within this deluge, there is bound to be a large amount of noise and repeated information, as well as important details containing information that is actionable or could increase overall situational awareness (Vieweg et al., 2010).

In a local wildfire or flood, the numbers of people tweeting about smoke, flames, or water levels from the affected area might number in the high tens or maybe hundreds, depending on population density. But thousands or even hundreds of thousands of people (in the case of a catastrophic event like the Haiti earthquake) watch and sometimes tweet from afar, sharing links to media articles about the event, sending their prayers, etc. During the Red River flooding in 2009, more than half of those tweeting about the event were not local to the area affected (Starbird et al., 2010).

Neither responders nor affected citizens have the tools yet to sift through this massive amount of information to find the signal within the noise. Even if they could define a way of homing in on tweets that were only coming from affected areas, they would still have to be able to manually read each tweet to understand its meaning. Though researchers are actively working on this problem (Palen et al., 2010), we do not yet have a deployable, robust computational solution for extracting key information from tweets automatically.

Tweak the Tweet: background and rationale

TtT is an idea that addresses the difficulty of using computational tools to make sense of Twitter data in real time. This idea was initially presented by Starbird and Stamberger (2010) at a Random Hacks of Kindness event (RHOK #0)[2] in November 2009 as a low-tech solution for leveraging Twitter for citizen reporting during crises. Extending the established hashtag convention, TtT encourages Twitter users who want to report information during a disaster to insert pre-defined hashtags *within* tweet text to make their tweets machine-parsable. The idea takes advantage of the public searchability of tweets, and describes a fairly simple remote computer program that could process tweets that use TtT syntax.

By placing TtT-specific hashtags in certain places within their tweets, TtT users tell the 'listening' machine how to classify the different pieces of information:

> #haiti #need food and h2o #name Villa Manrese #loc Haut Turgeau #info 1000+ ppl no aid 18 days #contact JL 555–5555

In this example, the #haiti tag tells the remotely located process that captures tweaked tweets that this tweet is about the Haiti earthquake event. The presence of the #need and #loc tags indicates that the tweet is using the TtT format. After the computer program identifies this tweet as TtT, it will create a 'need' record due to the presence of what is known as a 'primary' tag. The need will be recorded as food and h2o; the name of the entity in need will be Villa Manrese; the location will be Haut Turgeau; and the contact information will be JL at 555–5555.

Though computationally simple, the concept does not come without a cost. Its complexity arises on the user side, shifting the burden of communication and interpretation more heavily onto the Twitterers themselves. People who wish to report information must adjust their normal tweeting behavior to include new hashtags and specific word orders, while compressing lots of information into a single 140-character tweet. Significant deployment efforts for several events of different types (e.g. earthquakes, floods, fires, severe weather) over the previous 11 months have highlighted the inherent difficulty of this behavior-shaping criterion and illuminated a variety of usability issues in the initial TtT syntax that have since been addressed. In spite of these problems, these efforts have also brought insight into how structured data reporting can work and who is most apt to use it – the answer to which is different from the original vision.

TtT deployment for the Haiti earthquake: bootstrapping a nascent idea

On January 12, 2010, at 16:53 local time (EST), a 7.0 magnitude earthquake shook the country of Haiti, causing catastrophic damage.

Hundreds of thousands of lives were lost with many more casualties, and an estimated 1.5 million people were left without homes (*New York Times*, 3 September 2010). In the early aftermath of the quake, with the country's already vulnerable infrastructure almost entirely destroyed, thousands of people were reportedly trapped in the rubble of collapsed structures: electricity and phone services, where available before, were down. While foreign rescue teams attempted to reach trapped victims, relief agencies struggled to meet basic needs such as food, water, shelter, and medical care for other affected and displaced people. The *New York Times* (3 September 2010) referred to the relief effort as a 'logistical nightmare' due to the severity of need and the wide-scale destruction of the existing infrastructure.

Though we conduct research in disaster studies year-round, our move to assist in the Haiti event was based on a desire to help through one means we had available – Tweak the Tweet – not to use the event to conduct research on the proposed structured data format. In fact, we were not sure our dual involvement as researchers and helpers would enable appropriate research investigation. In the end, we learned a great deal about the deployment of a TtT instance as a process, which is what we report on here. Within hours of the earthquake, CrisisCommons,[3] an emergent organization comprising a coalition of largely technology-oriented individual, governmental and non-government organization volunteers aimed at assisting in crisis response, began to organize conference calls. The group invited our research team to participate, and during one of those calls, on January 14, someone listening in suggested the possibility of using TtT. Afterwards, our research team met locally to consider the moral and practical implications of operationalizing the nascent idea to assist in the Haiti relief efforts.

Our team was concerned about the readiness of the TtT syntax. The syntax had yet to go through a single round of usability testing. Our only use scenario was based on an affected person tweeting from the ground; we did not know how easy it would be to learn the syntax, especially for a person experiencing the stress of a crisis event. Also troubling was that, at that time, there was no infrastructure in place to *process* the tweets, though we were hopeful that the CrisisCamps[4] efforts planned for later that week would produce tools for digesting the data. Technology access was another issue. Even prior to the earthquake, very few people on the ground in Haiti were connected to Twitter, and use of other networked computing services was also limited. Would TtT be privileging the needs of people who had the means to access social media to the detriment of others who could not promote their needs in this way? And finally, as researchers, we struggled with the idea of taking an active role in an event; that an intervention of this kind would change the social landscape of the phenomena we were trying to study; and without certainty that it would be for the better.

After some debate, we concluded that the potential gains for the affected area outweighed the risks. We rationalized that the 'users' would probably not be affected Haitians communicating their needs, but international relief workers who could use the format to coordinate response efforts. We did not know if it would work, but we felt that if TtT could possibly help make the situation better, even for a single person, then it would be worth the effort to 'deploy' the syntax. At 19:51 EST on January 14, researchers at University of Colorado's Project EPIC[5] officially deployed Tweak the Tweet for the Haiti earthquake relief efforts, in collaboration with parallel efforts at CrisisCamps. A notable result of this decision was that the deployment itself was a multi-faceted and -staged project that required significant time commitment by seven researchers at Project EPIC, working in a variety of roles.

Prescriptive tweets

Following the initial concept as outlined by Starbird and Stamberger (2010), we began by tweeting out *prescriptive* tweets that modeled the syntax:

> #haiti pls tweet in format: #haiti #offering [list offers] #loc [location] #num [amount] #contact [@ or #]
> #haiti use 1 main hashtag per twt: #imok, #ruok, #need, #offer or #have, #open [road, store or other], #close [road, store or other]

To distribute the prescriptive tweets, we activated a Project EPIC Twitter account (@epiccolorado) and had researchers using their own personal accounts as well to bootstrap the creation of an audience. From the @epiccolorado account, automated scripts broadcast the prescriptive tweets at regular intervals. To reach as broad an audience as possible, and following the initial TtT suggestion for using formal response and mainstream media to distribute the messages, we direct-addressed the accounts of journalists and media outlets, response agencies, and other influential Twitterers, requesting that they retweet the prescriptive tweets. Table 3.1 shows statistics on the number of prescriptive tweets and the number of people who retweeted those tweets.

Table 3.1	Distribution of TtT tweets during the early aftermath of the Haiti earthquake

Type of TtT tweet	Total	Not including EPIC tweets	# of Twitterers who tweeted one of type
Total TtT tweets	5016	3083	295 (6 EPIC)
Prescriptive	907	37	16 (5 EPIC)
Prescriptive retweets	154	135	71 (3 EPIC)
Translated	1861	1040	74 (5 EPIC)
Original (from affected people and remote organizations)	46	39	10, 4 in Haiti (3 EPIC)
Retweets of translated and original TtT tweets	1860	1732	255 (5 EPIC)
Unknown altered form – cannot classify as retweet or translated	188	100	39 (3 EPIC)

Example tweets

We soon realized that prescriptive tweets were not enough to instruct people on how to use the TtT syntax and that we needed to further model communications behavior with 'example' tweets. These 'example' tweets contained real, current information that we found over e-mail listservs, and on mainstream media websites, blogs, and other tweets. Researchers reformatted the information using TtT syntax, and then tweeted the modified reports:

Original tweet:

Who has basic medical supplies for La Ku La Pe hospital Nan Pele (60–80 ppl normally) please contact me

Modified, 'example' TtT tweet:

#haiti #need basic medical supplies for #loc La Ku La Pe hospital Nan Pele for #num 60–80 ppl please contact @vrn_wa

TtT format update

Immediate feedback from both users and our research communities led to a move to simplify and clarify the TtT syntax from the original version published in Starbird and Stamberger (2010). We formalized the difference between primary, 'type of report' hashtags and secondary, 'data' hashtags while adding more flexibility for free text. For example, instead of writing '#need #water #food and other #supplies,' the more natural syntax supports this as '#need water, food, and other supplies.' Our revised instructions requested that users include only one primary tag (#need), so their tweet could be categorized, and then as many other secondary or 'data' tags as were necessary and could fit. This improved syntax with instructions was released late on January 18 – before any substantial adoption of the initial version – and received positive feedback among early adopters of the original form.

Wiki for language translation and syntax suggestion

Examining tweets and other information sources, we recognized several different languages in use, including three languages used by Haitians themselves (Haitian-Creole, French, and English) and many more languages by response agencies and relief groups located worldwide. We wanted to support TtT use for people using a wide variety of languages, but did not have access to professional language translators within our research group. Addressing this issue, we created public wikis that allowed anyone to contribute translations, tag ideas, and revised instructions that clarified ambiguities. This open resource strategy resulted in full translations for the TtT syntax, prescriptive tweets, example tweets and instructions in French and Haitian-Creole, and later, after the February 27, 2010 Chile Earthquake event, to Chilean Spanish.

Syntax editor

To further aid use of the TtT syntax, on January 22, we quickly developed and released a web application that allowed users to fill out a report form that generated a correctly formatted TtT tweet. Though the application was rapidly developed and not even connected directly to Twitter (i.e. it was not a Twitter client; to tweet, users had to copy and paste the generated text into their Twitter client), several users reported in follow-up studies that they found it helpful in the construction of tweaked tweets.

YouTube video

The effort also came to include video instruction on January 22. We created a video using screen-capture software to demonstrate and explain a process for creating tweaked tweets, which included how to locate relevant information, copy it into a Twitter client, add the correct syntactic tags, and move/edit text to create a tweet that fitted the 140-character limit.

Tool development: if you come, they will build it

One significant hypothesis embedded in the original TtT concept (predating the Haiti event) was that volunteer programmers would develop the technological resources necessary for processing TtT data as well as end-user tools for making sense of it. This hope was based on observations from previous research on the use of Twitter during the North American Red River flood in 2009 (Starbird et al., 2010), which described how several programmers from the Red River region voluntarily developed simple scripts to extract river height data from the US Geological Survey (USGS) website to publish over Twitter at regular intervals. TtT was designed to leverage and enable that same kind of volunteerism. Since all the TtT data were publicly available, anyone with programming skills could retrieve it via the Twitter Search APIs to create sense-making tools. When we deployed TtT for Haiti, we hoped that this volunteer programming would happen quickly.

Though some simple tools for TtT tweet identification emerged through CrisisCamps in January and February 2010, Good Samaritan programmers did not manage to produce a stable and robust system for filtering and parsing TtT tweets into value-added tools. The problem, perhaps, was that volunteers were not motivated to develop tools for a format that was not being heavily used. There was no proof that TtT would ever be used by enough people to render the developers' time well spent. At the same time, it was very difficult to ask Twitter users to adopt a syntax that had no tools to support it, and no apparent added value in using it.

We began to focus resources within our lab towards the development of TtT sense-making tools, including an RSS feed of identified TtT tweets made available specifically for the Sahana Foundation.[6] However, the suite of value-adding tools envisioned in the original TtT concept would not be fully developed until several months later, and that effort came almost entirely from within Project EPIC.

As public proponents of the syntax, we struggled with the almost daily decision to keep encouraging others to use it while there were no solid tools for digesting the data generated. The compromise was for us to manually support the syntax, using over-the-counter Twitter-search apps to identify TtT tweets, and then attempt to route those tweets to potential listeners as the event unfolded. Four people, operating the @epiccolorado account in shifts, covered as many hours of the day as possible (nearly 20 hours most days), making sure that any info tweeted by others using the TtT format was retweeted and/or directed to the Twitter accounts of agencies that we knew were listening. In an attempt to garner support for the syntax, especially once we realized that our user base was likely located *outside* of Haiti (see below), we sent out a press release as part of the effort to help in this new way, and accepted media interview requests for the same reason.

The work was emotionally exhausting and the dilemma of asking people to use a not fully supported syntax was never resolved. Ten days after the initial TtT deployment, we decided that we could no longer actively promote the syntax for this event, and we halted the distribution of prescriptive tweets. However, our team continued to use TtT to tweet new information that we learned and to route other TtT tweets to groups we knew to be listening.

Tweak the Tweet use during immediate aftermath of Haiti earthquake

Using Twitter data collected from January 14 to February 1, we saw adoption of the syntax by a small group of Twitterers and some willingness by others to help spread the format through retweeting (Table 3.1). Ten Twitterers used the TtT format to send 39 'original' TtT tweets about their own situation or the needs of their organization. Four of these ten Twitterers were in Haiti at the time. Though these numbers do not show significant adoption of the syntax, and certainly not by many of those directly affected by the event, they do suggest that knowledge about the syntax or the use of 'structured data' did have some reach. Perhaps the most interesting finding involves 74 remotely located Twitterers who used the syntax to tweet information they found in other places (e.g. e-mail, blogs, personal phone calls, Ushahidi[7] reports, etc.) Together they sent 1,040 TtT tweets, many of which contained actionable information.

These 'voluntweeters' in a sense translated information from a variety of sources into the structured data form of the TtT syntax (Starbird and Palen, 2011). Not physically affected by the event, but anxious to assist, these volunteers had the time and ability to understand a fairly technical concept and put it into action. Still other Twitterers assisted by promoting the TtT syntax, retweeting both prescriptive and 'live' TtT tweets, and linking to the instructions wiki on the Project EPIC website or to news media articles that described the syntax.

The revelation of volunteer Twitterers, along with the suggestion of a proxy user who tweets for someone who does not have a Twitter account, indicated that the original user scenario for TtT – that of an affected person on the ground of an event – was only one of several possible scenarios for using structured data in a mass emergency event. We recognized other deficiencies in the original vision as well. Initially, we felt that users would need value-added computational tools that filtered and mapped tweets to give them feedback and motivation for continued use of the format. However, in a follow-up study (Starbird and Palen, 2011), we found that several dozen people who assisted in the Haiti event had adopted the format, without the type of automatic tools we had initially described. Many TtT Twitterers were using the format manually, running searches on TtT hashtags using third-party Twitter applications to find actionable information, and then routing that information to others, just as we were doing from our TtT 'emergency operations center' in our lab. For some, the format was seen as authoritative in a chaotic information space. Some chose to tweet using the syntax to demonstrate to other Twitterers that they had verified the information.

Although our research group lamented that we did not yet have the tools we planned to build ready for the Haiti event, we were impressed that many in the Twitter community were able to find their own value in the syntax as they directed information to proper sources. As time went on, we were able to create more tools to support both the recovery effort in Haiti and other events that occurred later that year in 2010.

Chile earthquake: conceptualizing the deployment as a campaign

Less than two months after the Haiti quake, on February 27, 2010, an earthquake of magnitude 8.8 struck the country of Chile. Though an earthquake-prepared Chilean infrastructure prevented the kind of widespread and catastrophic damage that occurred in Haiti, hundreds of lives were lost not only from structural collapse but also from a tsunami that hit several coastal towns. Immediately following the earthquake, with more experience now about how to help propel such an effort, our team again went to work distributing messages about the syntax, asking for Chilean Spanish language translation help by hosting publicly editable wikis, and deploying new tools that we had recently implemented for supporting the format in the Haiti recovery efforts. On March 1, four days after the initial quake, we had a working TtT infrastructure that collected TtT tweet reports, in both English and Chilean Spanish, and published the records parsed from those tweets onto a public Google spreadsheet.[8] Spreadsheet columns included report type, report content, time, location, contact, status, and 'more info' (see Table 3.2). On March 25, when we ended that collection effort, we had recorded 228 TtT reports, which were mostly about missing people (#sebusca).

We felt that TtT deployment for the Chile earthquake was substantially more effective and efficient than for Haiti. We were now practiced at launching such an effort, and understood the deployment to be a part of a socio-technical 'campaign.' And critically, Twitter use in early 2010 was much higher in Chile than in Haiti. Additionally, as a result of the

Table 3.2	Examples of missing person records from tweets sent after the Chile earthquake

Type	Time	Name or need	Location	Contact	More info
#sebusca	3/1 18:34:54	carlos dominguez torres	parral	@martes	trabaja en peluquería morales pza de armas
#sebusca	3/1 10:19:35	silvia riveria	concepción	@marcomarco	
#sebusca	3/1 10:05:22	marisa cordoba	los angeles	9 55555555	profesora historia liceo de niñas 57 años
. . .					

Note: The titles in the first row are translated here from Spanish to English.

Haiti effort, we had publicly available tools (i.e. the spreadsheet) that demonstrated the added value for prospective users in the Chile response. However, the importance of a local advocate who can localize such a socio-technical effort cannot be underestimated: the influence of a single Twitterer, @Clandrea,[9] was significant.

@Clandrea is a woman living in Chile who had just survived the earthquake and who had been added to many Twitter Lists of popular media outlets during the event, including NPR News, Yahoo News, NY Times, HuffingtonPost, and CBS News. Twitter Lists are curated lists of users that another Twitter user can make, typically recommended sources, often associated with a specific topic. We identified @Clandrea as someone who had both international and local influence during the event and began to communicate with her through Twitter, asking her to use TtT and to retweet some of our prescriptive and example tweets. Analyses of tweet distribution showed that her activity was a significant factor in the adoption of TtT for this event. Therefore, an important component may not be how many prescriptive tweets are sent, but rather *who* sends them. Ideal messengers of the TtT format seem to be account owners who are recognized as having local authority during an emerging event. Though originally hypothesized as response agencies, effective TtT prescriptive tweeters may include influential local citizens as well.

Fourmile Canyon fire in Boulder, CO: unexpected local authority

On September 6, 2010, an emergency hit close to home for us at the University of Colorado, directly affecting our own community including many of our friends and colleagues. The Fourmile Canyon fire began burning at about 10am on Labor Day morning and would continue to burn for ten more days. Some 3,500 people were evacuated from their homes during the initial days of the fire, and approximately 9,000 more were put on evacuation notice later in the week due to a forecast of high winds (Eliot and Banda, 2010). By the time the fires were put out, 169 homes had been lost, though thankfully there were no serious injuries.

Seeing the smoke first hand, we began tweeting about the fire within the second hour of the event, and at 12:11pm, while the community was still settling on a standardized hashtag to report the event (eventually #boulderfire), we deployed an instance to collect and map TtT tweets to an interactive Google map,[10] a tool we had added to our suite during the

Deepwater Horizon oil spill. The deployment for the Fourmile Canyon fire was our most successful to date. We collected 811 unique TtT tweet reports in ten days and 161 different authors contributed a TtT tweet to our records. Locals tweeted photos of the smoke plumes, as well as reports of need and offers of help for those who evacuated during the fire. Twitterers outside Boulder who had volunteered and used TtT during previous events began to help from afar. Several people contacted us through Twitter and were added as editors to the public Google spreadsheet we created, which became a collaborative space where GPS locations were added and records were verified.

Hundreds of people accessed this spreadsheet and other emerging volunteer groups asked to tap the data to add to their own information resources. Our interactive map was linked to by several other websites and some media outlets.

We felt that this comparatively successful deployment of TtT stemmed from a perceived authority of Project EPIC by others, especially with respect to this local event, both in our community and afar. Though we were not the most important or influential individual Twitterers during this fire – those titles more likely belong to other Twitterers, namely @fishnette and @laurasrecipes,[11] who picked up more followerers and were more highly retweeted during the event – our collective effort to deploy the TtT syntax and its growing base of associated tools during the Fourmile Canyon fire generated information resources that were accessed by people wishing to gain more information about the event. This relatively successful effort was a culmination of many of the things we had learned in other deployments, and offered further evidence towards some of our emerging hypotheses about how to communicate TtT during a crisis event.

Other events

Over the course of 2010, Kate Starbird, the first lead researcher for project EPIC's TtT efforts, spent increasingly more time supporting TtT activities across several other events, which are described in Table 3.3. None of these other deployments involved large campaigns of prescriptive tweets, but instead relied on reconceptualizing a TtT effort as one that needed to be highly localized to evolving circumstances and language. Finding local advocates for a TtT instance sometimes ran in conjunction with remote 'voluntweeters' who could assist. The first author created another Twitter account dedicated solely to Tweak the

| Table 3.3 | | Volume of TtT tweets and unique records from TtT supported events in 2010 |

Event	Collection dates (all 2010)	# TtT tweets and retweets	# TtT unique records*
Haiti Earthquake	Jan 10 – Feb 1	5016	N/A
Chile Earthquake	Feb 26 – Mar 15	1932	230
Iceland Volcano Ash / Stranded	Apr 18 – Apr 22	204	114
Oil Spill	May 9 – Aug 4	N/A	805**
Pakistan Floods	Aug 15 – Sept 9	1050	235
Boulder Area Fires: Fourmile Canyon and Peewink Fire	Sept 6 – Sept 17	1854	811
Typhoon Juan	Oct 18 – Oct 22	114	39
Hurricane Tomas	Oct 22 – Nov 19	N/A	N/A
Haiti – Cholera and Political Unrest	Nov 19 to Dec 14	N/A	N/A
Midwest Storm (US)	Oct 26 – Oct 28	71	48
SF Giants World Series Celebration	Oct 2 – Oct 3	97	51
Pacific NW Snowstorm	Nov 19 – Nov 25	140	94
Pacific NW Floods	Dec 10 – Dec 15	143	108
CA and Utah flooding	Dec 17 – Dec 21	124	97
Astoria, Oregon Fire	Dec 19 – Dec 20	31	31

N/A, Exact numbers unavailable due to technical problems, unclear boundaries between events and other issues.

* Excluding records created from non-TtT tweets that had both imbedded GPS location and a photo.

** Researchers manually altered many non-TtT tweets to add them to the records and the map resource. This total number of unique records is therefore inflated for this event.

Tweet efforts, and began developing relationships with other Twitterers interested in social media and emergency response, including several digital volunteers and some practitioners. As these relationships and the tools to support the syntax evolved, towards the end of 2010, it became possible to launch TtT in a matter of minutes with only a few carefully placed prescriptive tweets and links to the activated tools.

One theme that emerged in our lab's initial discussion of TtT in November 2009, and then again repeatedly as TtT was deployed for

Figure 3.1 Tweak the Tweet client application, January 2011

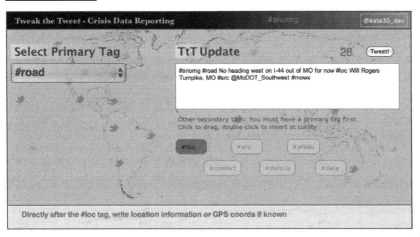

new events, was the clear need for a Twitter client application to help potential users create tweets in the 'correct' syntax – a development effort we are undertaking now and which, at the time of writing, is close to deployment.

Discussion: campaign to support diffusion of a socio-technical practice

The first year of deploying TtT 'in the wild' has provided insight into the potential of using TtT or another structured data reporting format to augment citizen-reporting and other digital volunteer activities via social media services.

We have had multiple opportunities to consider why TtT might not be ideal for citizen-reporting during crises. TtT reporting cannot be considered a replacement for traditional 911 services, as the open-ended nature of social media and lack of feedback make that type of functionality problematic. Additionally, there are many other viable tools for crisis data reporting, like Ushahidi, which uses SMS and web-form reporting, and other web-form reporting sites.[12] Unlike these form-based approaches, TtT can be hard to use in its raw form. Consequentially, we do not view TtT as *the* channel for reporting information via social media, but rather as one tool among several that can be useful during times of crisis for sharing information. We are encouraged by some success in the early deployments described here, and have learned much about how to support TtT use.

A lesson that has been clear from the start is that such an effort is in need of a campaign to raise awareness and offer instruction, both in advance of an event and while it is occurring. The TtT method is, in its entirety and well beyond the idea of the syntax alone, a *socio-technical innovation*. Because the method depends upon a change in individual as well as social interactive practice, it requires broad support through tools, instruction, example, and advocacy in the ways we have described here. As we think we will see with other social movements that rest on social media services, its success should be conceptualized as matter of *technological diffusion* (Rogers, 1995; Grudin and Palen, 1995).

Rogers' model of diffusion of innovations predicts some of the difficulties that we faced in pushing for TtT adoption, as well as some of the successes. For instance, Rogers claims that local peers are more important than mass media channels for persuading others to adopt, so we should not be surprised to find that a local advocate was critical to driving adoption during the Chile earthquake event. Conversely, our failure to address well what Rogers' terms *principles-knowledge* – the knowledge of how an innovation works, not just how to use it – may have hampered adoption and appears to have led to some discontinuing TtT use after a short trial, as Rogers warns.

Though the method may be too complex to become easily 'viral,' the deployment of support tools, instruction, and behavior modeling, as well as rapid adaption of these to particular events, expands the syntax into a method that could come to help organize parts of the information space in emergency response. Fortunately, the demands for adaption in communications arise during an emergency when people are willing and primed to learn new skills (Hughes and Palen, 2009; Kendra and Wachtendorf, 2003).

Though formal responders might adopt a structured data format – or certainly be compelled to if members of the public are organizing their vast communications in this fashion – it is clear in our findings that some spontaneous volunteers are looking for ways to make their communications matter, to make those transmissions rise to the top of the pool of the many communications that suddenly emerge during a mass emergency. The background and special circumstances of disaster may in fact make a complex innovation like this one possible.

Conclusion

Over the last year, we have led several efforts to deploy TtT and created prototype tools to show how the syntax might be useful for crisis events. Though several usability issues remain, we have made progress simplifying the syntax and creating supporting tools to increase the likelihood of structured data use during mass emergency events. We know that one key component is the matter of a 'campaign' to support diffusion of what amounts to a socio-technical innovation. However, some major questions remain, including who should lead such a campaign effort, if there should be a formal 'listener' to the data, and who that listener should be. We plan to continue our efforts to make TtT useful to citizens and responders during crisis events and generate more knowledge about both the nature of structured data use in crisis events and the matter of diffusion of these new forms of socio-technical innovation.

Notes

1. In this chapter we use the term *citizens* as a contrast to *first responders* or other emergency management personnel to enhance language fluidity. *Members of the public* is a more accurate (but unwieldy) phrase, as not all people are citizens of the countries they reside in or of the countries they are assisting.
2. *http://www.rhok.org/event/rhok-0.*
3. *http://crisiscommons.org.*
4. CrisisCamps are bar-camp style events organized by CrisisCommons to improve disaster response by connecting responders and other experts with volunteer programmers.
5. Project EPIC: Empowering the Public with Information in Crisis. *http://epic .cs.colorado.edu/.*
6. The Sahana Software Foundation provides software solutions and data services for assisting communication and coordination during disaster response. *http://sahanafoundation.org.*
7. Ushahidi is a specialized social media platform that enables citizen reporting during crisis. Arising out of the political unrest in Kenya in 2008, Ushahidi collects and processes SMS and web-form messages during events and generates a publicly available website with a 'crisis map' of the information reported (*http://www.ushahidi.com*).
8. This spreadsheet is available at *http://bit.ly/TtTsebusca* (accessed June 3, 2011).
9. Though other user handles in this paper are anonymized, @Clandrea's real name is used here with her permission.
10. Map for the Fourmile fire: *http://www.cs.colorado.edu/~starbird/boulderfire_ map.html* (accessed June 3, 2011).

11. These two user handles are actual Twitter account names, used with permission.
12. One good example is the WA State Department of Natural Resources website for reporting landslides: *http://washingtondnr.wordpress.com/2010/12/15/citizens-are-helping-dnr-keep-landslide-database-up-to-date* (accessed June 3, 2011).

References

American Red Cross (2010). *The case for integrating crisis response with social media.* Washington DC: American Red Cross.

Dynes, R.R. (1970). *Organized behavior in disaster.* Lexington, MA: Heath.

Eliot, D. and Banda, P.S. (2010, September 10). Colorado wildfire evacuees cautiously allowed back home. USA Today. September 10. Retrieved from: *http://www.usatoday.com/weather/wildfires/2010-09-10-colorado-wildfire_N.htm.* Accessed December 12, 2010.

Fritz, C.E. and Mathewson, J.H. (1957). *Convergence behavior in disasters: A problem in social control.* Washington DC: National Academy of Sciences.

Grudin, J. and Palen, L. (1995). Why groupware succeeds: Discretion or mandate? In H. Marmolin, Y. Sundblad, and K. Schmidt (eds.) *Proceedings of the 4th European Conference on Computer-Supported Cooperative Work (ECSCW '95)* (pp. 263–78). Dordrecht: Kluwer Academic Publishers.

Hughes, A. and Palen, L. (2009). Twitter adoption and use in mass convergence and emergency events. *Proceedings of the 2009 Information Systems for Crisis Response and Management Conference, ISCRAM 2009.*

Kendra, J.M. and Wachtendorf, T. (2003). Reconsidering convergence and converger: Legitimacy in response to the World Trade Center disaster. *Research in Social Problems and Public Policy,* 97–122.

Messina, C. (2007, October 22). Twitter hashtags for emergency coordination and disaster relief. [Blog.] Retrieved from: *http://factoryjoe.com/blog/2007/10/22/twitter-hashtags-for-emergency-coordination-and-disaster-relief.* Accessed November 20, 2009.

New York Times (2010). Haiti earthquake of 2010. *New York Times,* September 23. (Accessed September 3, 2010.)

Palen, L. and Liu, S.B. (2007). Citizen communications in crisis: anticipating a future of ICT-supported participation. *Proceedings of the 2007 ACM Conference on Human Factors in Computing Systems* (pp. 727–36). New York: ACM.

Palen, L., Anderson, K.M., Mark, G., Martin, J., Sicker, D., Palmer, M. and Grunwald, D. (2010). A vision for technology-mediated support for public participation and assistance in mass emergencies and disasters. *Proceedings of the 2010 ACM-BCS Visions of Computer Science Conference.* Swinton, UK: British Computer Society.

Rogers, E.M. (1995). *Diffusion of innovations,* 4th edn. New York: Free Press.

Shear, M.D. (2010). Twitter is Newark mayor's friend as he digs residents out. *New York Times,* December 29. Available from: *http://thecaucus.blogs.nytimes.*

com/2010/12/29/twitter-is-newark-mayors-friend-as-he-digs-residents-out. (Accessed December 28, 2010.)

Shneiderman, B. and Preece, J. (2007). 911.gov. *Science*, 315, 944.

Stallings, R. and Quarantelli, E. (1985). Emergent citizen groups and emergency management. *Public Administration Review*, Special Issue, 93–100.

Starbird, K. and Palen, L. (2011). 'Voluntweeters': self-organizing by digital volunteers in times of crisis. *Proceedings of the 2011 ACM Conference on Human Factors in Computing Systems*, New York: ACM.

Starbird, K. and Stamberger, J. (2010). Tweak the Tweet: leveraging microblogging proliferation with a prescriptive syntax to support citizen reporting. *Proceedings of the International Conference on Information Systems for Crisis Response and Management (ISCRAM 2010)*.

Starbird, K., Palen, L., Hughes, A. and Vieweg, S. (2010). Chatter on The Red: what hazards threat reveals about the social life of microblogged information. *Proceedings of the ACM 2010 Conference on Computer Supported Cooperative Work* (241–50). New York: ACM.

Suh, B., Hong, L., Pirolli, P. and Chi, E. (2010). Want to be retweeted? Large scale analytics on factors impacting retweet in Twitter network. *IEEE 2nd International Conference on Social Computing* (177–84). Los Alamitos, CA: IEEE Computer Society.

Vieweg, S., Palen, L., Liu, S.B., Hughes, A. and Sutton, J. (2008). Collective intelligence in disaster: an examination of the phenomenon in the aftermath of the 2007 Virginia Tech shootings. *Proceedings of the Information Systems for Crisis Response and Management Conference (ISCRAM 2008)*.

Vieweg, S., Hughes, A., Starbird, K. and Palen, L. (2010) Micro-blogging during two natural hazard events: what Twitter may contribute to situational awareness. *Proceedings of the 2010 ACM Conference on Human Factors in Computing Systems* (1079–88). New York: ACM.

4

Heritage matters in crisis informatics: how information and communication technology can support legacies of crisis events

Sophia B. Liu, Leysia Palen, and Elisa Giaccardi

Abstract: Information and communication technologies increasingly enable the capture of experiences that result from disaster and mass emergency events. The social and cultural value of such traces, when collectively generated and shared across people and over time, can enhance or even dramatically change how we remember crises. By drawing from several disciplines concerned with digital heritage, and using investigations from three historically significant disasters, we offer an agenda for how information science and human-centered computing communities might conceptualize digital heritage as an emergent research effort in the crisis domain.

Key words: Bhopal gas leak, computer-mediated communication, crisis informatics, cultural heritage, digital heritage, Hurricane Katrina, September 11 attacks, socially distributed curation, social media.

Introduction

Innovative uses of ubiquitous information and communication technology (ICT) such as social media (e.g., Facebook and Twitter) increasingly occur in the immediate warning and response phase of a crisis (e.g. Palen et al., 2009; Starbird et al., 2010). However, the role of social media for crisis events outside of the emergency phase is still not well understood.

What happens to the information space for historic crises a year later, a decade later, or even a generation later? Do these crises have an information space online via social media? If so, how are historic crises being commemorated through social media? These questions speak to the heritage of historic crisis events emerging in the social media landscape.

ICTs are creating new ways for capturing, curating, and preserving the heritage of historic crisis events. *Heritage* in its broadest definitional sense refers to not only the tangible artifacts that societies leave behind, but also their intangible features (Silberman, 2008; Smith, 2006), which include traditions, customs, values, and oral histories. Ubiquitous personal memory devices and social media applications and services (e.g. multimedia recorders, camera phones, online calendars, e-mail systems, online media sharing, and social networking sites) are changing the methods of capture, storage, management, retrieval, and distribution of digital traces. An imminent feature of these changes in capture and downstream activities is how future societies might experience today's digitally captured data as components of cultural heritage.

This chapter begins with an anthropological view of heritage and how this connects with other disciplinary views of heritage. Illustrations of narratives and other heritage-related activities drawn from our empirical study from three disaster events follow. We conclude with a provision of items that articulate a research agenda for considering digital heritage concerns in the context of crisis information management.

Disaster as a social process

Current research attention in the area of crisis informatics tends to focus on ICT-based activity during the emergency period (e.g., Hagar and Haythornthwaite, 2005; Landgren, 2006; Palen and Liu, 2007; Palen et al., 2009; Starbird et al., 2010). The emergency period is an important time period for such research study. However, the times before, after, and even long after a hazard impacts a region are periods when individual and social behaviors can also be influenced by new forms of computer-mediated interaction.

Furthermore, disaster anthropologists Oliver-Smith and Hoffman (2001) argue that disasters should not just be considered an event but also a socially constructed process with multiple interpretations of the crisis. By viewing a crisis or disaster as a social process, the 'historically produced pattern of "vulnerability," evidenced in the location, infrastructure, sociopolitical organization, production and distribution systems, and ideology of a society' becomes more visible (Oliver-Smith and Hoffman, 2001: 3). Recognizing these patterns of vulnerability strengthen a society's capacity to anticipate, mitigate, cope with, and recover from the impact of a crisis. Therefore, our aim is to take a long view of crises to uncover the ways in which social media is being used to communicate the multiple interpretations of a crisis event/ process, as well as to uncover the patterns of vulnerability that led to the crisis.

Living heritage and collective memory practices

Scholars from the heritage studies field conceptualize heritage in a similar way by considering the continuous nature of heritage. For example, contemporary heritage scholars view heritage as a 'living entity' (Kirshenblatt-Gimblett, 2004), which needs to be sustained through a continuous process of interpretation. We also consider Byrne's (2008) new model of 'heritage as social action,' where people are seen as 'active owners and modifiers of culture' (p. 162). The volumes *Theorizing Digital Cultural Heritage* (Cameron and Kenderdine, 2007) and *New Heritage* (Kalay et al., 2008) broaden the definition of cultural heritage in the digital media landscape by addressing its complex relationship to social, political. and economic issues. Giaccardi and Palen (2008) also elaborate on how new media are beginning to stimulate novel forms of cultural interpretation and production, thus enabling new categories of cultural objects to be imagined and created.

Human–computer interaction researchers have begun to discuss issues around collective memory that speak to how we might connect it to heritage issues. Churchill and Ubois's (2008) idea of a 'prospective retrospective' curatorial logic – that is, the ability to anticipate what we will want to remember in the future – speaks to the multi-temporal aspect of heritage. Similarly, Sas and Dix (2006) discuss issues concerning how we might design technology for 'collective remembering.' Friedman's call to design 'multi-lifespan information systems' (Friedman and Nathan, 2010) expresses a similar interest in preserving knowledge for the benefit of future generations.

In this chapter, we use the ideas of disaster as a social process, 'living' heritage, and collective memory in the digital context as the foundation for describing heritage practices taking place in the social media landscape.

Overview of the research project

To understand the heritage issues emerging from online social media culture around historically significant disasters, we conducted this research project in three phases. In Phase 1, we considered what types of social media services to focus on when studying the crisis domain. In Phase 2, we conducted a survey of social media presence for over 100 disasters (Liu, 2011). In Phase 3, we chose three crisis events based on the surveyed data and used virtual ethnographic methods to conduct an analysis of the narratives that are present in current-day communications of social media. In this chapter, we restrict our discussion to an overview of Phase 3.

For each of the three crisis cases, the first author conducted in-depth qualitative research using 'virtual ethnographic' techniques (Hine, 2005). As an online participant observer, she joined each social media service and observed the activity related to each crisis event. Cultural artifacts created by users of these services, such as a Facebook group's wall posts, Flickr photos, YouTube videos, and blog posts were collected and analyzed. She collected web-accessible information generated during noteworthy times of commemoration and cultural action activities, specifically around anniversary dates. The first author also conducted phone, e-mail, and instant messaging interviews with selected participants to better understand the reasons for their participation. Fifty people in total were interviewed: 18 for the Bhopal gas leak, 16 for the September 11 attacks, and 16 for Hurricane Katrina. We used Curio and MacJournal to organize the vast and varied data collected from each website and participant. For this paper, we asked participants if they did or did not want their names disclosed (some active online communicators prefer to have their comments attached to their online personas). We did not use names for those who could not be contacted or who wanted to stay anonymous.

During data analysis, we coded and categorized the data guided by theoretical concepts from literature in studies of heritage and disaster anthropology. In addition, other categories emerged during the analysis. Our aim was to understand how social media users participate in heritage-related activity with digital media, particularly in the crisis domain. This led to the documentation of the different narratives about each crisis event.

Three crisis cases

In this section, we present the findings for the three crises that exhibited a significant social media presence. We chose the Bhopal gas leak because it is a technological hazard that took place before the web was launched. We chose the September 11 attacks because it is a human-instigated event with a complex political backdrop that occurred before the rise of web-based social media. Lastly, we chose Hurricane Katrina because the crisis arose from a natural hazard that occurred at the beginning of the social media age. The different types of hazard agents and the timeframes in which they occurred vis-à-vis networked technological innovation yields insight about how historical events can be 'revived' or captured in real time using today's available ICT.

For each disaster, we present a simplified account of each disaster, followed by a more complex set of narratives as told by participants in social media venues. In this chapter, we focus on a reduced set of three types of narratives or themes as a matter of scope. We first present narratives from witnesses who experienced the tragedy firsthand. Second, we present narratives explaining the potential causes of the disaster. Third, we present narratives about how these disasters are understood to be ongoing.

The case of the 1984 Bhopal gas leak

On December 3, 1984, over 40 tons of gas leaked from the Union Carbide pesticide plant in Bhopal, India. The number of deaths remains debated; official estimates by the Indian Government are 3,787 immediate deaths and 11,000 casualties (Browning, 1993), but others estimate as many as 6,000 to 8,000 immediate deaths and as many as 200,000 people suffering from long-term health problems (Eckerman, 2005; Perrow, 2007). The current death toll is estimated to be around 25,000 and rising due to gas exposure to half a million Bhopalis. Many consider the Bhopal gas leak to be the world's worst industrial disaster.

Bhopal survivor stories of protective action and heroism

Stories from and about the survivors of the Bhopal disaster depict what happened on the night of the gas leak and its aftermath from a survivor's point of view. These stories are resurfacing on Facebook, particularly in the *Students for Bhopal* group's discussion board, as well as in some blog posts and YouTube videos. Such stories explain protective actions that were taken or could have been taken during the gas leak and even contain accounts of heroism.

In July 2008, Sachin Jain shared his survivor story in the Facebook group discussion topic he created called 'What's your story . . . on the fateful night of Dec 3, 1984?'[1] As his family ran from the gas, he remembered how 'somebody suggested to go near the lakes as the gas is soluble in water [and] so the amount of gas in the air there would be less.' Similarly, a medical officer who previously worked at the plant told people that night, 'If you have to go outside, go against the wind. To dissolve the gas, put a wet cloth on your face and along your doors and windows to prevent gas from leaking into the house.' Such protective actions could have saved thousands of lives, and this is arguably one reason people share and distribute such stories – to learn from the past. They are now recounted in Facebook posts and in the BBC's *One Night in Bhopal* docudrama, which can be found on YouTube.[2]

Jain also remembers a story about a night watchman at the Union Carbide plant who first noticed the leak. He writes:

> If he had gone to inform anybody, the amount of gas leaked by then would have killed everyone in the city . . . The only way out was to stop the outflow at the very moment. He put his finger in the valve [and] shouted for help . . . The man died. If that man would not have done this, I would not have been writing this. But to hide the facts, his deed was buried deep in the bureaucratic shit. But he's my personal hero.

Elsewhere, a 'heroic story of a station master' appeared on a blog post by Mani Padma entitled 'Survivor story – Bhopal Gas tragedy.'[3] Upon realizing the severity of the gas leak, the train station master 'valiantly attempted to signal all trains not to stop . . . [and] kept on at his post trying to contact stations to stop entering the city instead of fleeing and taking cover and in the process he lost his life.' Though such stories about the heroes that emerged from the crisis exist, they are not as frequent as the 'horror' stories from 'victims.'

Research on Bhopal gas leak in Wikipedia

For this study, we interviewed the main contributor of the 'Bhopal disaster' Wikipedia article,[4] Ingrid Eckerman, who made nearly

17 percent of the edits. In addition to being a family physician and having existing ties to the Bhopali medical community, she researched and synthesized known facts between the 1960s and 2003 about the disaster (Eckerman, 2005), which was the basis for her Wikipedia activity. In an e-mail interview, Eckerman explains the state of affairs before she began her Wikipedia work:

> There were very little facts about the disaster itself, the consequences etc. The interest was in compensation, legal issues and pollution – which started AFTER the disaster. Much of it was about the last years. The information about the disaster itself was rudimentary. The facts that were there were not always true, often exaggerated. Also, there was a mess of the references . . . It was not trustworthy; it was also considered 'POV' [point of view].

She used the content and structure of her book to contribute to the account of the pre-event phase, the gas leak 'impact' phase, and the immediate post-event phase of the disaster.

One question often raised about technological disasters is whether it was preventable (Perrow, 1999, 2007). The physical cause of the gas leak was water leaking into a methyl isocyanate (MIC) gas tank; it is still debated whether this was an operator error or an act of sabotage. Still, many warning signs have been documented indicating that a disaster would inevitably happen, with Wikipedia contributors listing such signs as appearing as early as 1976. Many explicit warnings occurred in 1982, when a safety audit by US engineers recorded the neglected condition of the plant. Some believe that the disaster could have been mitigated had warnings been heeded. Others argue that globalization is the root cause of industrial disasters (Eckerman, 2005; Perrow, 1999, 2007).

The unfinished story of Bhopal

Many consider the Bhopal gas leak to be an ongoing disaster. It not only killed three generations of people in some families but it also harmed subsequent generations: many of the children born of gas-affected parents suffer from chronic health problems. Adil Laiq Ahmed, a Bhopali born after the gas leak, treats the Bhopal tragedy as an ongoing disaster in the names he gives for his Facebook group and page ('Bhopal GaS Tragedy [25,000+ dead and counting]' and 'The Unfinished Story of Bhopal 1984'). An interview with Debosmita Nandy, who wrote a blog post[5] on the Bhopal Tragedy after a recent verdict, reveals that she thinks of this tragedy as 'a timeless disaster.' Just before the 25th anniversary of the disaster in 2009, The Bhopal Medical Appeal[6] advocacy group used Twitter to post: '20 days to go until 25th anniversary of the 1984 Bhopal disaster. It's not history. People still suffer.'

Some people try to communicate the ongoing suffering by providing statistics through social media. In response to one of the most-viewed YouTube videos about Bhopal, entitled *Bhopal Gas Disaster*,[7] one YouTube user comments:

> What facts do you want? 10,000 immediate deaths or the 30,000 who have died since then or the broken down rate of 15–20 MIC deaths per month or the 390 tonnes of remaining MIC that's left by Carbide as a gift for the future generation of bhopalis?

Such statistics express a message about how the impact of the gas leak has affected Bhopalis on a massive scale since the day it happened. Consider how Debosmita Nandy starts her blog post:

> For many of us, breaking news last a day or two and if we happen to be a part of it, then for a few years or may be a lifetime. But for many in the city of Bhopal, the breaking news of gas leakage on the eve of December 3, 1984 will haunt for generations to come.

While many Bhopalis face the ongoing effects of the disaster on a daily basis, these survivors and many of their supporters worldwide are leveraging social solidarity to argue for disaster mitigation by discussing the lack of safety and corporate responsibility issues that ultimately created and prolonged this disaster.

The case of the September 11 attacks

A series of coordinated suicide attacks in the United States took place on September 11, 2001. Four commercial airliners were hijacked: two planes crashed into each of the Twin Towers of the World Trade Center (WTC) in New York, one plane crashed into the Pentagon in Arlington, Virginia and one plane crashed into a field near Shanksville, Pennsylvania. These attacks led to the death of 2,973 people and the 19 hijackers. As a result, the United States launched the War on Terrorism.

Witnessing the 9/11 attacks and the missing person fliers

The September 11, 2001 attacks (aka 9/11) are often described as the 'most photographed and videotaped event in history.' As TV news stations began reporting the first plane crash into the WTC 1 (North Tower), eyewitnesses used their own digital cameras to record the event. While people were recording, a second plane crashed into the WTC 2 (South Tower). As a result thousands of 'born-digital' videos and photos were generated during the attacks, the first broad public documentary of its kind.

Many of these digital photos and videos now appear on YouTube in amateur and professional documentaries. For example, the amateur video called *September 11 2001: What We Saw*[8] – which has received over 7.3 million views and over 43,000 comments thus far – documents the attacks from the camerawoman's apartment home on the 36th floor of a building 500 yards away from the North Tower. The introductory caption states, 'Our unique perspective has an important historical value, and shows the horror of the day without soundtracks or hype often seen in other accounts.' Near the end of the film, she says, 'This is the documentarian in me that feels like I need to record this.' These numerous born-digital artifacts taken from multiple people and points of view are now prosthetic memories to those who did not experience the attacks firsthand. They also have been used in investigations to determine how the WTC buildings collapsed.

Some of most striking photos that emerged from those who witnessed the immediate aftermath of the attacks were on the missing person flyers posted around public spaces in New York City. They each were initially crafted to provide information to identify a missing person. They often included a personal photo, a physical description, work location in the WTC towers, or other information about how the missing person might otherwise be located. They appeared en masse at subway stops, in Union Square, along lampposts, and in other highly convergent places around the city. Over time they collectively became spontaneous memorials, giving tribute to the many who lost their lives on 9/11. Although these artifacts have now disappeared from New York City's physical landscape, the memories of the missing person flyers can still be found in the digital photos shared online on sites like Flickr and online archives like *Here Is New York: A Democracy of Photographs*.[9]

Revealing the pre-9/11 events and the 9/11 truth

In the immediate aftermath of the attacks, the source was deemed to be terrorism. Here we describe the narratives that address the pre-event conditions in the *History Commons* website, which allows people to create timelines about different topics. Each timeline contains multiple events to provide contextual details from vetted sources. We examined the 'Complete 911 Timeline,'[10] which contains 6,374 events preceding, during, and after the 2001 attacks. In the 'Before 9/11' category, it contains 754 events starting in 1976 with events associated with the Soviet War in Afghanistan, warning signs, insider trading, foreknowledge, US air security, military exercises, pipeline politics, and other pre-9/11 events. Derek Mitchell, the site's creator, explains in an interview that its purpose is to 'reclaim control of our story, our narrative.' The site explains it in this way:

> To provide a means for members of civil society to monitor the activities of powerful entities, such as governments, large corporations, and wealthy and influential individuals. In this capacity, the website should be regarded as an IT toolset that enables members of the public to operate as a sort of people's intelligence agency.

The use of ICT by a network of '9/11 Truth' groups, which ask, 'How did we get here?' illuminates how ICT platforms can serve as a message. They remind people of significant events that happened on September 11 as well as pre- and post-9/11, and they document their evidence. They believe that 9/11 was not an unexpected attack and was instead a 'false-flag operation.' Using blogs, DVDs with 9/11 documentaries, and online networking sites like Meetup and Facebook, they actively share their views.

The ongoing effects of the September 11 attacks

In a 'post-9/11 world,' the effects of these attacks continue to reverberate in ongoing narratives about the event. A blog post by Charles Scaliger called '9/11 Terror Attacks & Their Effect on America'[11] explains how the open-ended character of the phrase 'War on Terrorism' has 'the potential over a generation or two to undo much of the legal and constitutional fabric of our republic.' He urges that:

> We therefore ought to reflect as Americans on the potential long-term cost, both in lives and in laws, of the War on Terrorism.

As we remember the fallen on 9/11 and all those who have since given their lives to combat Islamic extremists, we should determine not to allow the power of such events to utterly overwhelm our heritage and our liberties. We should decide to give voice once again to that portion of our laws that we have permitted to fall silent.

People are using today's social media to examine implications that are becoming more obvious, including long-term health effects on those who were exposed to toxic debris. The 'Health effects arising from the September 11 attacks' Wikipedia article,[12] created five years after the attack, details how this crisis is appearing in the form of chronic health conditions like cancer and respiratory disease. This article is a collective account of this crisis using 81 sources. It breaks down the different types of political controversies surrounding the Environmental Protection Agency's statements regarding air quality in and around Ground Zero immediately after the attacks.

The case of Hurricane Katrina

Hurricane Katrina formed on August 23, 2005, peaked as a Category 5 storm on August 28, and then hit the US Gulf Coast on August 29. Hurricane Katrina became the sixth-strongest hurricane ever recorded in the Atlantic, the third-strongest in the US, and the costliest US hurricane with damage estimated at $81.2 billion dollars (Sylvester, 2008). About 1.2 million people were under an evacuation order, thus leading to 'the largest internal US diaspora of displaced people' (Brunsma et al., 2007). Katrina produced the highest storm surges ever recorded on the US coast, with some as high as 27.8 feet, resulting in 53 different levee failures (Knabb et al., 2005). The death toll reached 1,833 (Knabb et al., 2005), but some argue that about half of these deaths were directly due to the hurricane, with the other half resulting from inadequate emergency response (Sylvester, 2008).

Katrina survivor memories worth preserving and critiquing

Katrina survivor stories have appeared in Facebook groups like 'Hurricane Katrina Survivors.'[13] Some people will never forget the 'pain and death,' while others miss the loss of sentimental items like family pictures. Still many others emphasize how they 'miss the life' that they had pre-Katrina, especially those who are now displaced. In a story shared by one of the Facebook group members during the five-year anniversary, she explains how Hurricane Katrina 'was the day that I was torn away from the family and friends that I knew most of my life,' but goes on to mention how 'it is great that we have this page and we have Facebook to reconnect.' For some survivors, like Mary C. Theriot, Katrina taught her to 'never live that close to a levee or a lake like Pontchartrain, again.'

Amidst these survivor stories that explain the loss of their way of life and the lessons to be learned, analyses about how the media framed Katrina survivors' actions also arose. Just days after Katrina hit, social media users responded to a controversy around two news photos, one used the word 'looting' in its caption while the other one used the word 'finding.' On August 31, 2005, Flickr user Tricia Wang decided to upload a screenshot that included the two photos and explained this controversy in her caption. She titled this photo 'Finding-Looting: Comparing Representations in the Visual Reporting of Hurricane Katrina in New Orleans.'[14] A photo by an Associated Press (AP) photographer captures a dark-skinned man with the caption: 'A young man walks through chest deep flood water after *looting* a grocery store in New Orleans.' A Getty Images photo by an Agence France-Presse (AFP) photographer captures two light-skinned people with the caption: 'Two residents wade through chest-deep water after *finding* bread and soda from a local grocery store . . .' This Flickr photo received 129,000 views and 234 comments. Wang's caption emphasizes how word choice associated with the two photos affects the viewer's interpretation of survivors' actions. Such commentary within social media sites provides another interpretive layer to the collective narratives about Hurricane Katrina, which can play an important role in how Katrina survivors are remembered in the future.

Within two months of Katrina and the subsequent Hurricane Rita, the *Hurricane Digital Memory Bank*[15] was set up with the purpose of using 'electronic media to collect, preserve, and present the stories and digital record' of the hurricanes. It currently contains 43,300 artifacts including firsthand accounts, on-scene images, blog posts, and podcasts. A range of survivor stories emerged in this memory bank and in the social media landscape, such as stories depicting the intensity of the storm, the lessons of survival, and how one reacts to a crisis. But 'as colorful as these survival stories are there only seems to be a momentary thrill of morbid curiosity in it,' says Glenn E. Miller, a Katrina survivor and interviewee for this research. Miller believes that the recovery stories 'including the extraordinary charity that was offered' have a lasting value, and it is the stories that depict 'weird and unusual events, sudden acts of unexpected charity, moments of joy in the middle of struggle, strange coincidences, shocking moments, stories of intense improvising or funny, quirky events that brought humor to the middle of tragedy' that should be preserved.

Reviving the pre-Katrina history

One narrative that has emerged in the social media landscape is how Hurricane Katrina was not an unexpected disaster caused solely by a natural hazard, but rather a human-induced catastrophe as a result of technological and socio-political failures. Nearly a third of the events that appear in History Commons' 'Hurricane Katrina'[16] timeline project are categorized as 'Before Katrina.' The first event that appears is titled '1930–2005: More than 1.2 Million Acres of Louisiana's Coastal Wetlands Disappear' and includes numerous references to reports from official sources, such as the US Environmental Protection Agency, the US Army Corps of Engineers and the National Wetlands Research Center.

The following is an excerpt from a blog post by Fran Taylor explaining the significance of this wetland loss after interviewing Malik Rahim, the founder of the Common Ground Relief grassroots organization:[17]

> One reason Katrina so clobbered New Orleans was the damage that oil exploration and drilling had already done to the wetlands that used to buffer the mainland. Wetlands absorb the impact of a hurricane's storm surge like a sponge. The wall of water that produced most of Katrina's trail of wreckage reached almost 30 feet in places. Every square mile of wetlands reduces that storm surge by about a foot. 'Our wetlands are our first line of defense against hurricanes,' Rahim said.

Such blog posts depict how some people want to remind others of the symbiotic relationship between nature and society. Yet, other narratives arose about how Hurricane Katrina was a technological disaster because of the failure of the levee system. In a YouTube video entitled 'hurricane katrina banned footage'[18] with the description 'footage that george bush didn't want the public to see!!,' an ABC News reporter interviews local residents who believe that the city blew up the levees to save wealthier neighborhoods, as they had done in 1927. Although this deliberate act may not have happened in 2005, one blogger who created the 'Hurricane Katrina Pictures' blog[19] still emphasizes that 'The New Orleans flood was not a natural disaster. It was man-made. The Army Corp of Engineers under-engineered, falsified data, and ignored the facts of the real dangers of the levee system.'

Another narrative describing the socio-political aspects of Katrina explains the breakdown of the official response effort. This narrative emerges in many places, sometimes with extensive documentation of the political shift from the Federal Emergency Management Agency (FEMA) to the Department of Homeland Security as the basis for justifying this account.

Still surviving Hurricane Katrina

Hurricane Katrina hit the Gulf Coast more than five years ago but only some neighborhoods have rebuilt and recovered from the devastation. The *Repopulation Indicators for New Orleans* map mashup provided a visual indication of the neighborhoods and city blocks that are repopulating.[20] Those who were able to rebuild were hindered by the rise of 'exploiters,' a type of disaster converger (Kendra and Wachtendorf, 2003).

In the aftermath of Hurricane Katrina, some people began documenting contractor fraud; this type of fraud further victimized Katrina survivors. Although people began sharing their stories with neighbors and friends, it was not enough to get the word out. The blog 'Hurricane Katrina SOS: The aftermath was far worse than the storm . . .'[21] created a post called 'Contractor Fraud [and] FEMA Negligence' that includes a YouTube video to warn others about this danger.

Another way in which Hurricane Katrina is depicted as an ongoing disaster is through continuous updates on the rebuilding efforts by grassroots organizations like the St. Bernard Project,[22] a 'nonprofit disaster recovery organization in New Orleans dedicated to rebuilding the homes and lives of Hurricane Katrina survivors' by addressing 'the physical, emotional, and psychological devastation caused by the storm.' They use Facebook and Twitter to keep people updated on their recovery efforts. They created a Facebook fan page as a way for the volunteers to stay connected to each other after they leave. They also created Facebook pages for each house being rebuilt, which are updated weekly with pictures and a summary of the volunteers' work, allowing volunteers who helped earlier to see building progress.

We are beginning to see other grassroots disaster recovery organizations using social media outlets to publicize their activities. Such social media content has the potential of adding to the collective narrative about the ongoing repercussions of the disaster.

Discussion: a digital heritage agenda for the crisis domain

As these investigations of social media representation of crises indicate, multiple narratives become apparent with the advent of ICT. We can imagine that crisis narratives will continue to be produced, become accessible, and perhaps be adjusted as time passes and more is learned.

Crisis events expose how rich these collections of narratives can be, and how a participatory orientation to such crisis events continues long after the emergency. In addition, these disasters as described here highlight the emergence of visible, sharable memories that can be remixed, elaborated, and retold in ways that remind us of their processual nature, as well as their significance to our living heritage. Though the narratives are scattered across the Internet and require work to be found, accounted for, and interpreted, we can imagine a future where such accountings and voices are more accessible and even more vivid than they are today. This perspective, we believe, identifies new ground for research and development of digitally enabled heritage activities, which can then in turn be used to inform crisis information management efforts.

Make digital heritage a concern in cyberinfrastructure

As a first-order goal, digital heritage issues need to be integrated into the core mission behind cyberinfrastructure initiatives (NSF, 2007). Though the future of computing promises easier data collection and aggregation of vast datasets, which would seem to automatically enable heritage activity, we instead argue that much can be gained by making it a more formal design policy. Rather than rest only on post hoc processing solutions, there is a real need to design an infrastructure that will enable the kind of tools and services suggested by Sellen and Whittaker (2010) to support selective memory collection, recollection and retrieval.

The purpose of this goal can appeal to both analytical and emotional sensibilities. Preserving data to enable its treatment as heritage could reveal information about the cultural context for creating a national, or even global, 'picture' of disaster resilience from aggregated crisis data. Understanding the cultural context in conjunction with using mined heritage data from large datasets could help resolve why some regions or populations suffer from particular hazards or crises more than others.

The work here also shows how the accessibility of ICT makes it possible for untold numbers of 'voices' to contribute to the representation of how society experiences crises. To capture this would leave a compelling legacy and indeed might help heritage become widely valued as a production function of society. In other words, it is worth designing systems to support *prospective remembering*.

Preserve the medium through digital archaeology

It is not sufficient to preserve the accounts – the 'memories' of a crisis. We must also preserve representations of the media in which these memories were created. Heritage cannot be understood without an understanding of the limits and affordances of the media over which those stories were told. For example, in April 2010, Twitter donated their public database of tweets to the Library of Congress (LOC) to complement the Library's existing cultural heritage collection, but the LOC explicitly stated, 'The Library is not Twitter and will not try to reproduce its functionality.'[23] How might historians 100 years from now understand the value of Twitter if they are not able to experience the Twitter environment, which changes rapidly, as do its third-party clients? Similarly, many of the memories we gathered were from Facebook, but how might future generations learn from them if the contexts in which these memories existed are not also archived and preserved?

Link individual stories into collective narratives

As more people find ways to share stories about a crisis through emergent forms of ICT, future implementations will be needed to link these individual accounts together to construct collective narratives. Such narratives illuminate the themes and emerging voices that might not previously have been described as dominant but have momentum on the 'backchannel.' The narratives about the heroes during the Bhopal gas leak or the extensive history that led to the 9/11 attacks and the devastation of Hurricane Katrina are some examples of this. The key here is to collect enough individual accounts from a wide swath of society to appreciate the diverse set of interpretations.

Jesiek and Hunsinger (2008) explain how browsing and contributing to open digital memory banks allow 'people to create multiple and differential relationships to a given archive' where 'these relationships are the foundations of multiple and overlapping narratives.' Constructing collective narratives also allows people the potential to make 'connections between the tales' to tell a larger story, as exhibited in the MUVI project (Giaccardi, 2006). Supporting collective authorship must also be considered, especially since this is becoming more complex when using proprietary and commercial ICT (Van House and Churchill, 2008). How we design and guide the use of future information systems will ultimately determine who has the authority and ability to collect, store, and interpret the memories from our digital heritage around historic events, and so a conscientious egalitarian orientation is critical.

Support creative expression via story-sharing tools

Storytelling is a critical way in which the heritage of crises is constructed. Stories facilitate remembering and meaning-making because they weave together information and its context and emotion in meaningful and compelling ways. Shen et al. (2002) further argue for the need to support *story sharing*, a more conversational approach to exchanging stories. We should consider how ubiquitous social media (e.g. YouTube, Facebook, and Twitter) are facilitating innovative forms of story sharing throughout the entire life cycle of a crisis. For each of the crisis events we looked at, many people created YouTube commemoration videos that remixed publicly available photos with emotive music and captions, but the sharing of related stories then continued through the video's comments on YouTube and elsewhere. Story-sharing tools will need to support creative weaving of multiple types of content. Such tools also need to create a feedback loop in the story-sharing process to show distribution and evolution.

Support socially distributed curatorial activity

As we increasingly use prosthetic memory devices to consciously record and collect information about crisis events as they happen and over time, we all now face the problem of 'curatorial overload: too much information, too difficult to organize and retrieve' (Van House and Churchill, 2008). Here we view curation as an active process of engaging with and making sense of crisis-related digital memories to assess their value. Preservation and retrieval need to work in conjunction with 'mechanisms that stimulate participatory engagement,' lest the obsession to record everything will paradoxically increase 'amnesia' (Haskins, 2007).

Based on the fledging examples of curation identified in our past and current research, we anticipate the need for a suite of tools that support what the first author has termed *socially-distributed curation* (Liu, 2010), which would facilitate social aggregation, organization, interpretation, and re-presentation in a distributed way to support the active engagement of keeping the memories of historic crises alive. To consider how this behavior is presenting itself now, a common practice is the cross-pollination of online content from one forum to another. For example, Facebook user Adil Laiq Ahmed posted snippets from blog posts and tweets onto his Facebook group wall so that others could get a sense of what is being said about the Bhopal tragedy in forums to which they do not attend.

Cast heritage as social action

Lastly, information science communities can share in the move to cast heritage of crises as a form of 'social action' (Byrne, 2008). Heritage is a 'living entity' (Kirshenblatt-Gimblett, 2004) that triggers reflection in a way that has an opportunity to stimulate 'meaningful participation' (Haskins, 2007) rather than just spectatorship. Through active participation in heritage-related activity, we are reminded of the social and political benefits of keeping the heritage of these crises alive. As Byrne (2008) states, 'The implication is that we all – people in communities as well as heritage practitioners – are "heritage workers"' (p. 169). Designers need to consider the values being embedded in technologies; they have an opportunity to conscientiously design how digital heritage concerns can become a subject of a crowd-scale, participatory activity.

Conclusion

This chapter considers matters of disaster heritage in the changing ICT landscape by drawing across disciplinary fields and reflecting on how crisis events propel digital capture and remembrance activity. We examined a subset of the narratives that have emerged through social media representation in three crisis events. The narratives tell accounts of crises that extend long after and sometimes long before the impact of the event, and therefore illustrate the dynamic and continuous qualities of heritage-related activity. As people increasingly use ICT to document and curate the collective narratives that emerge from historically significant events, we must consider how we might design technologies, policies, and practices that will enable the sharing of digital artifacts not only with those who can immediately harness their value now for disaster mitigation purposes, but also with our descendants to strengthen their resilience to future crises.

Acknowledgments

This research has been supported by the US National Science Foundation (NSF) through an NSF Graduate Research Fellowship awarded to Liu, NSF grants IIS-0546315 and IIS-0910586, and by the Spanish Ministry of Science and Innovation for grant TIN2009–09687. Any opinions, findings, conclusions, or recommendations expressed in this material are those of the author and do not necessarily reflect the views of NSF.

Notes

1. *http://www.facebook.com/topic.php?uid=2206855545&topic=5690*   (NB. Websites cited in these notes were accessed on June 3, 2011).
2. *http://www.youtube.com/watch?v=uz73rcdSG80.*
3. *http://www.gingerchai.com/2010/06/17/survivor-story-bhopal-gas-tragedy/.*
4. *http://en.wikipedia.org/wiki/Bhopal_disaster.*
5. *http://debosmita.wordpress.com/2010/06/28/cover-story.*
6. *http://www.bhopal.org/.*
7. *http://www.youtube.com/watch?v=rmtN8NkMcmo.*
8. *http://www.youtube.com/watch?v=wNNTcHq5Tzk.*
9. *http://hereisnewyork.org/.*
10. *http://www.historycommons.org/project.jsp?project=911_project.*
11. *http://www.thenewamerican.com/index.php/usnews/crime/4572-911-terror-attacks-a-their-effect-on-america.*
12. *http://en.wikipedia.org/wiki/Health_effects_arising_from_the_September_11_attacks.*
13. *http://www.facebook.com/group.php?gid=2300824919.*
14. *http://www.flickr.com/photos/triciawang/38922728/.*
15. *http://hurricanearchive.org/.*
16. *http://www.historycommons.org/project.jsp?project=hurricane_katrina.*
17. *http://www.commongroundrelief.org/.*
18. *http://www.youtube.com/watch?v=Gtkuqf1w2Gc.*
19. *http://hurricane-katrina-pictures.com/555/5th-anniversary-of-katrina-today/.*

20. The map is unfortunately no longer available online. It was produced by the Greater New Orleans Community Data Center (*http://www.gnocdc.org*).
21. *http://katrinasos.wordpress.com/2009/10/24/our-story/*.
22. *http://www.stbernardproject.org/v158/*.
23. *http://blogs.loc.gov/loc/2010/04/the-library-and-twitter-an-faq/*.

References

Browning, J.B. (1993). Union Carbide: disaster at Bhopal. In Gottschalk, J.A. (ed.), *Crisis response: inside stories on managing under siege*. Detroit: Visible Ink Press.

Brunsma, D.L., Overfelt, D. and Picou, J.S. (2007). *The sociology of Katrina: perspectives on a modern catastrophe*. Lanham: Rowman & Littlefield.

Byrne, D. (2008). Heritage as social action. In Fairclough, G., Harrison, R., Jameson, J.H., and Schofield, J. (eds.) *The heritage reader* (149–74). London: Routledge.

Cameron, F. and Kenderdine, S. (eds.) (2007). *Theorizing digital cultural heritage: a critical discourse*. Cambridge: MIT Press.

Churchill, E. and Ubois, J. (2008). Designing for digital archives. *Interactions*, 15(2), 10–13.

Eckerman, I. (2005). *The Bhopal saga: causes and consequences of the world's largest industrial disaster*. Hyderguda: Universities Press.

Friedman, B. and Nathan, L.P. (2010). Multi-lifespan information system design: a research initiative for the HCI community. *Proceedings of the 2011 ACM Conference on Human Factors in Computing System* (2243–46). New York: ACM.

Giaccardi, E. (2006). Collective storytelling and social creativity in the virtual museum. *Design Issues*, 22 (3), 29–41.

Giaccardi, E. and Palen, L. (2008). The social production of heritage through cross-media interaction: making place for place-making. *International Journal of Heritage Studies*, 14(3), 281–97.

Hagar, C. and Haythornthwaite, C. (2005). Crisis, farming and community. *The Journal of Community Informatics*, 1 (3), 41–52.

Haskins, E. (2007). Between archive and participation: public memory in a digital age. *Rhetoric Society Quarterly*, 37 (4), 401–22.

Hine, C. (2005). *Virtual methods: issues in social research on the Internet*. New York: Berg Publishers.

Jesiek, B.K. and Hunsinger, J. (2008). The April 16 archive: collecting and preserving memories of the Virginia Tech tragedy. In Agger, B. and Luke, T. (eds), *There is a gunman on campus: tragedy and terror at Virginia Tech*. Lanham: Rowman & Littlefield, pp. 185–206.

Kalay, Y., Kvan, T., and Affleck, J. (eds.) (2008). *New heritage: new media and cultural heritage*. New York: Routledge.

Kendra, J.M. and Wachtendorf, T. (2003). Reconsidering convergence and converger legitimacy in response to the World Trade Center disaster. In Clarke, L. (ed.), *Terrorism and disaster: new threats, new ideas*. New York: Elsevier, pp. 97–122.

Kirshenblatt-Gimblett, B. (2004). Intangible heritage as metacultural production. *Museum International*, 56 (1–2), 52–65.

Knabb, R.D., Rhome, J.R., and Brown, D.P. (2005). Tropical cyclone report: Hurricane Katrina: 23–30 August 2005. National Hurricane Center.

Landgren, J. (2006). Making action visible in time-critical work. *Proceedings of the Human Factors in Computing Conference* (201–210). New York: ACM.

Liu, S.B. (2010). Trends in distributed curatorial technology to manage data deluge in a networked world. *UPGRADE Journal: 2010 – Emerging Information Technologies (II)*, 11(3), 18–24.

Liu, S.B. (2011). Digital commemoration: surveying the social media revival of historical crises. *Proceedings of the Human Factors in Computing Conference*. New York: ACM.

NSF (2007). Cyberinfrastructure vision for 21st century discovery. Retrieved from: *http://www.nsf.gov/pubs/2007/nsf0728/nsf0728_1.pdf*. (Accessed on October 17, 2010.)

Oliver-Smith, A. and Hoffman, S. M. (2001). Introduction: why anthropologists should study disasters. In S.M. Hoffman and A. Oliver-Smith (eds.), *Catastrophe and culture: the anthropology of disaster*. Santa Fe: School of American Research Press, pp. 3–22.

Palen, L. and Liu, S.B. (2007). Citizen communications in crisis: anticipating a future of ICT-supported public participation. *Proceedings of the Human Factors in Computing Conference* (727–36). New York: ACM.

Palen, L., Vieweg, S., Liu, S.B., and Hughes, A. (2009). Crisis in a networked world: features of computer-mediated communication in the April 16, 2007 Virginia Tech event. *Social Science Computer Review: Special Issue e-Social Science*, 467–40.

Perrow, C. (1999). *Normal accidents: living with high-risk technologies*. Princeton: Princeton University Press.

Perrow, C. (2007). *The next catastrophe: reducing our vulnerabilities to natural, industrial, and terrorist disasters*. Princeton: Princeton University Press.

Sas, C. and Dix, A. (2006). Designing for collective remembering. *Proceedings of the Human Factors in Computing Conference* (1727–30). New York: ACM.

Sellen, A.J. and Whittaker, S. (2010). Beyond total capture: a constructive critique of lifelogging. *Communications of the ACM*, 53(5), 70–77.

Shen, C., Lesh, N.B., Vernier, F., Forlines, C. and Frost, J. (2002). Sharing and building digital group histories. *Proceedings of the Conference on Computer Supported Cooperative Work* (324–33). New York: ACM.

Silberman, N. (2008). The quest for 'essence' in digital heritage. In Kalay, Y., Kvan, T. and Affleck, J. (eds.), *New heritage: new media and cultural heritage*. London: Routledge, pp. 81–91.

Smith, L. (2006). *Uses of heritage*. London: Routledge.

Starbird, K., Palen, L., Hughes, A.L., and Vieweg, S. (2010). Chatter on the red: what hazards threat reveals about the social life of microblogged information. *Proceedings of the Conference on Computer Supported Cooperative Work* (241–50). New York: ACM.

Sylvester, J.L. (2008). *The media and Hurricanes Katrina and Rita: lost and found*. New York: Palgrave MacMillan.

Van House, N. and Churchill, E.F. (2008). Technologies of memory: key issues and critical perspectives. *Memory Studies*, 1(3), 295–310.

5

Information needs and seeking during the 2001 UK foot-and-mouth crisis

Christine Hagar

Abstract: This chapter reports on the findings of a study which explored the multiple information needs that faced the Cumbrian farming community in the north-west of England during the biggest foot-and-mouth disease outbreak to affect the UK farming system. The findings of this study highlighted the importance of: the changes in information needs at different stages of the crisis; the context in which information seeking took place; the overlap of information and emotional needs; the formal and informal channels of information seeking; farmers as information providers as well as information seekers; the sense-making approach to information seeking during the crisis; trusted information sources; the need for a mix of ICTs; ICTs as a catalyst for innovation, place and space and new venues and meeting places for communities in a crisis; and providing a local response to a national crisis.

Key words: foot-and-mouth disease, information seeking, information needs, information and communication technologies, crisis.

Introduction

This chapter reports on the findings of a study which explored the multiple information needs that faced the Cumbrian farming community in the north-west of England during the biggest foot-and-mouth (FMD) outbreak to affect the UK farming system.[1] The main research questions were: what were the information needs of farmers during the FMD crisis?; how did farmers seek information during the crisis?; and why was it difficult for farmers to acquire the information they needed during the crisis? This study also addressed the role of information and communication technologies (ICTs) in the crisis by asking the questions: how did farmers use ICTs to meet these information needs?; and how did ICTs support the Cumbrian community during the crisis (Hagar, 2009a)? A mixed-method approach was used to collect the data, which were gathered via semi-structured interviews with farmers and their families, members of the farming community network Pentalk (*www.pentalk.org*) and personnel from BBC Radio Cumbria. As well as interviews, data also came from a number of publicly available resources. Triangulation, i.e. drawing on different accounts, produced a fuller interpretation and understanding of the situation, enhancing the ability to address the research questions. Documents[2] gave supporting data to the interviews; insight into the national FMD picture; and reports of events and the experiences of farmers in other regions of the UK. Data were analyzed for the types of information farmers needed during the crisis, the sources and providers of information, sources of trusted information, the methods used to access the information, changes in the use of ICTs during the crisis, and the impact of ICTs on community building.

Findings

The findings of this study highlighted the importance of:

- changes in information needs at different stages of the crisis;
- the context in which information seeking took place;
- overlap of information and emotional needs;
- formal and informal channels of information seeking;
- farmers as information providers as well as information seekers;
- a sense-making approach to information seeking;
- trusted information sources;
- the need for a mix of ICTs;
- ICTs as a catalyst for innovation;
- place and space and new venues and meeting places for communities in a crisis; and
- providing a local response to a national crisis.

Before discussing each of these issues, it is useful to summarize the characteristics of the FMD crisis for comparative purposes, as no two crises are the same. Crises are 'an interruption in the reproduction of economic, cultural, social and/or political life' (Johnston, 2002: 123–5). The FMD outbreak was an interruption of all four. It affected the rural economy including agricultural markets, farmers' channels for communication, and social life, and destabilized the UK government. The nature and scale of the epidemic was unprecedented in modern farming history. Although FMD was similar to other crises in having economic and emotional impacts, it was unique in other respects. Unlike many other disasters, the FMD crisis was an animal disease crisis, and although not transferable to people, it had a major impact on the lives of Cumbrian farmers. Unlike many disasters, such as 9/11, the Asian Tsunami, or Hurricane Katrina, where the length of the crisis event is short, the FMD crisis lasted for over six months. It was a crisis that spread and no one knew when it would end. Also unique to the FMD crisis was the simultaneous impact on farmers' work and home worlds, since these were in the same place.

Changes in information needs at different stages of the crisis

Farmers' information needs can be divided broadly into two parts. First, information was required at the different stages of the crisis: at the beginning of the crisis farmers were desperate to know about the origin of the disease; identifying the disease; finding out where the disease was spreading and whose farms had been infected; information on eradication including the slaughter and disposal of animals, and information about cleansing of the farm. Secondly, information was required on the complex system of biosecurity measures introduced by the government.[3]

Context in which information seeking took place

It is important to recognize the sociocultural and political contexts in which farmers were seeking information. Farmers live in close-knit communities and are very much an oral community, where information is passed on by word of mouth. Information is acquired from family, immediate farming neighbors and other farmers who often live in the same valley. In the sociocultural context, farmers were physically isolated, their daily routines disrupted, unable to exchange information, gossip and 'crack' in their usual meeting places. Farmers' means of accessing their usual 'ecology of sources' (Williamson, 1998) changed. Their normal channels of communication were disrupted from one which was primarily face-to-face to one in which technologies were the main methods of communication. Normally, farmers know where to go for their information: they exchange information at auction marts, at farmers' discussion groups, in the pub, and in meeting each other during their work. In the crisis this changed; they were seeking information in an environment where many diverse actors, networks, and agencies were responding to the crisis.

In a political context, farmers were seeking information in an environment where government disease control measures were complex: policies and strategies were continuously being adjusted to deal with the emerging situation; legal requirements and implementation on the ground were subject to continual change in order to address problems as they developed. Farmers' information seeking was hindered by the government response, one which was severely criticized for shortcomings in the information gathering and processing and methods of communication (Anderson, 2002). Information from the government was often not forthcoming, was not delivered at the 'right' time and at the 'right' place, and was often contradictory. This study adds to McConnell and Stark's (2002) work, which argues that the management of crisis is often driven by 'politics' as opposed to 'rationality.'

Formal and informal channels of information seeking during the crisis

When information needs are not being met, in the intense conditions of a crisis people seek information in formal and informal channels. Four stages can be identified in the FMD crisis: 1) the initial stages of the crisis when farmers sought information from informal channels, through friends and neighboring farmers, when information from the government was not forthcoming; 2) as FMD spread and legislation was implemented farmers sought information from the formal channels of government agencies and vets; 3) a return to informal channels as information from the government was lacking, not timely, or contradictory; and 4) desperate for information, farmers resorted to formal and informal channels. One of the major findings of this research is that when formal channels of information do not answer questions informal channels fill the gap. In a crisis, informal channels of information become even more important as people seek information from people whom they know and trust. In addition, a two-way exchange happens, as the people seeking information also become the providers of information.

Sense-making approach to information seeking during the crisis

The findings of this study add to Dervin et al.'s (2003) sense-making approach to information seeking, as farmers were seeking meaning, an understanding of the crisis, not knowing how the disease spread and why the outbreak had occurred. They wanted to know why the crisis was happening. Did it really have to happen? How did FMD spread? Why did one farmer get it and not another? How had the virus got there in the first place? There were many gaps in the information; it conflicted with earlier information or information from other sources; and it was disseminated and received too late. Farmers were trying to create a narrative that made sense and to fill in the gaps of their information needs, by trying to interpret rumor and gossip. The crisis was an extremely emotional time for farmers, and ambiguity was accentuated by the emotional tensions that often made farmers unwilling to accept the facts or consequences. This study highlights that in the extreme conditions of a crisis, making sense of information becomes even more critical. Also, as information is spread via rumor and gossip it becomes exaggerated.

Overlap of information and emotional needs

While the focus of this research was farmers' information needs, one of the findings of the study was the overlap of social and emotional needs with information needs and vice versa. For example, farmers often began seeking information about how to deal with a particular process and would find themselves seeking information and social support at the same time. Alternatively, when farmers were seeking information they often found themselves being provided with emotional support. This follows Chatman's argument that people cross information boundaries when information is perceived to be critical (Chatman, 1991). As Figley (1985) argues, social support plays a critical role in people's abilities to cope with and recover from disaster. In a crisis, information providers become the providers of social support, and those in positions providing social support become information providers. It is important for this change of roles to be recognized in order to prepare individuals and organizations for future crises.

Trusted information sources

One of the key findings to emerge in answering the question of why it was so difficult to meet farmers' information needs was the need for trusted sources of information (Hagar, 2010). In a crisis, trusted information takes on greater significance. Decisions have to be made about which sources of information and which information providers to trust. These decisions were critical, as by acting upon trusted information, farmers could shape and influence the nature of the crisis. As distrust of the government intensified, an existing trust divide between farmers and the government intensified. Generally farmers trusted anyone who had a local connection (except local government) and with whom they were familiar. Further, during a crisis, individuals must deal with information overload, from official and multiple unofficial sources. This increases uncertainty and the difficulty of making decisions about who and what are trustworthy sources of information.

As farmers distrusted much of the information that reached them, this lack of trust led to people making up stories, rumors and gossip. Consequently, much of the information that farmers were seeking and receiving was second- and third-hand. In a crisis, it is difficult to ignore rumors and gossip, as people seek information and explanations. Key questions are how do we distinguish between rumor and gossip and information, and how do we decide how reliable is the information content?

The information uncertainty of the crisis and the need for confirmation that farmers were doing the 'right thing' influenced their patterns of information seeking. Uncertainty brought about a need to compare different information sources. Even though farmers began to distrust the information about infected farms that was published on the Department for Environment, Food and Rural Affairs (DEFRA) website, some still felt the need to continue checking the website. We need to consider: Do people trust face-to-face contexts more than other environments, for example the Internet? This is discussed later in this chapter.

Need for a mix of technologies

Farmers' use of technologies, and the ability of the technologies to cope with a high demand for information and social support during the outbreak, highlights the need for a mix of technologies to be available in a crisis, and the importance of having multiple responses and multiple supports. A range of technologies is needed to disseminate and communicate information, and different technological choices are needed to accommodate different user communities and user preferences. This study adds to Dutta-Bergman's (2004) argument that users of a medium that satisfies a particular functional need also to use other media types to fulfill that need. His notion of channel complementarity suggests that new media forms co-exist with traditional media forms in fulfilling specific communicative functions. In this study, farmers needed a mix of technologies to meet their information needs and to provide more channels of communication to accommodate users' preferred choice of technology.

At the outset of FMD, farmers' access to technologies varied. Few farmers had access to the Internet and others were unable to receive local radio reception. During the crisis, access to technologies was interrupted, as the telephone infrastructure could not cope with the quantity of calls, but access to other technologies, the Internet, and e-mail increased. Television may offer significant broadcast capabilities for information, but as this research shows, during the crisis, isolated farmers preferred to use a technology where they could interact and receive an instant response. This mix of technologies in a crisis also needs to be considered in other contexts where there are different access levels to ICTs.

The crisis became a catalyst for ICT innovation as alternative means for exchange of information were set up, such as the Radio Cumbria website, interactive radio programs, new helplines, and online diaries. As technologies of memory storage change, cultural understanding of crises may also change. For example, in this research, online diaries allowed the collection of data that helped interpret the crisis, and also leave a more permanent and available record for others to read.

One of the major challenges for farmers in their information seeking was assessing the trustworthiness of information. An area of research focuses on the relationship between technology and trust (Guerra et al., 2003; Kuriyan, Kitner, and Watkins, 2010; Mital, Israel, and Agarwal, 2010), asking questions such as: What is the effect of ICTs on trust? What effect does the Internet have on trust? A key assumption has been that the Internet will undermine trust because it eliminates face-to-face interaction. In the FMD crisis the majority of farmers were in the early adoption stage of using the Internet and were assessing the trustworthiness of the technology. Making this assessment in the context of a crisis made this a complex process.

Trust in online sources can be enhanced by effectively making information accessible on the web and in chatrooms (Ben-Ner and Putterman, 2002). Farmers who had the appropriate skills to interpret online information could enhance their ability to authenticate the value of information, thereby encouraging trust. However, others could be overwhelmed by the mass of information, creating an increased risk of negative outcomes from using the Internet. This raises concerns about the inequalities caused by variations in the skills of different social groups (Guerra et al., 2003), such as farmers. There are strong arguments that trust can be enhanced by making effective use of online social networks available through Internet-based interactions (Ben-Ner and Putterman, 2002; Monika, Israel and Agarwal, 2010), such as the Pentalk Network.[4] Thus, in a crisis it is important for new spaces to be created where people can exchange information and provide social support.

E-mail gave farmers another medium through which to talk, and enabled the quick dissemination of rumors and gossip. In a crisis, the Internet, particularly the use of social media tools, also allows rumors and gossip to be spread rapidly and globally (Frost, 2000; Hagar, 2009b). These tools increasingly have the capacity and power to inform, but also to misinform. Governments need to be aware of the power of these tools, their ability to circulate gossip and rumours, and their potential to create panic during crises.

How would ICTs be used in a future FMD crisis? Farmers talk to each other on their cell phones, Internet use is widespread, and broadband is now more widely available. However, interviews revealed that in another crisis, farmers would still consider the traditional technologies of the telephone and radio to be important. One of the recommendations of the Anderson Inquiry (2002) stated:

In any future outbreak, the local media should be used to the full. DEFRA should provide tailored information to local radio stations or local newspapers in time for their deadlines, working with the Government Office network and the Government News Network.

Cohen and Willis (2004) contend that:

Radio audiences seek out the medium following national trauma as a way in which to help bridge the gap between self and others, local and distant, and to create and identify with interpretive communities of listeners through attention to a unified message. (p. 595)

Community radio played a crucial role in crises such as the 1995 Great Hanshin (Kobe) Earthquake and the 2004 tsunami, and is recognized by UNESCO (2008) as an important media for information dissemination. During the FMD crisis, local radio was an extremely important source of information and social support for farmers. As Gardner has remarked (2003):

Sometimes looked down upon as the 'poor relation' of television, and certainly old-fashioned compared to the Internet, radio today has become the one to watch ... [a] portable communication medium, the most widespread and the most economic; proving itself versatile enough to go hand-in-hand with the Web.

Some argue that radio will remain the most important media and what makes radio particularly appealing is its interactivity, its capacity to provoke dialogue and to solicit the participation of local populations (World Association of Community Radio Broadcasters, n.d.).

Place and space and new venues and meeting places for communities in a crisis

The FMD crisis certainly created a kind of placelessness, as well as a new place in cyberspace, necessitated as physical meetings became impossible while human contact became essential, and sustainable via the Internet. The farming community is naturally geographically dispersed but at the same time has strong local ties. Yet this move into cyberspace occurred against the background of a very real and immediate attachment to place.

The crisis created a greater attachment to place as the impacts of the disease targeted farmers' local, physical region, one that many had farmed as families for generations. Yet it created a detachment from place as farmers were cut off from contact with other farms, family, and the rural community, and found refuge in phone and Internet connections. The crisis created a strengthened identification with physical place at the same time it denied access to that place, and as new technologies offered placeless interaction.

As a result of the crisis new spaces of interaction developed, and a new sense of community (Bennett et al., 2002; Wall, 2002). Pentalk created a virtual space where farmers formed a 'new' community during the crisis, creating new connections at a local level. Not only did new spaces emerge for social interaction but also new associations were established; for example, the Pentalk coordinators, when they could, met face-to-face to discuss the development of the network, thereby providing a new dimension to the increasingly restricted movement of the offline community. The offline and online communities were separate but also integrated (Hagar and Haythornthwaite, 2005), each supporting the other.

Along with specialized communities, people also belong to multiple communities: of work, family, interest, practice, etc., some enacted locally, but also globally. Internet connections made it possible for Cumbrian farmers to create and maintain global communities. Pentalk enabled the farmers to extend their work community internationally. Again, paradoxically, the need for international contact was driven by geographically local conditions.

ICTs as a catalyst for innovation during the crisis

As demonstrated by the Pentalk Network, the Internet can be used to set up a rapid-response website, designed to centralize and aid the control of information flow during a crisis, and providing crisis response updates. The significance of a crisis lies in the fact that it may produce a new fundamental outlook; it can be both a danger and an opportunity. Crises can create imbalanced, disorganized chaos or serve as a catalyst for new and positive changes such as the Pentalk community network described here. This is a particularly interesting study because the Pentalk Network was one of the few positive initiatives to have emerged from the FMD crisis. Pentalk helped contribute to the survival of farming in Cumbria during the crisis and post-crisis.

Providing a local response to a national crisis

The case study of the Pentalk Network gives valuable insight into how a local community responded to a major national crisis, serving a population for whom work and home were in the same place. The network served as more than just an information dissemination mechanism; it acted as an important resource and site for interpersonal contact, information dissemination, and information discussion, each of which were particularly important during the crisis. Pentalk serves as an example for community leaders and administrators of a successful innovation and a sustainable one.

There is a degree of skepticism about how real some community networking projects are. The major challenge confronting local community technology installations worldwide is how they can be sustainable in the longer term (Gurstein, 2001; Simpson 2005). Pentalk, which emerged from a crisis, has become sustainable and still exists in 2011. When the crisis ended, not only did the network carry on but also it rapidly spread to the whole of Cumbria. The attention paid to the social, cultural, and organizational contexts in which the network was developed and used have contributed to this success.

Pentalk's success may be attributable to its focus on the specific needs of the farming community, first by reacting in response to a crisis, and second by continuing to help in ways that directly address community needs. Keeping the scheme purely for farmers and aiming at providing basic skills has contributed to its success. Current training that addresses government demands for online reporting, and a continued focus on farm needs and farm activity, have continued to encourage farmers to become involved. Also important has been the way work has moved from a central organizer to local coordinators, people embedded in the farming community and conversant with its needs and members. This provides Pentalk with a base of engaged participants who are close to local needs, and again are responsive to contemporary informational and technology needs.

Discussions have been held with representatives from other counties as to how similar schemes could be set up in other parts of the UK. If networks similar to Pentalk could be replicated in other areas, then the farming community would be in a much better position to deal with a future animal disease crisis, should one occur. A new space created by Pentalk, called VetCall, has the potential to act as an early warning system should there be another occurrence of FMD. The creation of this online space allows farmers to receive and discuss the latest information online on unusual cases. Thus, Pentalk could help by providing a direct link between farmers and vets in identifying a new outbreak of FMD.

Community networks can play an important role in disseminating information and providing social support in crises. Lessons learned from this study of Pentalk can be implemented by other community networks involved in crisis response.

Acknowledgments

Special thanks to Ann Risman (Pentalk Organiser at the time of the study), Steve Pattinson (Pentalk Co-ordinator at time of study), members of the Pentalk Network, the Cumbrian farmers and other people interviewed for this study. May you never have to suffer such a crisis again.

Notes

1. FMD is an infectious viral disease affecting cloven-hoofed animals, in particular, cattle, sheep, pigs and goats. FMD spreads rapidly and is serious for animal health and for the economics of the livestock industry.
2. Reports from independent inquiries (non-government inquiries): The Cumbria Foot and Mouth Inquiry (2002), a proceeding which was also transmitted in its entirety by BBC Radio Cumbria (*www.bbc.co.uk/cumbria*); The Anderson Report (2002); The Royal Society Report (2002); the National Audit Office report (Bourn, 2002); and the European Parliament Temporary Committee on Foot and Mouth Disease (2002).

    The Warmwell independent website (*www.warmwell.com*), set up at the beginning of the crisis, which provides an archive of articles, reports, parliamentary proceedings and commentaries from individuals.

    The FMD archives of Penrith Public Library. A collection of newspaper cuttings from local and national newspapers.

    Personal diaries and accounts written in local and national newspapers (Plummer, 2001) were particularly useful for relating the farmers' individual daily and weekly stories and for mapping the changes in their needs and responses as the crisis progressed.

    Recordings of local radio news reports and programs, such as the BBC Radio Cumbria *Nightline* phone-in program broadcast during the crisis.

    One interviewee gave access to a unique collection of supplementary data: a collection of documents which they had received in the mail and via fax during the crisis. This female farmer had kept the documents as memorabilia for her grandchildren. These documents came mainly from MAFF (the former

Ministry of Agriculture, Fisheries and Food, which was dissolved in 2002) or DEFRA (the Department for Environment, Food and Rural Affairs) and included: MAFF/DEFRA newsletters; information leaflets; Public Information Fact Sheets; licenses, e.g. for the movement of cattle and for moving silage; instructions for enforcement measures; list of approved disinfectants; and local National Farmers Union (NFU) newsletters. This collection was particularly useful and original copies of licenses were seen which farmers had referred to in the interviews. Also the documents from MAFF/DEFRA enabled the content of information sheets to be viewed, along with instructions etc. described in the interviews, and showed the method by which information was disseminated to farmers. Photocopies were taken of these documents, allowing me to refer to them during my research.

3. Restrictions were imposed on the movement of all animals and carcasses except under license, and on markets, fairs, 'gatherings of animals,' and hunting activities. Of particular note was the use of 3km-radius 'protection zones' and 10km-radius 'surveillance' zones,' in which there were various restrictions on the movement of animals, people, and equipment, as well as on other activities. Complicated licensing procedures were introduced to control animal movements. When farmers requested to move stock, for example for grazing purposes, vets had to issue licenses. The vet assessed where farmers wanted to move the animals and then MAFF/DEFRA approved or disapproved the movement. Another element of disease control was the introduction by farmers, individuals, businesses, and organizations (e.g. Cumbria County Council) of disinfectant footbaths or mats, usually situated at the entrance to a property.

4. The Pentalk Network was a community network constructed at a time of the FMD crisis with the aid of farmers. It was set up to provide computers and IT training (particularly e-mail and the Internet) for farmers and their families at the height of the FMD crisis. It was clear that farmers needed to become computer literate very rapidly and that, often, they could not afford to buy a computer. They needed to be provided with one and they needed to be taught to use it speedily, in a way that provided them with functional skills. Pentalk supplied re-conditioned computers to farmers free of charge for six months, after which they could buy them for approximately US $450 or return them at no charge. Initial funding for the scheme came from a start-up grant from the UK Learning and Skills Council, which was matched by the Rural Development Programme. Further funding came from the Department for Education and Skills (DfES). A Pentalk office was set up at the Penrith auction mart, which is normally the focus of the farming community. Pentalk served to connect farmers across Cumbria, by providing them with access to the Internet, e-mail, and links via their web pages, where farmers could access news and information available from government and other sources on the spread of the disease.

References

Anderson, I. (2002). *Foot and mouth disease 2001: Lessons to be learned – inquiry report*. No. HC 888. London: The Stationery Office.

Ben-Ner, A. and Putterman, L. (2002). Trust in the new economy. HRRI Working Paper No. 11–02). University of Minnesota: Industrial Relations Center.

Bennett, K., Carroll, T., Lowe, P., and Phillipson, J. (2002). *Coping with crisis in Cumbria: The consequences of foot-and-mouth disease.* Centre for Rural Economy Research Report: University of Newcastle upon Tyne.

Bourn, J. (2002). *The 2001 outbreak of foot and mouth disease.* Report by the Comptroller and Auditor General. HC 939 Session 2001–2002: 21 June 2002. London: The Stationery Office.

Chatman, E.A. (1991). Life in a small world: applicability of gratification theory to information-seeking behavior. *Journal of the American Society for Information Science,* 42(6), 438–49.

Cohen, E.L. and Willis, C. (2004). One nation under radio: Digital and public memory after September 11. *New Media and Society,* 6, 591–610.

Committee on the Internet under crisis conditions. (2003). The Internet under crisis conditions: Learning from September 11th. National Research Council. Retrieved 3 June, 2011, from *http://www.nap.edu/books/0309087023/html.*

Dervin, B., Loreman-Wernet, L., and Lauterbach, E. (eds.) (2003). *Sense-making methodology reader: Selected writings of Brenda Dervin.* Cresskill, NJ: Hampton Press.

Dutta-Bergman, M.J. (2004). Interpersonal communication after 9/11 via telephone and internet: A theory of channel complementarity. *New Media and Society,* 6(5), 659–73.

European Parliament Temporary Committee on Foot and Mouth Disease (2002). Draft report to control measures in the European Union in 2001 and future measures to prevent and control animal diseases in the European Union. (2002/2153(INI)). Retrieved June 6, 2011, from *http://www.europarl.org.uk/ section/2002-archive/foot-and-mouth-disease-european-parliament-debate-final-report.*

Figley, C.R. (1985). Traumatic stress: The role of the family and social support system. In C.R. Figley (ed.), *Trauma and its wake.* New York: Brunner/Mazel, pp. 39–56.

Frost, C. (2000). Tales on the Internet: Making it up as you go along, *Aslib Proceedings,* 52 (1), 5–10.

Gardner, C. (2003). The one to watch: Radio, new ICT's and interactivity. Retrieved January 26, 2011, from *http://comunica.org/1-2-watch.*

Guerra, G.A., Zizzo, D.J., Dutton, W.H., and Peltu, M. (2003). *Economics of trust in the information economy: Issues of identity, privacy and security.* Oxford: Oxford Internet Institute. Retrieved June 3, 2011, from *http://www. oii.ox.ac.uk/resources/publications/RR1.pdf.*

Gurstein, M. (2001). Community informatics for flexible networking. In L. Keeble, and B.D. Loader (eds.), *Community informatics: Shaping computer-mediated social relations.* New York: Routledge, pp. 263–83.

Hagar, C. (2009a). Technology: The information and social needs of Cumbrian farmers during the UK 2001 FMD outbreak and the role of information and communication technologies (ICTs). In B. Nerlich, Brigitte and M. Doring (eds.), *The social and cultural impact of foot and mouth disease in the UK in 2001: Experiences and analyses* (ESRC Science in Society Programme). Manchester: Manchester University Press.

Hagar, C. (2009b). Information in isolation: gossip and rumor during the UK 2001 foot and mouth crisis – lessons learned. *Libri*, 59(4), 228–37.

Hagar, C. (2010). 'Whom do you trust? Information seeking during the U.K. foot and mouth crisis', *Library and Archival Security*, 2(1), 3–18.

Hagar, C. and Haythornthwaite, C. (2005). Crisis, farming and community. *Journal of Community Informatics*, 3. Retrieved June 3, 2011, from *http://www.ci-journal.net/index.php/ciej/article/view/246/211*.

ISIC (Information Seeking in Context). (2010). Retrieved March 6, 2011, from *http://www.um.es/isic2010/*.

Johnston, R.J. (2002). *Dictionary of human geography*. 4th ed. Oxford: Blackwell, pp. 123–5.

Kuhlthau, C.C. (1999). Information seeking in context (ISIC). *Information Processing and Management*, 35, 723–890.

Kuriyan, R., Kitner, K., and Watkins, J. (2010). ICTs, development and trust: an overview. *Information Technology and People*, 23(3), 216–21.

McConnell, A. and Stark, A. (2002). Foot and mouth 2001: The politics of crisis management. *Parliamentary Affairs*, 55, 664–83.

Mital, M., Israel, D., and Agarwal, S. (2010) Information exchange and information disclosure in social networking websites: Mediating role of trust. *Learning Organization*, 17(6), 479–90.

Plummer, K. (2001). *Documents of life 2*. London: Sage Publications.

Royal Society. (2002). *Infectious diseases in livestock*. Policy document 19/02. London: The Royal Society.

Simpson, L.E. (2005). Community informatics and sustainability: Why social capital matters, *Journal of Community Informatics*, 1(2).

UNESCO (2008). Pioneering community radio: impacts of IPDC assistance in Nepal Retrieved April 5, 2011, from *http://unesdoc.unesco.org/images/0015/001585/158500e.pdf*.

Wall, M. (2002). Online lifeline for farmers. *Sunday Times*, November 10, 51.

Williamson, K. (1998). Discovered by chance: The role of incidental information acquisition in an ecological model of information use. *Library and Information Science Research*, 20(1), 23–40.

World Association of Community Radio Broadcasters (n.d.). Retrieved March 8, 2011, from *http://www.idrc.ca/uploads/user-S/11606750491Sheet12_Radio.pdf*.

6

The Ericsson Response – a ten-year perspective: in the light of experience

Sarah Gannon

Abstract: In this chapter we endeavor to draw some basic conclusions about the information and communication needs which emerge and evolve in the different stages of a humanitarian emergency or crisis and about the factors which inhibit full effectiveness of the aid agencies' response. We also include a critique of the role played by Ericsson Response and by commercial organizations generally in providing communications infrastructure and support at times of humanitarian crisis, identifying some systemic weaknesses and opportunities for improvement. Looking to the future, we advance some recommendations aimed at enhancing current response models to further improve performance in crisis information management, and speculate as to the potential for engaging some leading-edge and experimental technologies in transforming the effectiveness of disaster response from an information and communication perspective.

Key words: Ericsson, United Nations, disaster response, emergency response, humanitarian crisis, information and communication technologies.

A brief history of ER

Ericsson Response (ER) was established in 1999 with the aim of providing communications technology support to international aid agencies working in disaster recovery and humanitarian crisis situations. Ericsson's core expertise in the development and deployment of telecommunications systems, in both radio and fixed networks, was the bedrock on which the initiative was founded. A cohort of Ericsson Response Volunteers was assembled from the large and internationally diverse pool of Ericsson employees who were enthused by the concept and driven by a desire to 'make a difference'. ER's first director, Dag Nielsen, who held the post from 1999 to 2005, set about establishing strong links to UN aid agencies. Volunteers were trained and prepared for missions to deploy containerized GSM (Mobile Radio) Systems and the specially developed WIDER (Wireless Data Network) System into areas of natural disaster or humanitarian crisis where telecommunications infrastructure was disabled or lacking.

Some basic facts about ER today

ER today is a standby partner with the United Nations Children's Fund (UNICEF), the UN Office for Coordination of Humanitarian Affairs (UNOCHA), and the UN's World Food Program (UNWFP), operating on a par with other humanitarian governmental and non-governmental organizations (GOs and NGOs) such as RedR (Australia), the Norwegian Refugee Council (NRC), and the Danish Refugee Council (DRC). From an Ericsson corporate perspective, ER is an implemented and working example of strategic philanthropy. At the time of writing, Ericsson is the only commercial organization to have achieved this level of integration and successful inter-working with the UN agencies. ER has built up a track record of contributing to major humanitarian aid initiatives, including deployments during the aftermath of the Asian tsunamis in the Indonesian Province of Banda Aceh (2004–5) and more recently in response to the situation in earthquake-devastated areas of Haiti (2010).

ER operates through a basic concept of voluntary (and temporary) service by a pool of volunteers, internationally distributed, and with a 'light' headquarters function, taking care of internal and external communication, coordination, logistics, training, and equipment support. ER is today headed by a senior Ericsson manager, Rima Qureshi, who holds significant organizational responsibilities in the business dimension in addition to her ER role.

Number of volunteers: c. 140

Number of missions completed: c. 40

Largest single mission: Haiti

HQ staff: 3 (2 employees and one external contractor)

Equipment:

GSM Radio Systems: 7

WIDER Systems: 6

Ten years of learning

ER has been a learning organization at every stage of its development, as those involved have sought to make their contribution more effective and more relevant in complex, and sometimes confusing and cumbersome, international structures for the coordination of humanitarian response. In particular, the collective experience of volunteers in the field and of those involved in the coordination and management of the ER initiative has provided some key insights about information and communication needs and the associated technology requirements at the different stages of a mission. These insights, together with the experience of the Humanitarian Reform Initiative (2005), have provided a focus and an agenda for improvement efforts in the further evolution and refinement of response structures and activities.

Key issues in emergency response phase 1: first response (days 1–14)

Security prerequisites and self-sufficiency in communications

Common to all phases, and the number one priority, is security communications. The UN uses a formal set of definitions for levels of security risk. At each level there are clear requirements regarding the type of communication that must be available for all UN agencies. These requirements include radio (VHF/UHF) in the local area, all vehicles to be fitted with radios, and a radio room with satellite phone and/or basic data communications capability, for example satellite broadband (BGAN).

Today, satellite systems and private (i.e. closed user-group) radio networks are perceived to be the most reliable voice communication options. Public telecommunications systems tend to be problematic for the relief effort as emergencies routinely cause a significant increase in public communications, leading to congestion and an inconsistent service. Often, the public network suffers damage in the emergency event itself. For both these reasons it is best if the relief effort quickly becomes self-sufficient from a communications perspective.

The needs of first responders

First responders need accurate factual information about the current situation on the ground: the extent of the disaster; the number of people and geographical area affected; and the location, area of expertise, and capacity of other humanitarian organizations in the area.

In this context, voice communication capability in the immediate disaster area is the primary requirement. It needs to be rapid, frequent, and reliable to allow a valid situation analysis to be performed, immediate priorities for rescue and relief efforts to be defined, and new arrivals to be effectively integrated and deployed.

Another crucial consideration is that first responders on site need to quickly formulate and communicate their project plans and associated logistics so that these can be integrated into the all-important work of resourcing the operation, defining the mission's objectives and what is required to achieve them. If this information is not correct at the beginning, the inevitable consequence is that there will be loss of life. Agencies and their response teams will almost always have their own routines and protocols for internal communication and organization and will sometimes bring infrastructure components of their own, satellite phones and VHF radio being the most common.

Inter-agency communication

Inter-agency communication on site, to HQ, and to the outside world is best addressed by system solutions. Specifically, rapid access to and usability of shared systems, such as Local and Wide Area Voice and Data Networks, are major determinants of first-response effectiveness in the vital early days of the emergency. While pervasive and good-quality voice communication remains the *sine qua non* of Phase 1 response, the availability of data communication facilities offers an infinitely richer set of options to the agencies on site. The capability to transmit and receive images and text, such as maps, photographs, measurements, and technical data of all kinds (medical, engineering, topographical, etc.), can help the effectiveness of relief efforts to grow exponentially during the early days of the response.

Challenges: system establishment and ongoing management

Speed of deployment is critical and it is vital to minimize time lost in the approval and supply chain for the emergency telecoms response. On the one hand the coordinating agency needs to be prompt and decisive in requesting support while the provider needs to be geared up for the most rapid logistical response. The traffic-carrying capacity of the voice and data systems deployed also needs to be adequately dimensioned to sustain the services which the agencies require in the immediate area and with respect to global connectivity. Thus, pre-emptive capacity management activities need to be bundled into the response 'package' so that systems do not become overloaded and ineffective as demands increase.

Challenges: user competence

Two issues which can inhibit and dilute the positive impact of communications technology in the Phase 1 response, however, are compatibility between systems and the technical competence of users. This is particularly so in the area of data communications, where systems can rarely be deployed on a 'plug and play' basis and users often need a basic level of know-how to be able to troubleshoot the simpler, more common problems in connecting to and using a Wireless Data Network. Setting up shared data services is not easily achieved.

Where access to expert support is limited, agencies find themselves unable to benefit from the available infrastructure and are likely to fall back on 'old reliables', leaving the more advanced and functionally rich solutions unused. In this context the establishment of user support and help desk functions by the response providers can be of real and immediate benefit. One pivotal shift in the mindset, which has yet to be fully achieved, is the move from a reliance on paper-based communication to fully embracing electronic and paperless ways of working.

Challenges: interoperability

Inter-system compatibility is a further issue. Here we face one of the core technological dilemmas, in that the very diversity of systems and solutions that is such a driver of creativity and innovation in the commercial sphere becomes a handicap and inhibitor of effective wide-scale deployment in the more focused context of emergency response. De facto standards are helpful in this regard, in areas like database structures (e.g. SQL compatibility) and computer operating systems (e.g. Windows, Linux), but probably the most powerful emerging lingua franca of the telecommunications world for the second decade of the new millennium is IP, the Internet Protocol.

Focus on coordination

This matter of standardization is not limited in its operation and effect merely to the matter of technical specifications of equipment and systems, but extends also to the processes, information exchange formats, and ways of working employed by the vast array of aid agencies active in the world today. In this context, what is optimal for the individual organization or agency can become sub-optimal for the relief effort as a whole. Entities like UNOCHA play a major role here and work continuously to achieve a balance between the all-important freedom to act of the individual agency and the need to maintain effective cooperation and inter-working across the whole effort. Waste (whether in terms of time, energy, physical and technological resources or, indeed, money) is to some degree inevitable in the fraught and fast-changing environment of a disaster relief effort, but investment in structures for cooperation and standardization can offset the more negative consequences here.

Key issues in emergency response phase 2: establishment (days 15–30)
The needs of second-phase responders

In the Establishment phase, the emphasis shifts to stabilizing, interconnecting, and expanding the capacity and capability of the systems deployed during the First Response phase.

As the relief effort expands the number of responders increases, and while the requirements on communication technologies increase, the system used during the first phase must be scalable.

Responders in the second phase need to be concerned with supporting and facilitating this expansion, and will typically need to create a kind of 'back office' infrastructure to increase efficiency and effectiveness of the front line activities.

Challenges: data management

Volumes of communication and data flows increase rapidly during the Establishment Phase and rudimentary systems for organizing and sifting data and for producing summarized information for management and control must be quickly developed. Data on infrastructure, environment, displaced and missing persons, those requiring medical assistance, status and needs relating to supply and distribution of food, the provision of shelter, etc., are all part of the overall emerging picture.

For all of these data flows it is most helpful to have standardized protocols for frequency and content of reporting, supported by common data structures and transaction handling routines, shareable on an inter-agency basis. UN agencies by virtue of their experience and size tend to lead the way in this regard and it is the role of contributors like ER to provide expertise to deploy, fine tune, and support the chosen data management systems at the implementation level.

Challenges: user support and system optimization

One of the main ICT support challenges during the Establishment Phase is to operate a cycle of continuous improvement, adaptation, and relentless optimization of systems and infrastructure – and to do so at speed. This activity encompasses teaching and supporting users to make the most of the technology which is already available to them and can take the form of conducting 'just in time' induction and training sessions for new arrivals, distributing simple instructions, tips and techniques to get the most from available technology, and operating help desk type services for more complex user problems and requirements.

In parallel with this there is the constant need to expand system capacity, optimize system elements such as radio frequency and coverage, and maximize inter-operability between systems – often through the provision of Internet access and other IP-based services for data sharing and transfer.

Key issues in emergency response phase 3: consolidation (days 30+)

The needs of third-phase responders

By Phase 3, communications capability and infrastructure have typically returned to normal, meaning they have been restored to a level comparable to that before the emergency began. In developing countries, of course, this 'normal' status may still entail capacity limitations, service interruptions, etc., on an ongoing basis. Third-phase responders tend to be deployed in supporting follow-up operations dealing with some of the longer-lasting effects of the emergency (examples include reconstruction after a natural disaster, de-mining after a military conflict, etc.). For private sector contributors such as ER, the tasks involved and the applicable skill sets are often similar to those required in normal commercial operations.

Challenges: supply chain

The principal challenges in Phase 3 response relate to the supply chain for tools, equipment, and spare parts. Engineers are accustomed to having ready access to the materials they need to carry out their tasks, and when faced with uncertain and inefficient logistics will inevitably suffer a drop in effectiveness and output. It is often the case that simple component shortages will prevent time-limited mission objectives from being fulfilled.

Volunteers with the capacity to improvise and innovate, to some extent, will overcome these difficulties, but overall the effect will still be sub-optimal. Meticulous preparation and the bundling of tools and spares in the form of well-designed 'kits' is of assistance here, as is the collective experience and lessons learned from previous missions. Good advice is often to assume and prepare for the worst.

Challenges: sociopolitical context

It is a frustrating but unavoidable characteristic of disaster and emergency situations, particularly in developing countries, that the extent to which full recovery is possible is constrained by sociopolitical factors. The aid agencies and the technologists in organizations like ER cannot engage in social transformation and 'nation-building' initiatives as part of their response. Their mandate does not extend to social change or political reform and, accordingly, they will always be constrained by the prevailing power structure and sociopolitical norms of the large society around the disaster area. Diplomacy and an ability to access and act on the advice of local agencies and community representatives can mitigate, but not fully overcome, this constraint.

It's all about communication

'It's about communication between people; the rest is technology.' It's a truism, but one worth remembering and repeating, that communication is the vital enabler (and inhibitor) of all human endeavor. The ER experience affirms that the effectiveness of a disaster response increases in direct proportion to the quality of communication among all those involved. Other factors, such as readiness, equipment and logistics, security, etc., are hugely influential, but communication is the unifying theme which brings and keeps everything together. While ER is primarily a technology-based contribution, it is worth reflecting on the fundamental communication needs which this technology is deployed to serve.

Communication needs at the human level

These needs are the most consistent and easy to describe, remaining more or less unchanged at all times and in all places. They simply acquire a greater level of urgency and importance in an emergency context. At the level of the individual contributor in an emergency response situation, there is always an information and communication deficit. The setting is unfamiliar, often uncomfortable, sometimes dangerous, and always rapidly changing. The individual's efforts to function effectively are informed by continuous internal and external questioning on the fundamental themes of What, Where, Who, When, How, and Why.

Much of this information and communication deficit is improved by command structures and the team context in which the individual contributor operates. Accordingly, almost by definition, a command structure and team which is enabled to exchange information and instructions continuously, and in real time, will go a long way to meeting the needs at the individual level. However, consideration must also be given to the vital component of individual initiative, the power and the imperative of independent action. There are many aspects of the disaster and emergency context where the judgment on how to act and what to prioritize rest firmly with the person 'on the ground'. Disconnected from command structures and the team, the individual will still need to access information, draw conclusions, and inform about situations encountered and actions taken – the more varied and flexible the options, the better.

Communication needs at the institutional level

Communication needs at the organizational or institutional level pivot on two factors, namely scalability and control.

Scalability

The build-up of resources and capability at the site of a disaster or humanitarian emergency is a difficult balance between maintaining stability in the relief effort and its effects, while at the same time increasing, sometimes exponentially, the quantity and scope of activity. Frequent and accurate communication of status, emerging needs, and the impact of the ramping-up effort is essential for those who are controlling the inflow of people, equipment, and materials.

Equally, when it is time to begin ramping down the relief effort, whether because more pressing needs have emerged elsewhere or because the goals of the particular mission have been achieved, decommissioning must be done in an orderly manner. Ongoing activities and the rebuilding of indigenous communication systems must be taken into account.

Control

An emergency will require the relief operation to continuously reconfigure activities, scale up, down, or change location and focus in response to evolving circumstances. Individuals and teams, therefore, are often required to divert from proximate and well-understood local goals and apply their effort and expertise elsewhere in response to requirements which are not immediately visible to them. This situation generates two needs from a communication perspective at the institutional level:

1. The 'institution' (e.g. Agency HQ, inter-agency coordination function, etc.) needs a continuous flow of status information/situation reports

which from its central position can be integrated and evaluated to help prioritize and direct activities to maximum effect.

2. The individual or team relies on the institution for context, for the 'big picture' information, about where their activities fit in the overall jigsaw of response and most importantly for a coherent rationale for the instructions and directives they are receiving from the centre.

A note on stakeholders

An adequate and constant flow of funding is the necessary prerequisite for sustaining every relief effort. While structures for mobilizing inputs from donor nations and NGOs are well established, there is always the requirement that such stakeholders get regular, accurate, and (where possible) reassuring information on how their money is being spent. Situation reports – frequent, comprehensive, and integrated to form a clear and communicable picture of the progress of the relief effort – are therefore a core and consistent part of the communication needs at the institutional level.

Communication technologies: what they can and can't do

Communication technologies, given the state of technological development which has been attained today, can facilitate more or less any form and volume of interaction between any number of individuals and organizations active in a disaster zone or at the focal point of a relief effort. Practical limitations apply, however, and these mostly relate to what can be conceptualized as the base of the logistical pyramid by which the deployment of advanced communications systems is enabled.

The extent of the destruction and attendant chaos at the relief site itself, and the availability of skilled staff to deploy suitable communication systems to support the operation are all factors which potentially limit the effectiveness of the technological response. To this extent, when we speak of a response capability we mean not just the technology itself but the resources and expertise to deploy it, sustain it, and use it to maximum beneficial effect in the particular circumstance of the relief zone.

Opportunities for improvement

Overall, our ten years of experience in assisting at the front line of disaster relief and humanitarian aid initiatives have yielded some satisfaction that our capability in information and communications technology has delivered real benefits to the aid agencies and the people they serve, but at the same time we are left with the feeling that we can do better still. 'Do few things, but do them well' is advice often heard but not so often heeded, but in that spirit we offer some suggestions about where improvements could be targeted.

Improving partnership

Remembering that ER is an exercise in strategic philanthropy and corporate social responsibility, and not the company's core business, it is essential for ER to maintain alignment with the overall Ericsson market vision and supporting strategies. Communications technology, while recognized as a key enabler, is manifestly not the core business of the humanitarian agencies. Clearly, potential exists for mutually beneficial partnerships with providers from the private sector.

ER has succeeded in becoming a standby partner for many of the UN humanitarian agencies and, accordingly, has earned the opportunity to build cooperative initiatives with them in the formulation and deployment of communication technology strategies, based on Ericsson core competence, but informed by the experience and operational needs of the agencies themselves. For this possibility to bear full fruit, there must be more emphasis on collaboration and joint development, re-use of lessons learned in emergency crisis operations, and a better analysis and understanding of everyday communication needs. Essentially, the partnership needs to evolve. Unfortunately, such evolution is hampered by some natural, but not well-grounded, fears that commercial interests must in the end prevail and that the private sector always has a hidden agenda.

Within the defined boundaries of budget and ambition level which are a natural part of all commercial engagements, there is considerable room for flexibility and integration of effort. Topics worth exploring are numerous, but one immediately fruitful area to address would be the relatively short 'window of availability' (but coupled with high expertise) of the ER volunteer, typically limited to four to six weeks, compared to the typical four to six months' continuous commitment available from non-commercial GOs and NGOs.

Active and strategic partnership management in the ICT area will see agencies work closely with the standby partners to constantly monitor emergency response requirements, to encourage partners in new technology areas, and to synchronize volunteer competence to what is required by the missions. The evaluation and monitoring of volunteer competence and performance by the aid agencies is an underdeveloped area in the current stage of partnership evolution. Direct and candid feedback is essential to ensure improvement, and private-sector contributors will have no objection to meeting strict criteria on volunteer capability and field performance.

Improving organization

There are two main components here, namely volunteer coordination (rostering) and solution management (technology development). Volunteer coordination involves effective synchronization of the size and availability of the volunteer base in the standby partners with the mission needs of the partnering agencies. To ensure the quality and reliability of the volunteer roster, recruitment criteria need to be better defined and integrated with in-company employee development. Within the enterprise, this also means coordination with local management to maximize the positive impact of hosting volunteers in their organizations. Ways of measuring this positive impact also need to be examined.

Solution management involves improved and more active collaboration for emergency communication technology preparedness. Away from the white heat of the mission scenario, current and emerging communication requirements during a crisis response can be better aligned and understood, with respect to functionality offered by available and emerging technologies.

The Humanitarian Reform Initiative in 2005 created a new organizational structure to address deficiencies in the area of emergency response. One important outcome was the clarification and improved specification of roles and accountabilities during such operations.

Another significant outcome affecting ER was the birth of the Emergency Telecom Cluster, supported by clear statements about services to be provided and how the services should relate to each defined phase of the emergency response. Five years on, however, it is not clear how successful the cluster concept has been and additional changes introduced in 2010 have still to show their effects. Overall, the concept should lead to better communication, but old ways of working need to be reformed before the new approaches can become reality.

Improving information access

The rules governing information management in crisis situations are quite well defined, but there remains the problematic question of access. The challenge is not just to spread information but to do it in a secure way, being able to quickly adjudicate on what information can be open for all and what needs to be restricted so as not to compromise the affected population and the initial responders.

Most governments require that all communication is open, while among UN agencies the UN High Commission for Refugees (UNHCR) is the only UN humanitarian agency that has the mandate to protect its direct beneficiaries, and therefore can encrypt its communication. But even UNHCR cannot fully assure the privacy of its own access where it uses a third party to manage its information. The technology exists to provide effective information security at multiple levels while still respecting host government requirements, but close cooperative effort will be required between agency and standby partners to achieve an optimal implementation.

Improving technology

One stark and basic fact governs technology in an emergency context. If the technology cannot provide a reliable service during an emergency it will not be used. Reliability is paramount. Equally important is ease of use and familiarity. The most successful systems are those which conform to or mimic the everyday experience and basic technical competence of the non-technologist.

Most large-scale natural disasters occur in developing countries, and developing countries typically represent a worst-case scenario with regard to technology infrastructure. Hurricane Katrina, in the southern part of the USA, was an exception and a root cause analysis of communication failures during this emergency suggests that it was information management and not communication technologies that ultimately proved deficient. Most first-world countries will have geographically redundant networks and a certain level of disaster preparedness in place. The available networks have extra capacity to manage traffic peaks (New

Year's Eve being a routine example). This is not the case in developing countries, where most networks are under-dimensioned and under-funded. More often than not there is little in the way of network redundancy in place.

When disaster strikes, it is normal for all forms of communication to fail quickly and often completely during the first 72 hours. The humanitarian response must therefore rely on satellite and simple radio communication. Knowing this to be the case, the private sector can be encouraged to work via corporate social responsibility programs with disaster preparation in cooperation with local operators in at-risk areas. In parallel, work can proceed at the strategic level to define via the global humanitarian partnerships (e.g. the Emergency Telecoms Cluster, ETC) the most suitable technologies for use during an emergency response. Once such technologies are identified and agreed there should be a clear development roadmap, acceptance testing and proving program, etc., before it is introduced in the field. Solutions should demonstrably satisfy agreed performance goals with respect to reliability, coverage, speed, etc.

Pushing the boundaries
Self-imposed limitations

The scope of what is possible in the technology of information and communications today far exceeds that of the deployments which have thus far been attempted. It seems that there is a reluctance among technology providers, and not just in the ICT domain, to make available their very latest and most advanced components and services. Companies are prepared to deploy products which are 'leading edge', and in some cases not fully proven, in a variety of settings. These include in sport, in high-visibility trials and challenges of various kinds, in road shows and in proof-of-concept demonstrations, and in all kinds of customer field trials and marketing initiatives. This is sometimes risky, as the chances of failure are higher than when using exhaustively tested and mass-market-ready solutions.

Where rewards are high in terms of publicity, enhanced company image, and high profit potential, the risk is deemed to be very much worth taking. Indeed, it is often the case that only in extreme, stressed, and unpredictable conditions can the real quality, robustness, and capability of a system be fully exercised. It seems paradoxical that commercial organizations are reluctant to expose their most advanced technologies in the most challenging and unpredictable of all contexts, namely in disaster relief and emergency humanitarian assistance. There is arguably no single reason for this reluctance but rather a combination of at least two significant factors: cost and the fear of failure.

Limiting factors

Cost

Philanthropy has been described as 'the gift that keeps on giving,' but for a commercial enterprise, no matter how well intentioned and altruistic, there cannot be a limitless commitment. Companies dip into their corporate pockets certainly, some indeed dig deep, but the giving is calibrated and controlled as but one more component of the corporate cost base – budgeted, monitored, and routinely re-evaluated like any other expenditure. It is here that the concept of clusters (ER, for example, belongs to the ETC) is most beneficial. The cluster concept groups organizations, both commercial and non-commercial, according to the roles, disciplines, or technologies through which they contribute. Properly employed, clusters provide for sharing of effort and resources to sustain a more resilient capability, strength in depth, and a useful counterweight to donor fatigue.

Incidentally, the involvement of multiple organizations from a common business sector also engenders a benign form of competition where participants are naturally motivated to exceed each other's efforts, due to the normal competitive tendencies inherent in their status as commercial enterprises.

Reluctance to fail

Fear of failure is a more complex influencing factor. Advanced technologies form a continuum of stability, with those at the very leading edge being the most high-performing, but at the same time the most prone to failure. There is always the potential for negative publicity and impact on customer perception, resulting from system failures or from the exposure of technical or functional flaws. This makes technology providers naturally risk-averse in situations where there is high potential for reputational damage. Arguably, a disaster zone is a situation where it is safer to stick with the tried and trusted, with the older, more reliable but less functionally rich products and solutions.

There is also of course the very valid fear of inflicting damage on a relief effort, or of failing the victims in potentially catastrophic ways, through the deployment of unproven and unstable technologies. Yet, there is also the converse view, that in the crucible of a humanitarian crisis, the contributing organization should come equipped with the 'best of the best', sparing no effort to deploy all the potential at its disposal to support the relief effort.

Potential for exploiting the leading edge

Were we to put aside these self-imposed limitations and limiting factors and simply seize the available and emerging technology and deploy it, so to speak, 'without fear', then a rich range of possibilities emerges. We would use the full functionality of available systems today and, to take radio as an example, systems would move rapidly from 2G (typically voice and some data capability) deployments, through 3G (voice, full data, and some video capability), into LTE (Long Term Evolution) systems with rich multimedia capability based on data speeds an order of magnitude greater than those available today. We would also move increasingly from person-to-person to machine-to-machine communication. Two examples illustrate this.

Full video capability in the field

Consider the benefits of equipping first responders with communications devices (Smartphone or equivalent) enabled for interactive video transmission. Improvements in early situational assessments and a transformative impact on emergency medical response would be among the immediate benefits. Add GPS capability and Internet access and the first responder becomes intimately connected to an array of location-based services from a single, portable device routing support of all kinds directly to the point of need.

Intelligent, always-on collection of measurements

The telecommunications marketplace today pursues growth not just in terms of numbers of connected subscribers, but also in terms of numbers of connected devices. Indeed, based on currently available applications, the already identified market potential for devices exceeds that of human users in a ratio of 10:1. These intelligent, always-on devices, sending and receiving data continuously, can be used to collect and transmit data on a variety of physical and environmental characteristics of the disaster or emergency zone. Air and water quality, temperature, toxicity, etc. are examples of the data collectable by these static and mobile probes, creating the potential to multiply the effectiveness of the human teams deployed and to contribute to increased safety and a more rapid return to self-sufficiency for the affected populations.

Conclusion

While our ten-year experience of ER has been fruitful for us as contributors and beneficial to our UN agency partners, we are convinced that much more is possible in the years ahead. An increased focus on evolving and broadening the parameters of our partnerships, an increased emphasis on readiness and rapid response (moving from 'standby' to 'ready to go'), and a willingness to push the boundaries of our own technology are just some of the areas on which we could focus to good effect.

7

Information systems in crisis

Fredrik Bergstrand and Jonas Landgren

Abstract: The role of technology in crisis and emergency response organizations has drastically changed in the last ten years. Many of the challenges faced today are the results of organizational changes involving a move to more sophisticated technological platforms intended to improve existing work practices. Crisis and emergency response is also an area where lack of information has for a long time been a key ingredient. This notion still resides, even though much more information is available today. However, we believe the current information practice has much more potential. This chapter is an attempt to present and discuss possibilities for current and future information environments, and how these could be designed to better support ongoing work activities, organization, and situation awareness. The chapter presents insights into how key information sources such as verbal and visual information can be captured, stored, and used. It also discusses key components of an information environment.

Key words: crisis management, information systems, video communication, information environments, in-situ documentation, situation awareness.

Introduction

Government organizations responsible for emergency and crisis response today face challenges that did not exist ten years ago, when it was not uncommon that emergency and disaster response was colored by a significant lack of information. Today, there are still a majority of organizations that continue to experience a lack of information, despite recent developments in advanced information technology support. The rich use of mobile communication technology at a citizens' level means, in theory, that any important piece of information is only one phone call away. The rapid adoption of social software has shown that almost any critical situation will result in a quake of information from a massive crowd of individuals (Sakaki, Okazaki, and Matsuo, 2010). This development presents completely new challenges in terms of information systems support. Many systems currently in use by crisis response authorities have not been developed with this new world of massive information streams in mind. Software solutions are still based on a message and reporting idea that only to a limited degree meets the well-known design principles (Turoff, Chumer, Van de Walle, and Yao, 2004) for emergency and crisis response information systems.

We argue that many information systems are in crisis, due to the lack of capacity to provide support in this new crisis information landscape. This chapter is an attempt to present and discuss what future information environments should include in order to provide new capabilities for improved shared situational awareness (Harrald and Jefferson, 2007) based on a wide range of information inputs, both from response actors and from the general public. For response actors, being able to make use of information from the public has been highlighted as an important aspect in studies of social media use in wild-fire events and school shootings (Hughes, Palen, Sutton, Liu, and Vieweg, 2008). Designing and developing system support in order to establish shared situational awareness and providing material for a common operating picture (Harrald and Jefferson, 2007) is a complex task, with several important challenges that need to be addressed. We will present and discuss these challenges by describing and discussing the possibilities and challenges of some of the key information resources in future information environments. We will thereafter present fundamental components necessary to consider when designing and developing these components in information environments for crisis and emergency response settings.

Exploring key information resources

In this section, we describe and discuss three different key information resources that future information environments must address in order to provide support for improved situational awareness and material for a common operating picture. These key information resources include verbal communication, video communication, and in-situ documentation.

Making use of verbal communication

Verbal communication is fundamental in emergency response work and tends to increase in ambiguous situations (Dunn, Lewandowsky, and Kirsner, 2002). This means that how people talk and what they talk about says something about the situation they experience. In emergency response work, verbal communication is often seen as a problem and attempts have been made to further improve verbal communication technology (Camp et al., 2000). In large-scale disasters, we see how the restoration of the mobile phone networks is a prioritized activity due to their importance as an infrastructure for coordination between response organizations but also for the affected communities and their communication with the outside world. In Europe, significant investments have been made to establish dedicated national communication infrastructures based on the TETRA (terrestrial trunked radio) standard, allowing the police, fire brigade, paramedics, and other core response actors new means for secure and stable radio communication.

Despite the fundamental role of verbal communication technology in emergency and disaster response, there have been few attempts to provide new means to leverage the fact that verbal communication is now done in a digital format. One of the key problems with verbal communication in time-critical work is its ephemeral qualities, making it difficult for anyone to obtain the original content of a communication that has already occurred (Whittaker and Amento, 2003). One of the key functions of verbal communication in emergency response work is to provide situation reports and to communicate the ongoing actions of a particular actor. There is a risk that aspects of the information get lost, and it is also time-consuming to re-communicate information in a large network of actors. There is a need to transform verbal communication from an ephemeral state to a state of persistence in order to make information in such conversations digitally accessible. Studies of network technicians have shown that transformation of verbal communication into a persistent form decreased cognitive load and improved problem solving in dynamic situations (Rogers and Brignull, 2003) as well as the coordination of solving network failures (Whittaker and Amento, 2003). Here verbal communications were automatically transformed into text, enabling new possibilities of searching and sharing the content of the verbal communication.

Making use of verbal communication means in the most practical sense that the communication sequences are recorded, tagged (time, sender ID, receiver ID), stored as audio clips, and perhaps also transformed into text. Having large volumes of small fragments of verbal communication in a persistent state opens up for new ways of visualizing response work using a range of fresh perspectives. One could envision how these communication structures could become even more valuable than the content of the specific conversations. Making use of verbal communication will not only partially provide new ways to enforce accountability, but also provide means to structure the communication, and make it visible and accessible as part of the emergency response work. Collections of persistent verbal communication could be used to provide an evolving structure of communication that would correspond to, and make visible, the ongoing response work (see Figure 7.1).

These structures would allow new ways of making visible the work structure as a resource for sensemaking (Weick, 1995) as part of the ongoing response work. Visualized communication patterns would provide insights on which organizations have established contact, which roles seem to be core nodes, and if any organizations are missing in the ongoing response work. However, making use of verbal communication is not unproblematic due to its embedded consequences for privacy, responsibility, authority, and accountability. Few professional response organizations are ready for this type of openness and transparency. However, the future of emergency and disaster response will call for technology support that will embed similar or equivalent capabilities. A key challenge will be to explore the balance between the positive and negative effects with such hyper-transparency.

Making use of video communication

In everyday interactions we normally use different mediums for different types of communication. Each medium has its own characteristics, which will affect the effectiveness of the communication in different ways (Daft et al., 1987). A face-to-face discussion between two persons could be considered rich in content since the medium supports multi-modal communication, mainly consisting of talk and body language. Face-to-face also allows for quick reactions and responses. The discussion would not be as rich if the phone were used instead since the medium does not

Figure 7.1

Screenshot of VisualResponse (I): a prototype developed to demonstrate how multiple types and sources of information can be visualized in a set of views. This figure shows a communication pattern, based on mobile phone call records, between personnel at Fire and Rescue Services (FRS), the County Administrative Board (CAB), and the Police. The arrows indicate who made the call.

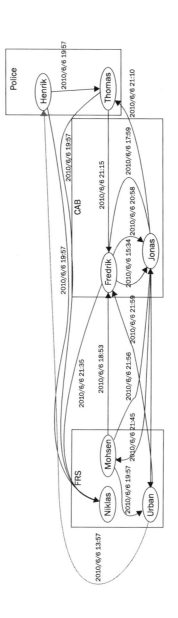

support translation of body language. E-mail would carry even less information. It is evident that different mediums have different characteristics; this is especially important to acknowledge when it comes to crisis and emergency response. The communication between the incident site and coordination centre most often consists of verbal discussion over radio and telephone. The communication between the actors is rich in information, most often rich enough to make well-grounded decisions on tactics and resource allocation. The remaining documented information from the communication may, however, not be as detailed. This creates problems related to backtracking and information handover. Stepping backwards in time often entails a rational line of facts, decisions, and events. However, this is probably not how the real event played out, and only a few people in the organization possess first-hand information about the situation. Leveraging video for documentation and communication could therefore improve how a current and a past event is comprehended as the information provided is contained in a rich and persistent format.

Video is currently used in many organizations, but the ways of using video vary. Almost all organizations leverage the streaming video feeds from news organizations during larger events; a growing number of organizations use video feeds generated by social media technologies to get instant and information rich situational updates. Some actors, especially law enforcement organizations, use CCTV technologies to either prevent crime or prove that a crime was committed (Tullio et al., 2010). A smaller number of early adopters in emergency and response organizations use video applications designed for their specific work practice (Bergstrand and Landgren, 2009). The major benefit is that the mobility and flexibility of such solutions are different compared to stationary CCTV camera systems. Using high-end mobile phones for video broadcasts provides new opportunities for communication and documentation in an information-rich and persistent format. The work conducted at command and coordination centres has long been based on a mental image of the situation, consisting of thoughts and notions about the event. New video technologies enable professional actors to get a better understanding of the event and place their view of the event in a more comprehensible form (Bergstrand and Landgren, 2009; Landgren and Bergstrand 2010).

The characteristics of videos are, however, not a suitable solution for all types of work practices and actors. An oft-portrayed problem with video use is that the details of a situation provided by the video make people shift their focus from a long-term to a short time perspective.

Depending on the role and responsibility of the organization receiving the video, there is a risk of a negative effect of video use. As people are removed from the front lines of the event to take on a greater perspective, video may bring much of the detail back into the command centre and create a shift in focus. A major risk in this case is that the timescale shrinks, from planning for hours or days in advance, down to minutes. This has been a concern with early adopters of video technology in law enforcement and the fire brigade.

Another concern of video use is related to the sharing of video information. The content of video clips is not known in advance and this creates a risk of subjecting people to undesired material and legal problems. Laws and regulations on how video can be used in response work differs between countries and states, and what is legal in one state may be highly illegal in the next state. Since video is rich in information, everything from license plates, patient information, or any other kind of sensitive information could be included.

Broadcast video is a powerful medium capable of rich communication in a persistent format. As the mobile infrastructure and handheld devices constantly evolve to greater capacities, new opportunities to utilize mobile broadcast video will become available. Video is making its way into more and more professions, and it is only a matter of time before it becomes a standard procedure in documentation practices.

Making use of in-situ documentation

In times of emergency situations or disaster events, response organizations produce large amounts of information in order to provide appropriate responses. Computer-based dispatch systems keep track of response units and accident locations, and provide detailed log-data of where units are and how long they have been at a specific location. Such data is transformed to valuable information in post-incident analysis in order to provide detailed reports of how the organization used specific resources. However, there is a type of information that in most organizations is completely forgotten, both during a response as well as afterwards. Such information is here termed as in-situ documentation, characterized by its short lifespan, strong contextual dependency, and informal use. This information is produced by the members of a response organization and materialized as paper notes and whiteboard sketches. In-situ documentation is often put in the recycling bin or wiped off the whiteboard after it has served its purpose. However, in-situ documentation is important information when it comes to understanding not only what activities the organizations undertook during the response work, but, perhaps more importantly, why, and what assumptions formed these actions.

By focusing on making in-situ documentation less ephemeral and more persistent, such information will become a valuable resource both during response work and for a larger professional community in post-incident analysis. In-situ documentation is produced in social interactions between personnel in the organization or in interactions across organizational boundaries. People make notes when they talk to someone over the phone (O'Hara, Perry, Sellen, and Brown, 2001), when people meet for a quick situation briefing, or at the whiteboard when they discuss a particular topic or situation. This means that in-situ documentation is highly social. It is produced in a social setting and reflects key aspects of the specific social interaction. Significant challenges when developing new means of making use of in-situ documentation are its short lifespan, strong contextual dependency, and informal use. Keeping in mind that in-situ documentation tends to be materialized in non-digital formats is yet another challenge. A key aspect for all response organizations is to acknowledge that in-situ documentation is a resource that should be handled with the same professionalism as documentation produced as part of formal reporting activities. This means that in-situ documentation must be archived during the response work. There are a few different strategies that could be deployed in order to make in-situ documentation persistent and thereby extend its otherwise short lifespan. These strategies are to: a) improve existing paper-based work practice; b) augment existing paper-based work practice; and c) transform existing paper-based practice into digital work practice. Each strategy has its pros and cons.

Improving existing paper-based work practice is a strategy that could be a first step for organizations that continue to work with pens and paper by making digital copies of the in-situ documentation that is produced. A key artifact in this approach is the mobile phone's digital camera. By making 'photo-copies' of the handwritten notes, and uploading the pictures to an information system, the paper-based notes could instantly be located on a time-line and assigned with a role-based metadata based on the caller-ID. This approach is far from perfect but can add important capabilities to an organization.

Augmenting existing paper-based work practice is a strategy that involves new digital artifacts, such as digital ink pens. There have been exploratory studies of such technology use in command and control centres (Khalilbeigi, Bradler, Schweizer, Probst, and Steimle, 2010). The approach means that the personnel continue to use pens and papers, but while using them a digital replica of the notes is automatically produced and stored. This means that the personnel continue to work with pen and paper but they gain detailed digital documentation without having to abandon fundamental artifacts in the existing paper-based work practice. However, switching to a digital ink pen infrastructure does not come without limitations. The personnel are required to use dedicated pens and often dedicated paper sheets.

Transforming existing paper-based practice into digital work practice is the most challenging strategy with its strong focus on abandoning the use of non-digital documentation artifacts. Here, the personnel are expected to make digital notes, digital whiteboard drawings, and only produce textual and graphical material using digital information technology. A major challenge in this strategy is to avoid the dependency of keyboard-centered input of information and instead open up to a variety of approaches to produce digital information. We currently see significant developments in new interaction techniques using multi-touch on mobile, handheld, and wall-sized displays (see e.g., Precision Information Environments, *precisioninformation.org*) which over time will change how in-situ documentation is produced. However, moving from a paper-based practice to a completely digital work practice is not just dependent on heavy investments in new artifacts but also requires a change in the underlying information systems to accommodate these new interaction modalities.

Whichever of the above strategies are deployed to extend the lifespan of in-situ documentation and make it persistent, there are still two challenges that must be addressed. Having a digital representation of in-situ documentation is just the first step; the second step is to make the documentation contextually relevant. Making documentation contextually relevant is related to a phenomenon that many have experienced, namely that paper notes and whiteboard drawings tend to fade from being insightful to meaningless over time. Further, reading someone else's notes from a meeting or looking at a whiteboard drawing from a discussion you did not take part in is often confusing. The reason for this is that the notes are contextually embedded and for additional people they lack context. In order to balance this fact, people must be able to assign context to the digital documentation. In its simplest form, this could include the capability to add notes to the digital documentation object. Such notes should cover more than just date/time and creator, but also information about who was part of the social context when the documentation was produced, who contributed to it, and what the underlying discussion was about. By adding such capabilities, the documentation will become a social object that people can share, comment upon, and rate.

The third and last step is related to the social aspects of in-situ documentation. In the paper-based work practice, in-situ documentation is informal and personal with limited reach. What we envision is how there will be a change from a personal focus to a social focus. This means that new mechanisms must be developed in order to allow the producer of in-situ documentation to determine an appropriate reach. Such a reach should not only be based on a traditional role-based model, but also along temporal and spatial dimensions. One could here envision an approach where in-situ documentation has a wide reach in the moment it is created and then slowly degrades, with limitations on who could access the specific piece of information. When the situation is over and the response work has been terminated, the information is again opened up with extensive reach for post-incident analysis. So far we have seen very few attempts at treating information in emergency and disaster events as social objects with extensive reach. It is reasonable that the future of emergency and disaster response will call for new mechanisms in order to provide some form of dynamic transparency to meet new demands on accountability and professional review of the actions conducted in response work.

Fundamental components of an information environment

In this section, we outline fundamental aspects of an information environment (Huber and Daft, 1987) that are necessary to consider when designing systems supporting situation awareness and providing material for a common operating picture (Harrald and Jefferson, 2007). The description is based on industry development efforts and academic research and inspired by the ongoing work at Swedish crisis response and management agencies.

Collecting traces of action

Many of our interactions with the world leave digital traces. The traces are generated from events such as swiping a credit card to the communications between friends and colleagues in social media. Digital traces are also created in emergency events generated from the computer-based dispatch systems, the production of documentation, the communication, and also by public bystanders. All data generated during an event is valuable information in both post-incident analysis and in the ongoing work.

Information and traces for a specific incident can be gathered from a wide range of sources. Some sources may be internal, from partner organizations and public sources. Information takes on a wide range of formats, from spoken words down to detailed data from sensor infrastructures. Phone calls, internal documents, event logs, transactions in internal business information systems, and whiteboard drawings are all digital traces of actions (Landgren, 2006) that can be collected and used in a meaningful way. Resource utilization, available personnel, and many other indicators of an organization's ongoing work can be collected and put into context. When looking into different organizations we often see vast amounts of data being generated, but only a small portion used in the practice. The general public and media also provide vast amounts of information, and citizens' reporting through social media can be a valuable input to an emerging situation (Starbird et al., 2010).

A component for collecting traces of actions must therefore include a set of flexible adapters that could be used to extract specific information from the organization's operational response information systems. Further, there must also be adapters that can extract information from public sources and social media infrastructures, such as Twitter and Flickr, without the need for traditional data integration techniques. Novel approaches for flexible collection of traces of actions must be developed to meet the demands of an ever increasing range of information sources, communication infrastructures, and social media platforms.

Structuring of data and information streams

As mentioned in the previous section, vast amounts of data are generated during a crisis or emergency situation. However, a structure needs to be applied to the information in order to create any sort of value. The lack of proper IT strategies often results in valuable information being scattered over several systems without the possibility of being connected. A proper systems architecture and an interconnected data structure is needed in order to access and query information extracted by collecting traces of the action component.

Information collected from other systems, such as Twitter tweets, cell phone call data, and Flickr photos, is of no or little use in the ongoing work if it only ends up on a server without anybody's knowledge. There needs to be meta-information available to make a connection between the ongoing situation and the extracted material. Structuring the data also implies added possibilities of connecting different instances of information. All systems generate information that could present a richer operating picture when brought together. An example could be the use of data from an emergency call center, extracting the location of recent callers and combining it with areas affected by an ongoing power outage. This would also form a new baseline to identify areas where emergency calls are no longer working. By structuring the information, new connections can be made and specific organizational properties can be put into context. The greater challenge is to look at their own organization, all the different systems used, what type of information they produce, and how it can become better connected along new baselines.

A component is needed in the information systems architecture that enables the structuring of information from a range of different systems. Further, this central component should be able to provide access to fragments of information from multiple sources in order to provide a better common operating picture. Access to fragments from multiple systems implies that the component is able to impose a system-wide structure on the information generated during specific emergencies or crises.

Visualization and exploration

Data visualization enables new forms of information to be brought into the work environment. 'The basic idea of visual data exploration is to present the data in a range of visual formats, allowing actors to gain deep insights from the data, elaborate and draw conclusions by directly interacting with the data' (Keim, 2002). When visualizing information, we are able to draw new insights and make new connections between the information and an evolving situation. Information overload is also reduced since generalizations are used when presenting the data. The number of rescue units, for example, could be presented as representations on a map instead of using a traditional detailed spreadsheet view.

Information in response work has many different characteristics that affect how it can be visualized. Typical characteristics include temporal, spatial, ordinal, qualitative, quantitative, or a combination of any or all of the above. Together the pieces of information create a construct depicting a stationary or mobile object, place, process, action, or relation (Andrienko and Andrienko, 2006). Each specific type allows for the information to be used in different types of visualization. Crisis response and management, however, is different from many other fields where information visualization is used. The main difference is the temporal relation between the onset of the event (when information is created) and when it is used. The information used in VISTA (King, 2006) for visualizing information for both strategic and operational decision-making in humanitarian relief work is gathered over weeks, months, and years, while a small-scale incident or crisis is only active for hours or days. The major challenge for information visualization in crisis management is not primarily related to the tools and methods for visualization. The challenge is related to the ability to extract and structure data in order for it to be used in visualizations.

Figure 7.2 Screenshot of VisualResponse (II): these views include the time and content of written reports, a temporal view of resource utilization, an actor network based on interactions over mobile phones, and a temporal and geo-spatial view of the state of readiness.

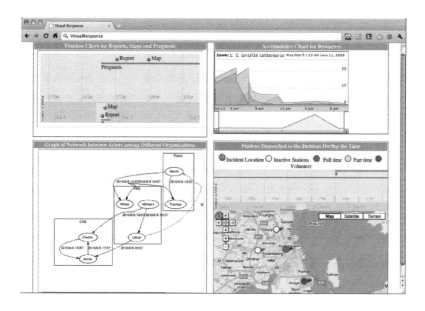

Information visualization is a key component since it brings the collected and structured information into context and makes it part of the work practice. Specific information content such as phone call meta-information, together with information about the caller, time, and the place of the call, forms a powerful set of data. By capturing and combining this type of multi-dimensional data, several types of visualizations can be created to explore the dynamics of a specific situation. Captured communications, in-situ documentation, location, and other forms of information and data can be combined into temporal geo-spatial 'event streams' depicting the unfolding of a situation as shown in Figure 7.2.

Collaborative problem-solving workspaces

Emergency and disaster response, by nature, is a truly collaborative activity, ranging from small-group collaboration to complex actor networks involving hundreds of different organizations. A common problem in any collaborative activity is coordination. According to Turoff et al. (2004), the coordination problem in emergency response has been largely ignored. One reason is related to the lack of technology support for people to dynamically form groups around an ongoing event, and by doing so allow a community of experts to interact and share insights across organizational boundaries. The main questions from a sense-making perspective in this activity are 'What is the story?' and 'What do we do next?' (Weick, 2005). However, due to the lack of technologies to support collaboration and coordination, the questions often change to 'What do others know?' and 'What are they doing?'. A collaborative problem-solving space must include a rich set of services for communication and information exchange in order to support the dynamics of collaborating with other actors.

Collaborative problem-solving workspaces are therefore an important component to allow small, as well as large, groups to dynamically formulate problems, discuss topics, and prioritize activities (Turoff et al., 2004).

Such workspaces will not only allow formal and informal groups to share expertise but also provide transparency and allow different expertise on different levels or from different organizations to observe, review, and provide input on the activities that are ongoing. Collaborative technologies have evolved greatly during the Web 2.0 era. The key component of collaborative workspaces is based on a range of well-known functionalities typically found in mainstream tools for activities such as collaborative writing, project management, live rich communication, discussion forums, event planning, and voting.

Communication platform

Communicating with the public is a critical task in emergency and crisis response. Updated information about ongoing events, instructions on how to act, where to find more information, and other key aspects need to be communicated. There are currently multiple channels used for this type of communication, ranging from actor-specific websites to distribution via traditional media, and even specific early warning systems to inform, warn, and move people out of danger. A major concern is that the information provided to the public is often sporadic, delivered late and with vague content (Sutton, Palen, and Shklovski, 2008). Improved means to capture and structure data would make it possible to provide the public with up-to-date and rich information. The channels of communication need to be redesigned as the use of traditional media has greatly changed during the last decade. Many organizations have incorporated new channels, such as social media, into their information dissemination protocols; however, more work needs to be done. One could imagine that the use of social media channels will increase and in turn will not only require functionality to push information to the public, but will also allow new means for more continuous interaction between authorities and the public. An important trend has emerged where the public, as well as automated sensor systems, provide more and more information into emergency response information systems. Detailed witness reports and sensory data are today published in social media channels, and these have proven valuable in response work (Starbird et al., 2010).

Interactions over the phone or through joint meetings are still the most common methods of information exchange. New systems for information sharing are constantly being implemented. The main problem with many of these initiatives is that they lead to 'yet another system', requiring additional manual documentation practices. Professional communication needs to be supported in the work practice and not become a burden of new tasks and responsibilities. The communication platform should be designed to accommodate a range of communication channels and provided as an embedded component in the information environment.

Conclusions

We have presented important challenges for designing, developing, and managing information environments that improve situation awareness and establish a common operating picture in emergency and crisis response. A primary challenge is to make use of the vast amounts of data and information generated as traces of actions from the current work practice. Specifically, we have shown that verbal communication, video, and in-situ documentation are key information objects that future software solutions should view and use as important resources. Making use of vast amounts of information in emergency and crisis response is not just a technical challenge but is also colored by social and organizational complexity. Designing and developing system support for emergency and crisis response is not a novel task, nor a task that is done without significant restrictions due to the existing installation base. We hope, however, that our chapter could be used to provide some guidance as well as inspiration for future initiatives striving to build systems that improve the information capabilities of emergency and crisis response organizations.

References

Andrienko, N. and Andrienko, G. (2006). Intelligent visualisation and information presentation for civil crisis. In: Suares, J. and Markus, B. (eds.) *Proceedings of 9th AGILE Conference on Geographical Information Science*. Visegrad, Hungary, pp. 291–8.

Bergstrand, F. and Landgren, J. (2009). Using live video for information sharing in emergency response work. *International Journal of Emergency Management*, 6(3/4).

Camp, P., Hudson, J., Keldorph, R., Lewis, S., and Mynatt, E. (2000). Supporting communication and collaboration practices in safety-critical situations. 2000 Conference on Human Factors in Computing Systems, The Hague, Netherlands.

Daft, R.L., Lengel, R., and Klebe Trevino, L. (1987). Message equivocality, media selection, and manager performance: implications for information systems, *MIS Quarterly* 11(3), 355–66.

Dunn, J.C., Lewandowsky, S., and Kirsner, K. (2002). Dynamics of communication in emergency management. *Applied Cognitive Psychology*, 16(6), 719–37.

Harrald, J. and Jefferson, T. (2007). Shared situational awareness in emergency management mitigation and response. 40th Hawaii International Conference on System Sciences 2007, Waikoloa, HI.

Huber, G.P. and Daft, R.L. (1987). The information environments of organizations. In Jablin, F. et al., *Handbook of organizational communication: An interdisciplinary perspective*. Thousand Oaks, CA: Sage, pp. 130–64.

Hughes, A., Palen, I., Sutton, J., Liu, S., and Vieweg, S. (2008). 'Site-seeing' in disaster: An examination of on-line social convergence. Information Systems for Crisis Response and Management Conference, Washington DC.

Keim, D. A. (2002). Information visualization and visual data mining. *IEE Transactions on Visualization and Computer Graphics*, 7(1), 100–7.

Khalilbeigi, M., Bradler, D., Schweizer, I., Probst, F., and Steimle, J. (2010). Towards computer support of paper workflows in emergency management. International ISCRAM Conference, Seattle, WA.

King, D. (2006). A visualization analysis tool for humanitarian situational awareness. International ISCRAM Conference, Newark, NJ.

Landgren, J. (2006). Making action visible in time-critical work. SIGCHI Conference on Human Factors in Computing Systems, Chicago.

Landgren, J. and Bergstrand, F. (2010). Mobile live video in emergency response: Its use and consequences. *Bulletin of the American Society for Information Science and Technology*, 36(5), 27–9.

O'Hara, K., Perry, M., Sellen, A., and Brown, B. (2001). Exploring the relationship between mobile phone and document activity during business travel. In B. Brown and N. Green (eds.). *Wireless world*. New York: Springer-Verlag, pp. 180–94.

Precision Information (n.d.). Precision information environments. Retrieved January, 2011, from *http://precisioninformation.org*.

Rogers, Y. and Brignull, H. (2003). Computational offloading: Supporting distributed team working through visually augmenting verbal communication. 25th Annual Meeting of Cognitive Science Society, Boston, MA.

Sakaki, T., Okazaki, M., and Matsuo, Y. (2010). Earthquake shake twitter users: Real-time event detection by social sensors. *19th International Conference on World Wide Web*, Raleigh, NC, 851–60.

Starbird, K., Palen, L., Hughes, A.L., and Vieweg, S. (2010). Chatter on the red: What hazards threat reveals about the social life of microblogged information. *2010 ACM Conference on Computer Supported Cooperative Work*, New York, 241–50.

Sutton, J., Palen, L., and Shklovski, I. (2008). Back-channels on the front lines: Emerging use of social media in the 2007 Southern California wildfires. Conference on Information Systems for Crisis Response and Management (ISCRAM), Washington DC.

Tullio, J., Huang, E., Wheatley, D., Zhang, H., Guerrero, C., and Tamdoo, A. (2010). Experience, adjustment, and engagement: The role of video in law enforcement. 28th International Conference on Human Factors in Computing Systems, Chicago.

Turoff, M., Chumer, M., Van de Walle, B., and Yao, X. (2004). The design of a dynamic emergency response management information systems (DERMIS). *Journal of Information Technology Theory and Application*, 5(4).

Weick, K.E. (1995). *Sensemaking in organizations*. Thousand Oaks, CA: Sage.

Weick, K., Sutcliffe, K., and Obstfeld, D., (2005) Organizing and the process of sensemaking. *Organization Science* 16(4), 409–12.

Whittaker, S., and Amento, B. (2003). Seeing what you are hearing: coordinating responses to trouble reports in network troubleshooting. *8th Conference on European Conference on Computer Supported Cooperative Work*, Helsinki, Finland, 219–38.

8

Community media and civic action in response to volcanic hazards

Mario Antonius Birowo

Abstract: Awareness of the importance of community media in disseminating information related to natural disasters has encouraged people to use community radio. This chapter discusses the role of Indonesia's Lintas Merapi Community Radio in emergency situations caused by natural disasters. In response to the eruption of the Merapi volcano, Lintas Merapi has applied a convergence of traditional media (radio) and newer media (the Internet and social media). The central argument is that people use their media to fulfill their communication needs and to find solutions for their problems, especially during the occurrence of a natural disaster such as a volcanic eruption.

Key words: community radio, natural disaster, volcanic eruption, ICT, Lintas Merapi, Indonesia.

Introduction

A natural disaster seriously disrupts the economic and social progress of any society. The United Nations Educational, Scientific and Cultural Organization (UNESCO) states that a natural disaster is the combination of hazards, vulnerability of people, and their capability to respond to risk. Natural disasters have a serious effect on a community or region and are caused by the impact of a naturally occurring, rapid onset event, such as earthquake, volcanic eruption, landslide, tsunami, flood, or drought (UNESCO, n.d.).

Merapi volcano, with a height 2,980 meters above sea level, is located on the border between the provinces of Yogyakarta and Central Java. The volcano is about 30 kilometers north of Yogya, the capital city of Yogyakarta province. Merapi literally means 'mount of fire.' Surono, the Head of the Center for Volcanology and Geological Disaster Mitigation (PVMBG), says that Merapi is known as the most active volcano in the world (Seputar Indonesia, 2010). In the last decade, there were two big eruptions in 2006 and 2010.

People on the slopes of Merapi in 2010 suffered from the eruption. Badan Nasional Penanggulangan Bencana (BNPB), the National Agency for Disaster Management, reported that Merapi's activities in 2010 killed 259 people and destroyed hundreds of houses in the affected areas (BNPB, 2010). The eruption of 2010 was the biggest since 1872, according to Subandriyo, the Head of Balai Penyelidikan dan Pengembangan Teknologi Kegunungapian (BPPTK), the Volcanic Technology Development and Research Center. In 1872 pyroclastic flows from Merapi reached 11–12 kilometers; after Merapi's most recent eruption (2010) pyroclastic flows reached 15 kilometers (Syaifullah, 2010; Seputar Indonesia, 2010). Pyroclastic flows are fluidized masses of rock fragments and gases that move rapidly in response to gravity (Riley, n.d); they are in effect heat clouds created by a volcano. Local people call the flows *wedhus gembel*, which literally means 'trash sheep' (referring to the name of a native sheep).

The Indonesian government set up an early warning system to alert people to a Merapi eruption. There are five observatory posts, sirens, gas detectors, and loudspeakers surrounding the volcano (Wirakusumah, 2003). Although the government provides an early warning system, it can only be effective if people in the risk areas support it. The role of local media, particularly community radio, in providing information to those affected is crucial for coordination among the local people, government, and aid agencies (see Gillham, 2000).

Lintas Merapi Community Radio is an example of a grass-roots people's initiative that uses local resources to manage and disseminate information in their environment. This chapter discusses the role of Lintas Merapi Community Radio in emergency situations caused by volcanic activity. The material for this chapter was written in response to my observations of eruptions of Merapi in 2006 and 2010. In emergency situations community radio has shown more flexibility, in terms of mobility and adaptability of formats and content, as compared to mainstream media.

This flexibility is related to its focus on people-oriented programs, as its mission is to serve the people's interest. In emergencies caused by natural disasters, people in affected areas need adequate information. Awareness of the importance of information related to natural disasters has encouraged people to use community radio. In several cases of natural disasters in Indonesia people used community radio to supply information to the affected areas (Birowo, 2010).

The strength of community radio is that there are contacts and networks within communities and among community radio activists. As a part of civil society, activists also have links with non-governmental organizations (NGOs) and academics (see Allen, 2006). Lintas Merapi Community Radio has demonstrated the importance of networks in supporting its activities, especially in dealing with natural disasters.

Natural disasters create new situations which lead to uncertainty among people. People need information to adapt to the situation, resolve uncertainty, and make decisions about how to survive. Information is also useful in helping people to face hardship, physically and psychologically. For example, the role of communication can be seen in the case of Hurricane Katrina in New Orleans. Prior to the hurricane, it was important to prepare people to cope with the disaster by providing information about safety strategies and evacuation routes. Mass media gave weather predictions which were useful for people to make decisions on how to survive the hurricane. Following the hurricane, information giving recommendations about living accommodation, updates on affected areas, and safety tips on returning to homes, helped people understand their new situation.

Living with natural disasters

While Indonesia was recovering from the devastation of the tsunami in Aceh and from the Nias earthquake, which both occurred in 2004, further earthquakes in Java (in the Bantul and Klaten regencies on May 27, 2006) and a tsunami in Java (Pangandaran Beach on July 17, 2006) shocked the country. The World Bank and the Asian Disaster Reduction Center reported that more than 5,000 people were killed in these latter disasters (ADRC, 2007). Indonesia experienced several other natural disasters over the following years: a landslide in Manggarai, East Nusa Tenggara province (2006); Merapi's eruption in Yogyakarta (2006); floods in Jakarta (2006, 2007); an earthquake in West Sumatera (2007,

2009); a landslide in West Java (2010); a landslide in West Papua (2010); an earthquake in West Java (2010); an earthquake in West Sumatra (2010); volcanic activities of Mount Bromo in East Java (2010); and Merapi once again in Yogyakarta (2010).

Many of these natural disasters were related to the location of the Indonesian archipelago. Indeed, Indonesia is a country that experiences many natural disasters since it is located in a tropical region along the Pacific 'Ring of Fire,' sandwiched between three continental plates: the Eurasian Continental Plate, India–Australian Oceanic Plate, and Pacific Oceanic Plate. This is a setting with the potential for various natural hazards such as earthquakes (volcanic and tectonic), volcanic eruptions, tsunamis, floods, landslides, and droughts. Wirakusuma, a PVMBG geologist, said that 20 percent of the Indonesian population was living in high-risk areas prone to geological hazards (2003). The Center for Hazards and Risk Research at Columbia University (2005) gave the historical data on disasters in Indonesia from 1907 to 2004 (excluding the Aceh Tsunami in 2004); this information illustrated that over almost 100 years Indonesia experienced 10 cyclones, 11 droughts, 78 earthquakes, 93 floods, and 43 volcanic eruptions. Given these circumstances, many say that Indonesians should be familiar with natural disasters and should be prepared to anticipate them.

Studies of the effect of natural disasters on communities show that low-income or marginalized communities are the groups that suffer the worst impact. The loss of infrastructure has a significant impact on the poor, especially in terms of access to sanitation, electricity, and clean water (Buckland and Rahman, 1999; Pyles, 2007; Asian Disaster Reduction Center, 2007; Freeman, n.d.). As Mathbor (2007) emphasizes, the most vulnerable people suffer the worst effects of disaster since they have limited resources, which also may also delay emergency action.

In the context of Indonesia, Tanesia (2007) shows that in the early days after natural disasters victims often have to manage the impact with very limited resources, since governments need time to coordinate activities and provide funding. In Bantul, Yogyakarta Special Region, for instance, victims of the earthquake in 2006 stayed for more than two weeks in the emergency accommodation that they built themselves with the debris from their homes. Additionally, they had limited access to drinking water and sanitation, which affected their health. Contaminated drinking water and lack of sanitation can create diarrheal diseases Hepatitis A and E (Watson, Connolly, and Gayer, 2006).

Lintas Merapi: radio for people living in a high-risk area

Since Merapi is a very active volcano, people living in its vicinity always face the risk of a potential eruption. Aware of the dangers of Merapi, they use resources such as their indigenous knowledge, their community organization, and their communication systems to reduce risk to life and property. In 1995 Pasag Merapi was developed, an organization established by villagers to improve the people's capacity to manage their environment and develop strategies to reduce the risk from natural disasters (BBC Indonesia.com, 27 February 2007). According to Sukiman, a founder of Pasag Merapi (interview, 17 September 2007), although the group was founded by only a few villagers, Pasag Merapi became a center of activity for the village people living on the slopes of Merapi. Although people had organized training for risk-reduction since 1995, Merapi's activities during April and May 2006 raised awareness of the need to improve the methods to protect life. That action was strengthened after Merapi's eruption at the end of 2010.

People on the slopes of Merapi understood that information is important in reducing risk of suffering caused by disaster. For this reason they established a communication system that was supported by the use of a community radio, named Radio Komunitas Lintas Merapi (Lintas Merapi Community Radio), meaning 'Crossing Merapi.' This radio station was set up to distribute information about the Merapi volcano quickly. It served 70,000 people living on the slopes of Merapi, especially Deles sub-district, Central Java.

The radio station was established in 2001 as a result of the people's need for an effective, but cheap, communication device. The studio was located in the house of a farmer (named Sukiman) in Kemalang village, Klaten regency, strategically located beside a village road so easily accessible by villagers. The village is only four kilometers from the top of Merapi. The radio station was created with very limited funds as an 'emergency' service. In the early days it only worked on 20 watt power and used very simple, hand-built equipment. The station did not have a soundproof studio but was positioned in a room in Sukiman's house. He reported that only a few people were interested in the purpose of the radio station when the service was initiated.

In 2006 two events occured that caused people in the Deles sub-district to rethink the importance of community radio. First, in April of 2006, Merapi erupted and people were evacuated by the government to refugee camps for months. Many of the evacuees were farmers who were worried about their crops, livestock, and their houses, without which they could not make a living.

One month after the eruption, a 5.7 magnitude earthquake in Yogyakarta and Klaten, 30 kilometers to the south of Deles, occurred, with its epicenter in Bantul. The earthquake destroyed Bantul (Yogyakarta province), Klaten (Central Java province), and their surrounding areas on May 27, 2006. More than 5,000 people were reported dead, and 60,000 houses, buildings, and public facilities were damaged or destroyed by the earthquake (United Nations Office for the Coordination of Humanitarian Affairs, 2006). Damage to electricity, telephone, and transportation facilities isolated the affected people from other regions for three days after the disaster. Chaos ensued because there was no power in the location and mobile phone networks were overloaded. Inhabitants were faced with uncertainty as they did not know what would happen to their lives and their environment. Rumors that there would be another, bigger earthquake or tsunami spread throughout the region. Just an hour after the earthquake, roads filled with people running or driving to find a higher place in the north of Yogyakarta to avoid a tsunami; people panicked, remembering the tsunami in Aceh on December 26, 2004.

As a result of these unfortunate experiences, people in Deles began to reconsider the importance of community radio for disaster risk reduction. They agreed to improve their radio station and in 2008 a new studio was built outside Sukiman's house. It was equipped with a mixer, an audio compressor, handy talkies/HT (two-way radio), a desktop computer, a phase-locked loop/PLL (a closed-loop frequency control system), and a tower. Although located in a remote area, the radio station included an Internet link supported by a local non-profit organization. At the back of the studio, a patrol post was built to monitor Mount Merapi as an early warning system in the village.

Furthermore, based on their daily experience in anticipating Merapi's hazards, the people set up a standard operational procedure for monitoring the environment of the volcano. Because there was no telephone line, local people distributed HTs to 14 *pos ronda* (patrol posts). Pos ronda were observation points to visually monitor the activities and environment of Merapi. People in charge at these posts reported emergency situations to the studio of Lintas Merapi and the announcer would then broadcast the information to all inhabitants. To complement their monitoring, they cooperated with BPPTK (a government institution responsible for monitoring volcanoes in Indonesia). Information from BPPTK ensured the accuracy of the radio's report about Mount Merapi's activities.

Information from Lintas Merapi Radio was not only used by local people, but also by people living along the 'rivers' that flowed from Mount Merapi. The 'rivers' were lines of hot and cold material (stone and sand) that usually occurred after heavy rain on the slopes of Merapi. Many people utilized materials from Merapi, such as stones and sand, for building materials. They dug sand and stones from these rivers and sold them in the surrounding areas. Since their lives and livelihood depended on the condition of the rivers, they listened to Lintas Merapi Radio's reports on the situation in the upper parts of Mount Merapi, thus avoiding the impact of flood material brought by the rain. The radio announced emergency information to its listeners if there was potential risk from conditions on Merapi.

The volunteers agreed that whenever there was an emergency the radio would be activated. This agreement was put into action on one such occasion when there was particularly heavy rain in the early hours of one morning. Volunteers went immediately to the Lintas Merapi studio to broadcast live reports about the situation on Mount Merapi. The radio was also set up to broadcast information about evacuation paths and refugee camps as needed.

To enable participation, Lintas Merapi Community Radio invited everyone to be a volunteer, declaring the station to be media for all people. The operation of Lintas Merapi was financed by donations from individuals and from local organizations, such as Forum Klaster Lereng Merapi (Clusters of the Slope of Merapi). To maintain transparency, all budgets were posted on the wall of the studio for everyone to read. To maintain community orientation, the radio did not accept any commercial advertising. However, it did broadcast public service advertising to promote villager productivity. To further this goal, it was also used to support programs of agriculture and home-industry, such as handicrafts, and production of local delicacies and traditional snacks.

Volunteers of Lintas Merapi invited outside institutions to work together in the development of the radio station. For instance, starting on August 23, 2007, its services were offered to local government and the wider public, including non-profit and people's organizations, to be used as a part of the early warning system in the vicinity of Mount Merapi.

Living as refugees

The risk of potential volcanic damage cannot force people to relocate. A similar situation is also apparent in Hawaii, where people living in the

Puna District on the volcano Kīlauea do not want to move to another area since their present location supports a good livelihood, which is more important than the volcanic risk. For those people, benefits from natural resources are more attractive than the risk (Gregg et al., 2004).

Uncertainty is a problem for people in a risk area. When there is a volcanic eruption, there is no knowledge or technology to predict how long the eruption will last (James, 2007). When Merapi's volcanic activity increased in 2010, the government asked people living in *kawasan rawan bencana* (KRB, i.e. risky areas) to move from their villages. The risky areas covered a radius of 15 kilometers from the top of Merapi. Many moved without preparation so that when they evacuated, they could not take clothes, food, and other property. Suddenly they faced a new situation: living in camps with limited facilities.

Relocated people were in the refugee camps for months, which seriously impacted their lives. Since most of refugees were farmers, being away from their fields and their houses threatened their livelihood. They did not have any information about how long they should stay in the camps. This situation made people return to their houses to feed their livestock: a dangerous activity. For people on the slopes of Merapi, livestock was their only wealth, so it can be understood why they wanted to take the risk.

Living in uncertainty in the refugee camps increased people's frustration; they believed that Merapi did not erupt according to the forecasts. They thought that the decision of the government to evacuate had been enacted too early. In fact, before the evacuation they had expressed their preference to stay in their villages but the government decided to evacuate them as soon as the activity of Merapi increased. There was a conflict between the government's policy and the people's interest. On one side the government thought that they had a responsibility to save local people from volcanic hazards, but on the other side people wanted to stay in their houses to protect their property. In this case, people thought that their voices were not considered in the decision making and they resisted. This situation is reflected in Pearce's argument (2003: 217) that people will challenge policies and actions that do not involve them in the disaster management process.

People living on the slopes of Merapi had a belief that they would be protected by God from the hazards of the volcano. This feeling of safety was observed by De Coster in 2002 (Lavigne et al., 2008). Local people thought that they would not be affected by Merapi's eruption. As a result of this belief, the people of Kemalang village were still in their village when the government announced a Level IV alert, the most dangerous level of Merapi's activities. This level means that all people living in a radius of 20 kilometers from the top of Merapi should be evacuated.

Social capital

Where government expenditure and preparedness to take action in disaster management is limited, it is important to consider the potential for the community to take an active role, as it is the community that suffers the effects of disaster (Allen, 2006). Given these circumstances, the people are on the front line in dealing with emergency situations; they are affected by the disaster and should respond to the situation. It is necessary to enhance community participation in disaster risk management. Through communication, people can raise public awareness about risk as a collective problem. Community members are invited to mitigate risk and to find solutions. This process of understanding ultimately encourages community action to address the risk (Flint and Luloff, 2007).

In the case of Merapi's eruptions, community initiatives were organized spontaneously to help victims. Lintas Merapi and two other voluntary community radio stations around the slopes of Merapi developed civic engagement as part of their activities. At the time of the 2006 Merapi eruption, community radio stations founded a network, named Jaringan Informasi Lingkar Merapi/Jalin Merapi (Merapi Rim Information Network). This network provided a communication system between the communities on the slopes of Merapi. Supported by the Combine Resources Institution (CRI), a local NGO, they published information on the web at *http://merapi.combine.or.id*.

Volunteers working in community radio contributed articles to this website, reporting the situation from within. They wrote of their anxiety concerning the future of farmers, criticizing economic policies which did not support the farmers. Prior to the 2010 Merapi eruption, this website was a tool for volunteers to voice their interests about the environment of Merapi and their concerns over the environmental destruction of their villages caused by sand mining.

Another contributor suggested a project that would preserve water by planting casuarina trees, potentially attracting people outside Kemalang village to give donations. In another example, the villagers planted hundreds of guava trees to provide food for monkeys from the forest that surround their village, preventing the monkeys from attacking the village fields. In 2007 Lintas Merapi Community Radio received an award from the BBC for this contribution to risk reduction management and natural conservation.

On September 24, 2010, Merapi showed increasing volcanic activity. The Indonesian government warned those on the slopes of Merapi of the potential risk from the volcano. The government categorized Merapi's activities as Level 3 (on a scale of levels from 1 to 4; this level allowed people to stay in their village). In response to the government warning, volunteers from Lintas Merapi helped to monitor the activity of the volcano and gave information to people via radio. Through this media, Lintas Merapi prepared its community to be aware of the activities of the volcano. Because of the increased activities of Merapi, volunteers created a team to watch the volcano intensively. They continuously gave reports to the local people on the development of the volcano's activities.

On October 26, 2010, Merapi erupted. The government (BPPTK) declared Level 4 status for the volcano's activities, advising local people to leave their villages. This forced people living on the slopes of the mountain to evacuate to refugee camps. In the last minute before leaving for a safer area, volunteers of Lintas Merapi Community Radio still broadcast information based on their visual monitoring and seismographic data from BPPTK.

Due to the evacuation, Lintas Merapi Community Radio could not continue to broadcast its programs. Although they could not operate their radio station, volunteers did not stop working but switched their focus, giving attention to refugees. They took action by observing refugee needs, collecting and distributing aid.

Merapi's eruption of November 5, 2010 forced people within 20 kilometers of the top of the mountain to leave their homes. There were 602 camps surrounding Merapi for more than 270,000 refugees, spanning the seven regencies: Sleman, Bantul, Kulonprogo, Gunung Kidul, Magelang, Boyolali, and Klaten (Jalin Merapi, 2010). The people of Kemalang village preferred to be independent refugees. They did not go to the government's refugee camps, but went instead to Manjung village, Klaten regency, 25 kilometers from their village.

A huge number of refugees needed food, clothes, mattresses, and drinking water but unfortunately, in the early days, supplies were not available for all of them. Thanks to mass media, many people outside the affected areas provided food, drinking water, masks, medicine, and clothes for refugees. Since the camps were spread over more than five regencies, distribution of supplies was a problem and although some camps had a surplus, many did not have enough provisions.

To support supply distribution and collection, volunteers of Jalin Merapi built ten posts to serve refugee camps, supported by a communication system coordinated by CRI. They revitalized the Jalin Merapi website as a hub of information for volunteers. Starting from a desire to give information about day-to-day developments in Merapi's activities and the situation in affected areas, volunteers shared information concerning victims' needs and about the distribution and collection of aid. Potential donors could use information from Jalin Merapi to find out what refugees needed and identify the location of refugee camps so they could determine what to donate.

The Jalin Merapi website consisted of messages from Twitter, SMS, Facebook, and radio streaming. Messages were created by volunteers who wanted to coordinate with other volunteers. People outside Jalin Merapi could send messages to ask about the situation in a certain area or the needs of refugees.

During the emergency response phase in November 2010, Jalin Merapi became an 'organization' of more than 3,000 volunteers. Since volunteers came from various backgrounds, Jalin Merapi declared the network independent, with no religious or political party affiliations. All people who wanted to help victims were welcome. Volunteers understood that they worked for humanitarian purposes; there was no space for discrimination.

Working to help victims in emergency situations is not simple. Volunteers must manage many activities, such as coverage areas, collecting and distributing aid, and monitoring situations in affected areas and refugee camps. In disaster areas there is always an urgent need for information to evaluate the situation, find out how to get aid, and how best to use the aid (Tanesia, 2007). To fulfill this need, a convergence of old and new media is helpful. Many volunteers used Facebook as their means of communication. To accommodate them, Jalin Merapi created five groups in Facebook consisting of 1,245 members (a group in Facebook has a maximum of 249 members). On Twitter, Jalin Merapi had thousands of followers. On November 5, 2010, the day of a big eruption, the number of followers increased up to 36,000 (Dewi, 2010). The contents of messages consisted of information about refugee needs.

Jalin Merapi used the Internet to access data from authoritative government institutions such as PVMBG and BPPTK. Communication with official sources was important to ensure the accuracy of information before Jalin Merapi delivered it to the people.

On December 3, 2010, the government downgraded the status of Merapi volcano from Level 4 to Level 3, allowing refugees to move back to their homes. The people of Kemalang village used this information to confirm that they could go back to their village. Volunteers from Jalin Merapi could operate their community radio again and begin observing the volcano, especially the flows of cold lava. Lintas Merapi Community Radio celebrated with a recovery campaign, inviting people to plant trees to replace those destroyed by pyroclastic flows. To indicate that Merapi was no longer dangerous, several people climbed the mountain on December 31, 2010, departing from Lintas Merapi Community Radio's studio.

The disaster management of Merapi's eruption illustrated the importance of social capital, especially social networks. The core idea of social capital theory is that social networks have value that can help people coordinate their activities. In his book *Bowling Alone: The collapse and revival of American community*, Putnam (2000) notes that a social network is important in community-building because community sustainability is built by interrelations among its members. The networks of social connection are used for a specific event, but following that community members have a willingness to communicate with each other in daily life. Hence, communication plays an important role to maintain civic engagement, which in turn can be seen as a basis for volunteering, philanthropy, and spontaneous 'helping.'

Van Vuuren (2001) notes that social capital is related to the motivation of volunteers to work in enterprises such as community radio. Volunteers see their activities as valuable to community life and they are inspired to participate when they see the benefits of radio in pursuing the community's common interests, such as providing information.

On the front line

A consequence of the close relationship between media, such as community radio, and the community is that those involved understand the local problems of the community. Community radio volunteers became frontline reporters in an emergency. In several disaster-affected areas in Indonesia, volunteers had the advantage over journalists from the mainstream media – they lived in the affected areas, were close to the victims and knew their people and environment well. In addition, as victims, volunteers could understand the reality victims faced and could voice victims' interests accurately. Community radio stations have proved that they can provide specific information for particular communities, especially in areas affected by natural disasters.

Conclusion

This chapter has argued that people at the grassroots in Indonesia use their community media to satisfy their communication needs and find solutions for their problems, especially during the occurrences of natural disasters. Community radio can be seen within the framework of the people's initiative of collective action in order to respond to an emergency situation caused by a natural disaster. The collective response to a natural disaster has often involved the establishment of community radio stations, especially to fulfill the communication needs in affected areas. With the continual exposure to natural disasters, Indonesian people have become aware of the potential hazards constantly presented by their environment. Thus, a general awareness among the population of the importance of community media for the dissemination of crucial public information relating to natural disasters has encouraged people to use community radio in such situations.

Furthermore, the chapter has demonstrated that in the chaotic and uncertain circumstances caused by recent natural disasters, the public dissemination of information was crucial for people to understand their recently changed situation. Limited equipment was not a barrier to community radio volunteers fulfilling the people's need for information. The ability of community action to provide information through radio in the affected areas originated from their solidarity with the community. In other words, social capital was essential for the development of community action as a response to sudden disasters, and community radio stations had already played a vital role in strengthening relationships among community members. Community radio was also an important link to people outside the disaster areas.

Finally, this chapter has shown that the uniqueness of community radio's response to natural disasters was that it represented the events from the perspective of victim experiences, since the sources of information – interviewees and reporters – were mostly insiders. In this context, the initial role of community radio stations in disaster areas was that of responding to the state of emergency. In addition, in some areas community radio stations have also supported community-based strategies of disaster preparation by broadcasting timely warning information.

References

Allen, KM. (2006). Community-based disaster preparedness and climate adaptation: local capacity building in the Philippines. *Disasters* 30 (1): 81–101.

Asian Disaster Reduction Center (ADRC). (2007). *Natural Disasters Data Book 2006: An Analytical Overview March 2007*. Asian Disaster Reduction Center. Available at: *http://www.adrc.or.jp/publications/databook/DB2006_e.html* (accessed July 29, 2008).

Birowo, M.A. (2010). Community radio and grassroots democracy: A case study of three villages in Yogyakarta Region, Indonesia, Media and Information. Curtin University of Technology, Perth.

BNPB. (2010). Perkembangan Pengungsi Bencana Merapi. Available at: *http://www.bnpb.go.id/irw/cetak.asp?id=163* (accessed June 4, 2011).

Buckland, J. and Rahman, M. (1999). Community-based disaster management during the 1997 Red River flood in Canada. *Disasters* 23(2): 174–91. Available at: *http://www.blackwell-synergy.com.dbgw.lis.curtin.edu.au/doi/abs/10.1111/1467–7717.00112* (accessed November 1, 2007).

Center for Hazards and Risk Research, Columbia University. (2005). Indonesia natural disaster profile. Available at: *http://www.ldgo.columbia.edu/chrr/research/profiles/indonesia.html* (accessed June 4, 2011).

Dewi, A.S. (2010). Menolong Lewat Kicauan: Kisah Relawan Admin Jalin Merapi. In M. Nazaruddin, Sulistyawati and B. Hermanto (eds.) *Relawan Berbagi*. Yogyakarta: Jalin Merapi.

Flint, C.G. and Luloff, A.E. (2007). Community activeness in response to forest disturbance in Alaska. *Society and Natural Resources* 20 (5): 431–50.

Freeman, P.K. (n.d.). Infrastructure, natural disasters, and poverty. International Institute for Applied Systems Analysis. Available at: *http://www.iiasa.ac.at/Research/RMS/june99/papers/freemansolo.pdf* (accessed June 4, 2011).

Gillham, B. (2000). *Case Study Research Methods*. London: Continuum.

Gregg, C.E. et al. (2004). Community preparedness for lava flows from Mauna Loa and Hualalai volcanoes, Kona, Hawai'i. *Bulletin of Volcanology* 66 (6): 531–40.

Jalin Merapi. (2010). Info Posko Pengungsian. Jalin Merapi and Combine Resources Institution. Available at: *http://merapi.combine.or.id/posko* (accessed December 29, 2010).

James, B. (2007). *Disaster Preparedness and Mitigation: UNESCO's role*. Paris: UNESCO.

Lavigne, F., De Coster, B., Juvin, N., Flohic, F. Gaillard, J.-C., Texier, P., Morin, J., and Sartohadi, J. (2008). People's behaviour in the face of volcanic hazards: perspectives from Javanese communities, Indonesia. *Journal of Volcanology and Geothermal Research* 172 (3–4): 273–87.

Mathbor, G.M. (2007). Enhancement of community preparedness for natural disasters. *International Social Work* 50 (3): 357–69.

Pearce, L. (2003). Disaster management and community planning, and public participation: How to achieve sustainable hazard mitigation. *Natural Hazards* 28(2–3): 211–28. Available at: *http://www.springerlink.com.dbgw.lis.curtin.edu.au/content/x4447nm175642784/fulltext.pdf* (accessed November 1, 2007).

Putnam, R.D. (2000). *Bowling Alone: The collapse and revival of American community*. New York: Simon & Schuster.

Pyles, L.P. (2007). Community organizing for post-disaster social development. *International Social Work* 50 (3): 321–33.

Riley, C.M. (n.d.). Pyroclastic flows. Available at: *http://www.geo.mtu.edu/volcanoes/hazards/primer/pyro.html* (accessed June 4, 2011).

Seputar Indonesia (2010). Rekor Baru Letusan Merapi. Available at: *http://www.bnpb.go.id/irw/cetak.asp?id=129* (accessed June 4, 2011).

Syaifullah, M. (2010). Letusan Merapi Terbesar Dalam 100 Tahun Terakhir Tempo Interaktif. Available at: *http://www.tempointeraktif.com/hg/jogja/2010/11/05/brk.20101105-289637.id.html* (accessed June 4, 2011).

Tanesia, A. (2007). Women, community radio, and post-disaster recovery process. Isis International. Available at: *http://www.isiswomen.org/index.php?option=com_content&task=view&id=891&Itemid=200#up* (accessed June 4, 2011).

UNESCO (n.d.). Disaster risk reduction. Available at: *http://www.unesco.org/new/en/natural-sciences/priority-areas/disaster-preparedness-and-mitigation/disaster-risk-reduction* (accessed June 4, 2011).

United Nations Office for the Coordination of Humanitarian Affairs (2006). OCHA situation report, No. 6: Indonesia earthquake. Geneva: OCHA.

van Vuuren, K. (2001). Beyond the studio: a case study of community radio and social capital. Australian Community Broadcasting Series (4). Available at: *http://tranquileye.com/free/files/Beyond_the_Studio.pdf* (accessed June 4, 2011).

Watson, J., Connolly, M., and Gayer, M. (eds.) (2006). *Communicable diseases following natural disasters: Risk assessment and priority interventions*. Geneva: World Health Organization.

Wirakusumah, A.D. (2003). Early warning system for geological hazard in Indonesia. Paper presented at the Second International Conference on Early Warning, Jakarta.

9

Public libraries and crisis management: roles of public libraries in hurricane/disaster preparedness and response

John L. Brobst, Lauren H. Mandel, and Charles R. McClure

Abstract: The hurricane damage that the United States Gulf Coast has sustained over the past decade was a catalyst for this study of the service roles public libraries provide in hurricane/disaster preparedness and response. Libraries have taken major steps to better meet community needs arising from these emergency situations. This chapter identifies new public library service roles, and discusses successful technology solutions and communications programs that public libraries can employ to assist local communities prepare for, and recover from, hurricanes and other disasters.

Key words: public library, disaster planning and response, hurricane, service role, emergency.

Introduction

The past decade has seen heightened hurricane activity in the United States, with more than $150 billion in damage in 2004 and 2005 (Pielke, 2008). Florida has experienced 53 hurricanes or other severe storms since 2000, resulting in over $64 billion in damage and 149 related fatalities (List of Florida Hurricanes, 2010). In 2007, reacting to this history of hurricane damage, the State of Florida created the Florida Catastrophic

Storm Risk Management Center (*www.stormrisk.org*) at Florida State University. This center 'supports the state's need to prepare for, respond to and recover from catastrophic storms' (Florida Catastrophic Storm Risk Management Center, 2010, para.1).

In 2008, the Information Use Management and Policy Institute (Information Institute; *www.ii.fsu.edu*) at the Florida State University was awarded a grant from the Florida Catastrophic Storm Risk Management Center to investigate *Hurricane Preparedness and Response by Utilizing Florida Public Libraries* (*Hurricane Preparedness and Response*; McClure, Mandel, Pierce, and Snead, 2010). Since 2004, the Information Institute has collected data that describe the roles and services that public libraries along the US Gulf Coast (i.e. Texas, Louisiana, Mississippi, Alabama, and Florida) have played in hurricane/disaster preparedness and response. These data come from annual national surveys of technology use and deployment funded by the Bill and Melinda Gates Foundation and the American Library Association (Bertot, Jaeger, McClure, and Langa, 2006), the Florida Division of Library and Information Services (McClure, Mandel, Snead, Bishop, and Ryan, 2009), and from numerous interviews conducted by staff at the Information Institute (Bertot, McClure, and Jaeger, 2006). These data revealed a number of cases where individual public libraries joined together as partners to create local hurricane/disaster preparedness and response teams. By working together, these libraries were able to leverage resources and contribute a range of skills and knowledge to handling information management and various communications prior to, during, and after such storms. Public libraries also have joined forces with local government agencies and community organizations to create integrated emergency response teams. This teamwork has placed public libraries at the forefront of emergency management networks, a position further supported by public recognition of libraries as trusted and effective government agencies. Individual public libraries have proved to be effective team members in supporting state and local government preparation for, and response to, hurricanes and other disasters.

The *Hurricane Preparedness and Response* project's intent was to reduce the state's overall disaster risk by raising the readiness level of all public libraries to meet the challenges posed by these weather-related catastrophes. Specifically, this project:

- identified and organized relevant public library hurricane-related information resources, services, roles, and best practices;

- identified, assessed, and organized successful individual public library experiences and best practices related to hurricane preparedness and response;

- developed model plans, standards, guidelines, and recommendations, making them widely available via print and through an interactive web portal;

- offered strategies to assist state and regional public library and government officials with disaster coordination and organization responsibilities; and

- disseminated information resources, services, experiences, best practices, plans and guidelines to coordinate public library managers and government partners in order to better prepare for and respond to hurricanes.

Collectively, these project activities served to improve the state's overall hurricane disaster preparation and response, reduce risk, and contribute to the mitigation of these crises.

This chapter begins by providing a brief overview of the background and methodology of the Information Institute's *Hurricane Preparedness and Response* project, as well as a summary of the public library hurricane/disaster service roles. Then, the chapter details how libraries can coordinate and collaborate with other government agencies, specifically with local emergency operations agencies, to better assist their communities in managing crises. The chapter concludes with next steps and recommendations for how libraries can implement identified service roles and become more involved in community crisis management.

Background

Several significant efforts have examined the contributions made by libraries during times of disaster. An oral history project developed a knowledge base of stories about the roles that librarians performed during and in the aftermath of disasters (Featherstone, Lyon, and Ruffin, 2008). This knowledge base described service roles and activities related to emergency and disaster planning, preparedness, response, and recovery. The study identified eight service role categories:

- institutional supporters
- collection managers

- information disseminators
- internal planners
- community supporters
- government partners
- educators/trainers, and
- information community builders.

The study concluded that librarians, particularly health sciences librarians, made significant contributions to disaster preparedness and recovery activities. The study noted the value of establishing collaborative relationships between libraries and local, state, and federal disaster management agencies and organizations.

The success with which libraries can perform these service roles greatly depends on being prepared for emergencies, and part of that preparation involves having formal and detailed disaster plans. Oelschlegel (2008) makes the point that disasters are low-probability, high-impact events, and perhaps because of that low probability, the Heritage Preservation (2005) survey of public, academic and special libraries found that 78 percent of libraries had no local disaster plan. Oelschlegel (2008) notes the importance of planning and preparedness, but urges a more comprehensive and community-involved approach to the planning process, highlighting the importance of planning for situations where the library may become part of a coordinated response to a disaster in which it is not directly involved. Some examples of such disasters where library services are important in responding to local area emergency situations include local fires, train wrecks, and plant explosions. In such situations, the nearby libraries provide critically important and timely information to the community, thereby increasing the credibility of the library as the place to turn for information in times of crisis.

Disaster planning is not simply about restoring services to the public; it extends to offering support to a disaster relief effort that may meet broader community needs. Zach and McKnight (2010) identify the differences between traditional disaster planning and planning for responsive information services. Most library emergency plans assume that a disaster will affect only a single institution or perhaps a small area in a city (i.e. a few blocks), further assuming that systems that have been disabled are available elsewhere within the community to provide temporary backup during the emergency. These assumptions quickly fall apart when the disaster is a wider community-based event during which 'it is very possible that 90 percent of the best library emergency and disaster plans will be irrelevant' (Davis, 2000: 341). Library disaster planning must be comprehensive, while retaining the flexibility to react to unforeseen emergencies. A formal planning effort provides the foundation that helps ensure that the library is ready to be an active participant in the community's recovery efforts by engaging as a vital link in the larger emergency response scenario. In responding to disasters, service roles evolve and come to the forefront of the library's service to the community.

In the US Gulf Coast region, libraries have demonstrated outstanding efforts towards providing services and support when hurricane events devastated their communities (McClure, Ryan, Mandel, Brobst, Hinnant, Andrade, and Snead, 2009). Welsh and Higgins (2009) interviewed library workers who had experienced Hurricane Katrina on the Gulf Coast. They found that those libraries that could open after Katrina prioritized their efforts to offer essential services, including access to computers and information via computers; assistance in filling out necessary relief aid forms; listening; providing comfort; and providing volunteer support to the community recovery efforts. Also, Jaeger, Langa, McClure, and Bertot (2007) conducted a number of interviews with public librarians and state library officials along the Gulf Coast regarding their activities, roles, and services during the 2004 and 2005 hurricanes. This study found that public libraries successfully provided a range of disaster preparedness and recovery services that were unique, as other government agencies were not providing and could not provide such services. The public libraries clearly played roles in both providing information and facilitating communication, illustrating the unique value that public libraries offer to their communities during and after disasters.

With over 2,200 public library outlets in the Gulf Coast states, virtually every community in that region has access to a nearby public library (National Center for Educational Statistics, 2005). To varying degrees, each of these libraries has the potential to contribute to or assist in emergency preparedness and response. These public libraries are exceptionally well positioned to provide emergency preparedness and response services, but they need access to information as to how to organize in order to assist their local communities effectively in emergency preparedness and response.

By developing plans, guidelines, and recommendations, as well as documenting best practices for how libraries can serve in these roles, the *Hurricane Preparedness and Response* project is designed to contribute to the overall success with which the Gulf Coast states can manage and respond to hurricanes and other disasters and reduce the impact of these crises on Gulf Coast residents. Armed with such tools, public libraries, in partnership with other agencies, can mitigate some of the damage and destruction that these emergencies bring to the region. In this way, the project supports the region's need to prepare for, respond to, and recover from catastrophic storms and other disasters.

Project overview

Research by the Information Institute shows that libraries have responded to hurricanes and other disasters by taking steps to better prepare for the information needs of the libraries themselves and the communities they serve (McClure, Ryan, et al., 2009). Libraries have adapted their service roles to provide information services tailored to emergency support and assistance to hurricane victims (Bertot, Jaeger, Langa, and McClure, 2006; Jaeger et al., 2007; McClure, Ryan, et al., 2009). The project design specifically addressed the aforementioned need to conduct a systematic investigation of how libraries have responded to community needs during hurricane-related emergency management actions. Major activities to support that objective included:

- finding the best available recovery and preparedness information;
- conducting interviews with seasoned professionals to gather best practices;
- building a user friendly web portal to provide easy access to this information; and
- disseminating research findings and promoting the public library service roles to the Gulf Coast public library and emergency management communities.

The web portal provides an effective means of organizing and disseminating a range of information on how public libraries can assist local communities in preparing for and recovering from hurricanes and other disasters. That portal is available at *http://hurricanes.ii.fsu.edu*. Included within the portal is a more extensive discussion of project findings, which centers on eight critical service roles that libraries play in hurricane/disaster preparedness and response (described in the next section of this chapter).

Overall, the goal of this project was to work with public librarians to better assist their communities in preparing for and responding to hurricanes and other disasters. Individual public libraries provide a range of useful hurricane and disaster preparation and recovery services to their communities, but their discrete efforts are often isolated and unavailable to the rest of the library community. Fundamental to the project was the objective to identify the roles, best practices, activities, tools, and resources developed by local public libraries for their communities and to make them available to the larger library profession. All public library managers could help their communities respond better if they had the benefit of some portion of their fellow library managers' disaster experiences. The project had three critically important tasks: first, to identify useful information; second, to make that information available; and finally, to build awareness of the existence of that information to the user community.

Public library hurricane service roles

The project team interviewed over 200 public library managers and emergency management officials who had aided their communities to prepare for or recover from a hurricane or other disaster. These interviews revealed eight possible service roles performed by hurricane-affected libraries:

- *Safe haven*: The public library is the community's living room before and after a storm with secure buildings, relaxing space, light, air conditioning, bathrooms, and comfortable chairs.

- *Normal service*: The community counts on normal library service before and after the storm to provide hope, re-establish government presence, reduce stress, return normalcy, and offer recreation and distraction.

- *Disaster Recovery Centers (DRC)*: DRCs attempt to assemble under one roof all agencies providing disaster benefits, possibly as a Federal Emergency Management Agency designated DRC, a state, county or municipal DRC, a point of distribution (POD) of aid, or simply a place for neighbors to talk about their experiences and provide each other with aid.

- *Information hub*: The community counts on the library before and after a storm to offer access to various communication equipment, be a trusted provider of accurate, reliable information, produce needed information aids where they do not exist, and deliver this information using whatever technology the community uses and can afford.

- *Cultural organizations liaison*: Public libraries may serve as liaison points between emergency management agencies and the community's cultural organizations.

- *Evacuee resource*: Evacuees count on the nearest public library for a safe haven, normal service, disaster recovery center, and information hub.

- *Improvise*: Should a disaster strike, the community counts on the public library to improvise and do what is needed to assist in the community's recovery, which requires the library to be flexible, innovative, and creative to efficiently and effectively meet the needs of those impacted by this type of disaster.

- *Get to know your local EOC*: Getting to know your local Emergency Operations Center (EOC) can result in the public library and EOC working together to provide best for the community's needs.

These key public library community hurricane/disaster response roles appear in greater detail, along with best practices and examples, within the project web portal: *http://hurricanes.ii.fsu.edu*. The eight service roles categorize and define the functions performed by public libraries during hurricane/disaster preparedness and response, a specific type of crisis management.

Joining the emergency response network

Before disaster strikes, library managers have an opportunity to focus on what they can control and manage. This includes preparing the library facility and staff, finding partners to help with preparation and recovery, and coordinating emergency response activities with local emergency operations leaders and government agencies as much as is reasonable. The team approach has proved to yield rewards greater than individual agency independent efforts. As one library manager noted, 'If I can build a relationship with directors of [local, state, and federal] agencies, it brings credibility of libraries to the table' (personal communication, October 15, 2009).

The first step in managing disaster response partnerships is to gain a better awareness of what each potential partner does to support community-wide hurricane/disaster preparedness and response. Open and frank discussions need to be held with a range of local emergency responders and others about the resources necessary to provide services to the community while meeting partners' needs. The next step is to plan and coordinate what the library can contribute, what the library needs from each partner in order to do so, and how the library's activities can mesh with other partners' activities; as far as possible, the library and its partners should prepare and test these new arrangements prior to an emergency. Working out the details in advance saves time, significantly improves response time and quality, and helps form bonds of trust and understanding among partners.

The director of one county emergency management agency identified several areas where libraries have directly assisted local emergency responders during the hurricane season (personal communication, December 3, 2009). Libraries have served as recruitment centers to solicit volunteers because typically they are located centrally within a community or offer several convenient locations from which to recruit seasonal participants. The library can provide rooms for organizational meetings, including serving as a Volunteer Reception Center, coordinating and organizing newly recruited volunteers, and conducting training sessions. Also, the library can serve as a coordination point for scheduling volunteer activities and for last-minute recruiting of volunteers. Community rooms can support various emergency operations and recovery programs, and library technical staff and personal computer resources can support the information and communication needs that facilitate the emergency activities. Emergency agencies often recruit library staff members to help as volunteers, because library staff members tend to have excellent people skills, organizational skills, and information retrieval skills.

After a crisis occurs, it is useful to assess what worked and what did not, and then determine what other efforts can assist the community in the future. In initiating these collaborative efforts, the library and its partners should keep in mind that making arrangements to aid each other and to coordinate these activities takes time, and that what is possible may vary from location to location due to local situations and library-county or library-city policies. Other organizations can make significant disaster response contributions, such as Multi-type Library Cooperatives (MLCs), state library agencies, larger library systems, libraries adjacent to hurricane-affected libraries, library vendors, library membership organizations such as LYRASIS (LYRASIS, 2010) and other regional library consortia. The key, however, is for the public library (1) to clarify relationships, responsibilities, and activities with other community, state, and federal emergency agencies prior to a hurricane or disaster, and (2) to understand which of the service roles it has the capacity and knowledge to offer the local community.

Benefits of partnering with emergency management organizations

Libraries need to become an integrated element in the overall network of emergency response that prepares for and reacts to disasters. Libraries can assist local, state, and federal emergency response efforts during each phase of emergency/disaster preparedness: planning, preparing, responding, and recovering. The following section addresses each of those phases and outlines specific activities that the library can undertake to better integrate the library into the local community's overall emergency response network, resulting in the provision of higher levels of service to the local community.

Planning phase

Libraries should take the initiative to introduce themselves to key officials and agencies involved with emergency management. This introduction will afford the library the means to promote the unique services that it can provide towards assisting in the overall disaster preparedness and recovery picture. Such services could include offering to display and distribute information, including print materials and electronic media. Through its reference services, the library can identify useful resources that the public can access in their efforts to gain information about planning for a disaster.

As an example, libraries often provide hurricane planning resources on the library's website before and during the hurricane season. To complement this, the local emergency management agency's website could add an active link to the library website, or the library could develop a special section of its website that addresses emergency preparedness. That special section would be a valuable asset to the public and would be another resource that the local emergency management agencies could promote or utilize. The special section of the website could include the identification of informative resources or practical guides that indicate how to develop disaster plans, for both individuals and for businesses. It also could include such helpful resources as links to the local emergency management agency's website, assistance programs, evacuee services, and even online tutorials on texting, as this is often the only means of communication when there are widespread power outages (American Library Association, 2010).

Preparing phase

Once libraries have introduced themselves to the emergency management organizations in their area, they should update and review their own disaster plans with staff. Activities would include identifying and inventorying supplies needed for various disaster scenarios as well as beginning to develop materials for display and distribution. During this phase, the library should reach out to local emergency response agencies to obtain informative brochures and materials for public display and access. These materials may need to be available in English and also in other languages, as determined by the demographics of the local service area. At this point, the library can expand the website developed in the Planning phase as a valuable tool in helping to provide informative resources.

More intensive efforts during this phase could include developing library-sponsored programs tailored to address specific emergencies such as hurricanes, epidemics, terrorism, and chemical spills. Promotional and awareness-building activities can help the public recognize the role of the library as a source for emergency preparedness and recovery information, and can build awareness of how well the library integrates into the overall emergency response network. Building this awareness before a disaster hits will help the public respond to and recover from a disaster event.

Responding phase

Several beneficial steps can help prepare and inform the public upon notification of a disaster. In the case of hurricanes, there may be days of advance notice before the disaster strikes. During this time, the library can update its website to provide more targeted information that will enable the public to make last-minute preparations or to decide whether to stay in an area or evacuate it. By monitoring local emergency communications and staying abreast of ongoing developments, this information could be disseminated using the library website or library-sponsored social networking sites.

Building an awareness of the library as a vital resource during this emergency situation could include efforts to publicize the library's role on its website and arranging on-camera interviews in the local news media. When disasters strike suddenly, such as tornadoes or earthquakes, the library can respond by posting relevant content on its website and providing links to key emergency agencies and relief organizations. As Internet connectivity may be sporadic, contact information should include telephone numbers and physical addresses.

Recovering phase

Once the immediate danger or disabling effects of a disaster have passed, the library should continue to provide ongoing updates to its website.

These updates could include information on library openings and closures, and provide current information on where to get help. Once the library is back to normal operations, local emergency management agencies should be informed as to which library outlets are open and what relief services they can provide. This approach of informing the emergency management agencies is the preferred procedure, as these organizations have priority access and are in a better position to prioritize the information that needs distributing. The library should initiate efforts early on to identify the appropriate officials who will handle such news releases. To maintain a steady and accurate stream of information to the emergency responders, the library should hold daily management briefings to provide updates on all recovery efforts and the availability of library outlets throughout the community.

The library also needs to have an emergency communications plan in place to ensure that information flows quickly and accurately throughout the organization. This plan could incorporate use of listservs, e-mail, texting, blogs, or social networking sites (such as Facebook, MySpace, and Twitter) to connect to and update library staff and library users. Many individuals can now access these social networking sites on their cell phones, should the library's Internet access remain down due to service interruption caused by the disaster.

These are just a few examples of the ways in which the library can integrate itself more effectively into the larger emergency response network that springs into action when a disaster becomes imminent. Many of these efforts rely on early preparation to contact and coordinate with local emergency management officials. By starting early and building the necessary relationships, these activities will help the library to be better prepared and to be organized earlier in advance of a disaster, and then to operate more smoothly after a disaster. Additional guidance on integrating the library into the local emergency operations management organization is available via the *Hurricane Preparedness and Response* web portal (*http://hurricanes.ii.fsu.edu*; Information Use Management and Policy Institute, 2010).

The web portal: a technology for crisis management

A web portal provides a means to gather together a wide range of information in a single location, in a way that is conveniently accessible to users and easily obtainable with just a few mouse clicks. Implementation of web-based technology has become a popular application in libraries, which already organize a wide range of information to make it accessible to users in a variety of locations. Examples of successful library portals abound, such as the highly localized SkokieNet from the Skokie Public Library (IL) and numerous MyLibrary portals like MyLibrary@NCState from North Carolina State University, BUILDER Hybrid Library Demonstrator at the University of Birmingham (UK), and MyLibrary@ LANL service at the Los Alamos National Laboratory, among others (Buhmann, Greenwalt, Jacobsen, and Roehm, 2009).

The Information Institute began this project by conducting a formal needs assessment, which included interviews with over 200 hurricane-experienced librarians, emergency management officials, and other experts in the field. This user-centric assessment indicated the need for a one-stop, comprehensive collection of hurricane and other disaster information. Interviewees indicated that such a consolidated resource would greatly improve the services librarians provide their local communities in hurricane/disaster preparedness and response. The needs assessment also indicated that librarians and emergency management officials required mechanisms to share information, collaborate, and communicate with each other. Web portal technology could provide these capabilities, and, as an emergent technology, the web portal had matured to the point where it had a track record of solid reliability and high performance. The project team determined that this need for a comprehensive collection of information and a collaborative communication platform would be met best by the creation of a *Hurricane/Disaster Preparedness and Response* web portal.

What the portal offers the practicing librarian

A guiding principle in the design of the web portal was to ensure that the information, resources, and best practices were readily available to all public libraries and their staff. With that principle in mind, the portal design provided an easy-to-use resource for librarians, containing valuable information on all aspects of hurricane preparedness, such as guidance on developing effective hurricane plans, integrating efforts with governmental agencies, and identifying best practices for public librarians. The completed web portal is dynamic, content-rich and delivers timely and relevant information to librarians, including emergency information, web-based resources, and informative links for multiple resources.

Interactive features such as the project blog and wiki promote effective collaboration and information exchange as libraries prepare for and react to emergencies. In addition to serving the needs of the librarians, these interactive tools provide effective communication mechanisms for integrating library efforts with the various local emergency response organizations.

Employing the web portal approach provided the Information Institute with the capability to consolidate and organize numerous resources in an easy-to-use structure while providing timely and relevant content. The portal (available at *http://hurricanes.ii.fsu.edu*) provides a wealth of information for practicing librarians, including the following:

- a consolidated set of resources that provides everything librarians need in one place, including plans, workbooks, and success stories from disaster-experienced libraries;

- best practices for response and recovery that detail how libraries can prepare for and respond to disasters; and

- detailed service roles that explain how libraries can function as integral parts of the emergency response network.

In providing these resources to the library community in a consolidated and easy to use format, the web portal was very successful in supporting the project's intention, which was to reduce the state's overall disaster risk by raising the readiness level of all public libraries to meet the challenges posed by these catastrophes.

The coordination, management, and integration of information resources through the project web portal are important contributions to public library hurricane/disaster preparedness and response. In addition, the portal offers fast searching for resources on a variety of topics, with the best resources for each of the identified service roles through additional project data collection and analysis. Part of the original project plan was to evaluate the use of the portal before, during, and after a major hurricane. However, the 2009 hurricane season was relatively quiet for Florida and the Gulf Coast region, and this was not possible. Therefore it is not possible to include any examples of real use of the portal during an actual hurricane.

Value of the portal

The project team conducted interviews with practicing librarians to ascertain their views on the utility of the portal. The librarians indicated that they were pleased to have access to the wiki and blog to communicate directly with one another regarding requests and needs. Interviewees indicated that many times in the past they had problems exchanging ideas and sharing information quickly, and that the project blog provides a solution for that issue. The librarians also appreciated that they do not have to reinvent the wheel when it comes to creating library policies that would apply during a hurricane/disaster event, since the portal includes 'real-life' library policies. One librarian said, 'It seems that everything you need to set up a plan and execute it is here and it is great to go to one place and find it all rather than hopping around from library to library and different organizations' [websites] with less information than is included here' (personal communication, November 18, 2009).

Many librarians appreciated the Web 2.0 Tools section of the portal as a means to communicate amongst librarians and emergency responders, saying things such as 'this could be a one-stop-shop for anyone who is a librarian' (personal communication, November 5, 2009). Also, one remarked on the Web 2.0 tools' usefulness for members of the library's community, saying: 'There's a part for residents? I am curious about that. I can see that being extremely useful to people, they would be thrilled. When you are busy at the desk and you have 20 people asking you [to] set them up on a computer so that they can browse and get information. People can get practical information from people who have already done the research. Rather than a librarian saying "Maybe you could do this, or maybe you could do that." A person could see that this person found groceries here, and they found ice there' (personal communication, November 18, 2009).

Although no major hurricanes hit Florida or the Gulf Coast in 2009, the librarians already see the value of the portal to their work in hurricane preparedness and response. Helen Moeller, then Director of the Leon County Public Library (Tallahassee, FL), summed up the overall librarian viewpoint:

> After disasters, people flock to their public libraries for information, computers, a safe place to be with other people, to relax, to read, and to borrow materials. Your website will provide much needed information in a standard framework that is not readily available elsewhere. Great job! (personal communication, May 29, 2009)

This and similar comments by other librarians suggests that the portal addresses an important service need.

Next steps: public librarians as crisis managers

This project included interviews with numerous hurricane-experienced librarians, emergency management officials, and other experts in the field. From these interviews came success stories and findings that indicate how librarians can undertake several general activities that will allow them to execute their critically important roles in hurricane/disaster preparedness and response more effectively. These activities center on efforts to build community awareness of the value that the library can offer before, during, and after disasters and to clarify the service roles that have proven to be successful in aiding recovery and rebuilding efforts. Such activities include:

- enhancing services, information, resources, and expertise to assist local communities and their residents during emergency response events;

- taking the initiative to work more effectively in their local communities and with the state for hurricane/disaster preparedness and response;

- improving communication, planning, and response among various government and other agencies regarding emergency preparedness and response; and

- building awareness and educating local community members, government officials, and others about the roles public libraries can play in disaster preparedness and response.

When libraries undertake these activities, they greatly improve the ability of Gulf Coast residents to better survive and cope with the results of a hurricane or other disaster by leveraging and coordinating the expertise of public librarians in working with other government agencies for disaster preparedness and response.

There are several specific steps librarians can take to help their libraries and communities manage crises. First, librarians can review the service roles, best practices, and guides as outlined on the project portal. As a first step, a library can select one practice to develop this season. For example, if you want to improve your role as Safe Haven, a likely best practice to adopt is to have an emergency or Continuity of Operations Plan (COOP). Decide which components of the plan to work on this year and do them. The underlying message is: do not try to do everything all at once. It is easy to get overwhelmed. Pick one small thing and do it well.

Second, librarians can coordinate their efforts with other responders in advance of a storm. Key partners are local emergency management and government agencies, but also important are local utilities, police, fire, church groups, and local businesses. Librarians should learn what these organizations intend to do and acquaint them with the role(s) the library intends to play. The goal should be to find ways to strengthen your community's ability to respond through collaboration.

Third, the library should prepare its staff. Library managers should communicate with library staff, telling them what is expected of them, why their work matters to the community in emergency situations, and giving details of disaster response roles and responsibilities. Reviewing this information annually should become standard operating procedure.

Finally, the library should publicize its role in emergency preparation and response. Public libraries can make certain that community members are aware of the services that the library can provide should a hurricane or other emergency situation occur. This should take place periodically so that community members are aware, and remain aware, that they can take advantage of the librarians' knowledge and skills in an emergency situation.

Public libraries are essential service points in times of crisis, providing a range of uniquely valuable services that extend beyond traditional roles. Libraries must now build an awareness of this important value in the community, and make that case to federal, state, and local agencies in order to gain recognition as essential service providers during disaster recovery. Improving awareness will help libraries better integrate into the overall emergency response network, making libraries a key component in a community's reaction to a crisis situation. This enhanced awareness is necessary to ensure that others see that it is a priority to provide library directors with quick access to their facilities after disaster strikes, not only to assess the library's damage, but also to provide access and services to the local community that the library serves.

Acknowledgments

The Information Institute acknowledges the generous help and support from project partners, the Florida Division of Library and Information Services, and LYRASIS, as well as Florida Multi-type Library Cooperatives, librarians, and state library staff who participated in the various data collection efforts, and emergency management personnel who shared their time and experiences. We also acknowledge the assistance and involvement from the state library agencies in Louisiana, Alabama, and Mississippi. We are especially grateful to the Florida Catastrophic Storm Risk Management Center at the Florida State University, which funded the project. The project team also acknowledges the contributions of the entire Information Institute staff for their work on this important project.

References

American Library Association. (2010). Disaster response: A selected annotated bibliography. Chicago: American Library Association. Retrieved June 4, 2011 from *http://www.ala.org*.

Bertot, J.C., Jaeger, P.T., Langa, L.A., and McClure, C.R. (2006). Public access computing and Internet access in public libraries: The role of public libraries in E-government and emergency situations. *First Monday, 11*(9), n.p. Retrieved June 4, 2011 from *http://firstmonday.org*.

Bertot, J.C., Jaeger, P.T., McClure, C.R., and Langa, L.A. (2006). *Public libraries and the Internet 2006: A special report on public libraries and the 2004 and 2005 hurricanes for the Bill and Melinda Gates Foundation and the American Library Association*. Tallahassee, FL: Information Use Management and Policy Institute, College of Communication and Information, the Florida State University. Retrieved June 4, 2011 from *http://www.ii.fsu.edu/plinternet*.

Bertot, J.C., McClure, C.R., and Jaeger, P.T. (2006). *Public Libraries and the Internet 2006: Survey results and findings*. Tallahassee, FL: Information Use Management and Policy Institute, College of Communication and Information, the Florida State University. Retrieved June 4, 2011 from *http://www.ii.fsu.edu/content/view/full/15176*. Additional annual reports from the *Public Libraries and the Internet* series are available at *http://www.plinternetsurvey.org/?q=node/13*.

Buhmann, M., Greenwalt, T., Jacobsen, M., and Roehm, F. (2009). On the ground, in the cloud. *Library Journal netConnect, 134*(12), 35–7. Retrieved June 4, 2011 from *http://www.libraryjournal.com*.

Davis, D. (2000). Disaster and after: the practicalities of information service in times of war and other catastrophes. *Library and Information Science Research, 3*(22), 341–43. doi:10.1016/S0740-8188(00)00045-1

Featherstone, R.M., Lyon, B.J., and Ruffin, A.B. (2008). Library roles in disaster response: An oral history project by the National Library of Medicine. *Journal of the Medical Library Association, 96*(4), 343–50. doi:10.3163/1536-5050.96.4.009

Florida Catastrophic Storm Risk Management Center. (2010). *About the Center* [Website]. Tallahassee, FL: Florida Catastrophic Storm Risk Management Center, College of Business, the Florida State University. Retrieved June 4, 2011 from *http://www.stormrisk.org/index.cfm?page=2*.

Heritage Preservation. (2005). *A public trust at risk: The Heritage Health Index report on the state of America's collection*. Washington DC: Heritage Preservation. Retrieved June 4, 2011 from *http://www.heritagepreservation.org*.

Information Use Management and Policy Institute. (2010). *Improving Florida public library utilization in community hurricane response* [Website]. Tallahassee, FL: Information Use Management and Policy Institute, College of Communication and Information, the Florida State University. Retrieved June 4, 2011 from *http://hurricanes.ii.fsu.edu*.

Jaeger, P.T., Langa, L.A., McClure, C.R., and Bertot, J.C. (2007). The 2004 and 2005 Gulf Coast hurricanes: Evolving roles and lessons learned for public libraries. *Public Library Quarterly*, *25*(3/4), 199–214. doi:10.1300/J118v25n03_17.

List of Florida hurricanes. (2010, February 5). *Wikipedia*. San Francisco, CA: Wikimedia Foundation. Retrieved from *http://en.wikipedia.org*.

LYRASIS. (2010). *LYRASIS* [Website]. Location: LYRASIS. Atlanta, GA: LYRASIS. Retrieved June 4, 2011 from *http://www.lyrasis.org*.

McClure, C.R., Mandel, L.H., Pierce, S., and Snead, J.T. (2010). *Hurricane/disaster preparedness and response by utilizing Florida public libraries: Final report*. Tallahassee, FL: Information Use Management and Policy Institute, College of Communication and Information, the Florida State University. Retrieved June 4, 2011 from *http://www.ii.fsu.edu*.

McClure, C.R., Mandel, L.H., Snead, J.T., Bishop, B.W., and Ryan, J. (2009). Needs assessment of Florida public library e-government and emergency/disaster management broadband-enabled services. Retrieved November 10, 2010 from *http://www.ii.fsu.edu*.

McClure, C.R., Ryan, J., Mandel, L.H., Brobst, J., Hinnant, C.C., Andrade, J., and Snead, J.T. (2009). Hurricane preparedness and response for Florida public libraries: Best practices and strategies. *Florida Libraries*, *52*(1), 4–7.

National Center for Educational Statistics. (2005). *State education data profiles* [Data file]. Washington DC: National Center for Education Statistics, U.S. Department of Education Institute of Education Sciences. Retrieved June 4, 2011 from *http://nces.ed.gov*.

Oelschlegel, S. (2008). Emergency preparedness and the role of information services. *Tennessee Libraries*, *58*(2), n.p. Retrieved June 4, 2011 from *http://www.tnla.org/displaycommon.cfm?an=1&subarticlenbr=17*.

Pielke, R. A. (2008). Normalized hurricane damage in the United States: 1900–2005. *Natural Hazards Review*, *9*(1), 29–42. doi:10.1061/(ASCE)1527-6988(2008)9:1(29).

Welsh, T.S., and Higgins, S.E. (2009). Public libraries post-Hurricane Katrina: A pilot study. *Library Review*, *58*(9), 652–9. doi:10.1108/00242530910997937

Zach, L., and McKnight, M. (2010). Special services in special times: Responding to changed information needs during and after community-based disasters. *Public Libraries*, *49*(2), 37–43.

10

Academic libraries in crisis situations: roles, responses, and lessons learned in providing crisis-related information and services

Stephanie Ganic Braunstein, Jenna Ryan, and Will Hires

Abstract: Although all major libraries in a community can potentially serve as sources of assistance during a crisis, academic libraries in particular have much to offer both to their institutions and to their communities. Disaster situations can be ameliorated by the expertise of academic librarians with their special capacity for information organization and management and service. Thus, academic librarians can and should take the initiative to get the library involved early in response efforts and at a high priority.

Key words: academic libraries, community service and support, crisis situations, disaster response.

How academic libraries compare to public libraries in a crisis

Roles of public libraries

Public libraries are generally considered to be community focal points and places where people gather to consume information. From offering casual reading for personal pleasure to providing intensive research in support of a specific project, these libraries satisfy people's need to explore their personal interests and crystallize their ideas. Public libraries collect material of general interest in popular formats and can potentially serve everyone who comes through their doorways. In addition, when fulfilling their function as a part of a free society, public libraries offer information without judgment about its intended use.

The public library is also deemed a necessary part of the structure of a civilized society; it serves the community at large and represents an integral component of communal organization. As a result, all residents of a typical community are almost automatically members of the local public library and form its potential user base.

Most, if not all, of these community libraries function so organically as a fixture in their respective communities that one might expect their status to remain largely unchanged during periods of crisis or emergency. However, the perception of community libraries is affected by the library's actions and involvement with crisis situations (Jaeger, Langa, McClure, and Bertot, 2006). During emergency conditions, the library can adjust its schedule of operations and even add additional temporary staff that has specific expertise to respond effectively to the emergency. Already places where the association with information is a natural occurrence, public libraries may need to modify specific functions and expand or repurpose them according to the dictates of the crisis and the urgency of response to it. The functions of acquiring information, analyzing and categorizing its content, and organizing it for potential use, are typical functions that can be made more urgent during a crisis situation. In times of crisis, public libraries increase efforts to protect and preserve information and to serve patrons. It is probably worth remembering that not only do some of the special response requirements of disasters include the need for wide and efficient dissemination of health and safety information, but they also include the need for dealing with the grieving, survival, and psychological effects experienced by a traumatized populace. A community library can often provide this type of support with emphasis on specialized collections and even programs designed to promote communal healing.

Based on interviews with librarians who engaged in activities during and after disasters, Featherstone et al. (2008) identified eight specific roles for libraries in disaster response, concluding that libraries can function as institutional supporters, collection managers, information disseminators, internal planners, community supporters, government partners, educators and trainers, and information community builders. Although most librarians routinely engage in activities associated with collection management, dissemination of information, and education and training, these roles are typically expanded during crises according to the perceived specific needs.

Roles of academic libraries

Public libraries are, by their public nature, highly accessible venues; they are usually spacious, with accommodating meeting rooms, and unrestrictive with respect to the populations they serve. In contrast, academic libraries are typically not located close to main roadways, do not necessarily cater to the needs of large groups, and require affiliation with their parent university as qualification for full access to services. Nevertheless, academic libraries can play a distinct role during a crisis situation by focusing on securing the special needs of the university campus, by enhancing their special connections with extra-regional agencies and organizations, and even, paradoxically, by supporting local public libraries with the academics' frequently stronger and more reliable communications networks that easily and quickly acquire, disseminate, and exchange information extra-regionally, nationally, and even internationally.

During a crisis, public information quickly becomes a critical part of the effort to understand, act, and marshal a response (Will, 2001). Because many academic libraries have relationships with governmental bodies to assist with research and the delivery of information, those relationships can be easily enhanced during crisis situations. Crises demand quick and thoughtful responses but, as emphasized by Van Scotter, Pawloski, and Cu (2010), it is absolutely necessary that organizations and agencies work together to minimize conflicts over jurisdiction, authority, control of resources, and potential liability as well as responsibility. The academic library can assist with the planning, training, identifying, and establishing of a chain of command and communication. These are particularly important tasks with which academic librarians, as handlers of sophisticated information, are familiar and experienced, and it is imperative that all efforts be consolidated and channeled in ways that best accomplish the recovery objective.

According to Block and Kim (2006), librarians often lead the way on the long journey to recovery and rebuilding. Academic librarians can be most effective during crises by quickly and deliberately transforming their posture from being passive members of a disaster response team to one of being enthusiastic and active participants. For example, the academic library can potentially be an immediately effective and invaluable ally to local businesses and non-profit organizations. Bringing together the various agencies, institutions, and organizations that will be needed to coordinate the recovery plan is an important function, and libraries are natural places where this kind of organization and enhanced coordination activity takes place (Will, 2001). Businesses affected by the disaster would be keen to identify other businesses that may be unaffected or minimally impacted so that they can enlist their assistance to rebuild, re-establish industrial supply lines, or repair networking connections. Libraries affiliated with universities having business schools and programs would be in a perfect position to assist with the development of these processes as well as to help establish links with business and commercial resources in adjacent communities.

Some academic libraries already serve as archives or depositories for government information and thereby have established connections with state and national agencies. Just as public libraries accumulate and disseminate information in support of local community organizations, academic libraries typically do the same for student organizations, administrative projects, and related off-campus activities such as educational forums. Academic libraries are expected to provide support to institutional interests in these ways and then, typically, to find ways to expand these services to the greater community at times of crisis. Thus, in their highly trained and experienced staff, academic libraries have the expertise and capacity to positively influence a recovery effort in ways that can complement the similar endeavors made by public libraries.

Further consideration of the specialized role of the academic library

When a disaster occurs in a community served by one or more universities, the research faculty of those universities becomes an invaluable resource for expert information on the local geography, ecology, social dynamics, and often on the disaster itself. As an example, when Hurricane Katrina hit New Orleans, faculty from Louisiana State University's Hurricane Center, Earthscan Lab, School of Coast and Environment, and many other academic units and departments worked closely with federal and state officials in responding to the disaster. In contrast, as faculty and university administrators rush in during a crisis to lend their expertise to the recovery effort, the potential role of the university library is often overlooked. This apparent oversight of a campus resource misses a vital point: the library houses a wealth of information – something that is often in short supply in the immediate aftermath of a disaster. Besides the millions of books, journals, newspapers, government documents, dissertations, multimedia, and other forms of physical information sources, academic libraries also make available hundreds of electronic databases with access to the latest research in almost any given field. In addition, the library can often negotiate with publishers and vendors to provide temporary emergency access to materials not normally available at a given institution.

Academic libraries are often centrally located within a campus, and in emergency situations, the academic library can become a gateway through which all the information and resources of its faculty, as well as of local, state, and federal organizations, other academic institutions, and of course the library's own resources can be centralized, managed, and efficiently distributed (Sheldon and Hendrickson, 1987). Another resource often unnoticed when it comes to academic libraries is the librarians themselves. Academic librarians may or may not have expertise in a particular field of study, but what they do have is expertise in the art of searching for, locating, obtaining, organizing, and disseminating information.

Despite the obvious potential for academic librarians to take major roles in disaster responses, they often miss those opportunities, sometimes through their own lack of vision. Library disaster plans, when they exist, essentially focus on the security of the staff and building, and the conservation of the collection (Zach and McKnight, 2010). Outside of the university environment itself, academic libraries are perceived as serving only the faculty and students of their particular institutions (Sheldon and Hendrickson, 1987). As such, it may not occur to emergency managers to approach the library for assistance. Thus when the library wants to take a leadership role in disaster response, both within its institution and within its community, it is frequently incumbent on the librarians to proactively offer their services.

Case study: Louisiana State University

When the Deepwater Horizon rig exploded on April 20, 2010, spewing oil into the Gulf of Mexico, the potential of the spill to become a major disaster was grasped almost immediately by local residents. At Louisiana State University in Baton Rouge (LSU), there was no question that this institution, with experts in petroleum engineering and coastal ecosystems, among others, would be heavily involved, and the library was determined not to be an exception. Almost immediately, the Web Development Coordinator at LSU's Middleton Library recognized the need for dissemination of reliable information to students, researchers, and the community alike and created an information page to guide students and faculty to dependable sources of information. The initial guide, consisting simply of a list of important numbers and basic information, went up on April 30 (Louisiana State University, 2010). The Web Development Coordinator then recruited a group of other interested LSU librarians to begin putting together a full subject guide dedicated to the oil spill.

LSU Libraries used a subject guide format powered by the Internet bookmarking tool Delicious (Kelsey and VandenBroek, 2010). The 'Oil Spill Subject Guide,' which went live on May 5, 2010, provided an interface through which patrons could browse, search for, and access web-based resources identified by the librarians working on the project. A tag scheme was created, including tags for the affected states; federal, state, and local government resources; format (such as maps, multimedia, etc.); and category tags such as health effects, engineering, environmental impact, economic impact, etc. Over the following months, the librarians participating in the project, which had been named the Louisiana Libraries Oil Spill Information Service (LLOSIS), continually updated the subject guide with reliable sources of information as these new sources became available. The Delicious tagging scheme allowed patrons to combine tags to narrow the growing list of resources to more specific topics – economic impacts on tourism in Florida, for example. In addition, each link was provided with a descriptor of a few sentences, and the titles and descriptions were fully searchable from the subject guide page. Later additions to the subject guide included self-updating RSS feeds from both Twitter and Yahoo News, and contact information for the various members of LLOSIS, along with their subject specialty.

The oil spill guide was publicized on the library's website, on monitors on the first floor of the library, and on the library's Facebook and Twitter accounts. Links to the subject guide were placed on LSU's main page for the oil spill response, as well as on the webpages of the various participating schools and programs. A number of individuals, organizations, and libraries also spread the Twitter and Facebook announcements to their own audiences; and the subject guide was featured in an article in *The Reveille*, the LSU student newspaper. In addition, LLOSIS members reached out to a number of student groups, including SCHOLR (Student Coalition to Help the Oil Leak Relief), and encouraged liaison librarians to make the faculty in their departments aware of the new resource. Many faculty members responded, praising the subject guide and/or offering suggestions for additions.

Two members of LLOSIS took primary responsibility for adding resources to the subject guide, although resources were also added by other members of the group. In the beginning, the focus of the project was to provide as exhaustive a collection of resources as possible; as a result, a good many popular sources such as newspaper and magazine articles were added, although the tags always clearly labeled them as such. At its height, the subject guide included over 450 tagged and searchable resources. In October 2010, the decision was made to streamline the subject guide by removing many of the out-of-date news articles and popular sources and to focus on more scholarly content, a process that can continue as oil spill research evolves.

Because the LLOSIS subject guide was unique, the members wanted to make sure it would be archived for posterity. LSU does not currently have the resources to do this; but the LLOSIS members spoke with a representative from the California Digital Library, who added the entire contents of the subject guide to their Oil Spill Archive and will continue to do so as the subject guide is updated (Seneca, 2010).

LSU was not the only academic institution to respond to the oil spill crisis by taking on the responsibility of organizing and publicizing information. The Florida State University System, in partnership with several private universities in the state, created the Oil Spill Academic Task Force (OSATF). Much like LLOSIS, their mission was to provide a central repository of information and expertise to serve those responding to the crisis in Florida (State University System of Florida, 2010). In addition, the University of South Florida created the Gulf Oil Spill Information Center (GOSIC) to archive information related to the oil spill (University of South Florida, 2010). While the focus of the LLOSIS Oil Spill Guide was on web-based resources, both OSATF and GOSIC focused more on document libraries and data. Other universities in the affected states, such as Mississippi State University, University of Texas at Austin, and University of South Alabama, also posted subject guides or informative websites related to the oil spill (Mississippi State University, 2010; Texas A&M University, 2010; University of South Alabama, 2010).

The success of the Oil Spill Subject Guide encouraged the members of LLOSIS to think about establishing a collective body of oil spill-related research for future generations. It has long been desired to establish an institutional repository at Louisiana State University; during 2010, attempts were made to provide information to and start the discussion among interested and affected scholars, researchers, and potential users. In 2011, an appeal was made before the LSU Faculty Senate to enlist the support of the faculty. In addition, as a result of the Gulf oil spill incident, a decision was made to write a grant proposal to the LSU Board of Regents to get funding for the hardware and software needed to establish an institutional repository. It was felt that the specific research connected with the ramifications of the Gulf oil spill would offer a timely opportunity to appeal for a repository. Yet another opportunity to appeal for the establishment of an institutional repository is the National Science Foundation (NSF) requirement that, from January 2011, all fund recipients will be obliged to provide evidence of specific arrangements for data management and storage of the products of their research (National Science Foundation, 2010). LLOSIS members approached the LSU Office of Research and Development (ORED) to ask them to encourage researchers to work with the library on data management for their projects and to contribute the final results to the proposed institutional repository.

A secondary effect of these activities by LSU librarians is the hope that their participation with the oil spill crisis will provide an opening for the library to become more directly involved in the research being done at LSU and to promote library services among the faculty, as well as serve as an example to other academic libraries on how to get more involved on campus at any time – not just during crises.

The academic library as locus of disaster: response deterred and deferred

A final consideration of how academic libraries function and/or respond during a crisis is the proximity of the library to the locus of the crisis. Clearly, a library directly affected by a crisis on-site will function differently from a library indirectly affected by a crisis off-site – possibly many miles away. Many of the differences in function will by necessity involve basic safety and preservation concerns.

It is a wry observation that if you want to write about disasters, you would be lucky to live in the state of Louisiana. Between hurricanes and oil spills, most Louisiana institutions are exposed to a seemingly never-ending series of crises. Taking advantage of this preponderance of crises, the authors would like to point out that the hurricanes of 2005, which wrought havoc on southern Louisiana, can provide one model for contrasting the functions of an academic library located at the epicenter of a disaster with the functions of an academic library located at a safe distance from a disaster.

Case study: Tulane University's Howard-Tilton Memorial Library

In late August 2005, hurricanes Katrina and Rita were responsible, either directly or indirectly, for an unprecedented amount of damage to southern Louisiana, especially New Orleans. When Katrina precipitated the failure of levees, and large sections of the city went underwater, Tulane University's main library, Howard-Tilton Memorial, took on approximately nine feet of water in the lower-level areas – areas that held substantial collections of government documents and music resources. In its October 2005 issue, *American Libraries: The Magazine of the American Library Association* (ALA) quoted Tulane's Government Documents Librarian, Eric Wedig, reporting that around 90 percent of the Government Documents collection was destroyed by flood waters in the basement (Eberhart, 2005: 22).

In February 2006, Tom Diamond, Head of Reference and Collection Development Services at Louisiana State University's Middleton Library in Baton Rouge, a city an hour away from New Orleans and relatively untouched by Katrina, interviewed administrators and staff from libraries directly affected by Katrina and Rita (Diamond, 2006). One of the interviewees was Lance Query, Dean of Libraries and Academic Information Resources at Tulane's Howard-Tilton Library. Dean Query's answers to Diamond's questions reflect the difficulties that an academic library, used to being the source of helpful information as a service-providing entity, encounters when it is so damaged that it cannot easily fulfill its mission of providing service.

The first question in Diamond's article, while not explicitly about service, sets the tone for the rest of the piece and addresses those previously mentioned basic safety and preservation concerns: 'Did your library have an emergency or evacuation plan in place to deal with external contingencies such as hurricanes? How well was the plan implemented?' (Diamond, 2006: 192).

Query's response, that a plan had been in place for almost a year before the 2005 hurricanes, concludes that no plan – no matter how well conceived – could have anticipated an event like Katrina: 'There are no disaster planning documents that deal with this type of disaster. What we talked about [in the September 2004 disaster plan for Howard-Tilton Memorial Library] were pipe breaks or fires. We don't deal with a whole city that is underwater' (p. 193).

Query goes on to explain that the university's plan was implemented in lieu of the library's plan: the crisis was greater than what the library's plan could handle, so the university's risk management division was called upon to pick up the responsibility. Interestingly, Query mentions that until it was needed, he was not aware of this university-wide 'large-scale disaster' plan (p. 193). Fortunately it was in place, but the lack of knowledge of its existence points out a potential communication problem for any academic library. Optimal circumstances would dictate that an academic library have a disaster/emergency plan that is seamlessly linked to a university-wide disaster/emergency plan and that everyone concerned, especially management/administrative personnel, be aware of this twofold plan.

Another question posed by Diamond addresses the problem of communication, communication being essential to an academic library's internal – and external – reason for existence. Diamond asks, 'How did the library staff maintain communication channels? What improvements can be made?' (p. 196). Query laments the fact that there was no formal backup system for communication. With IT systems down, the library eventually relied on a Yahoo.com discussion board, but only about 20 percent of library staff participated. This low level of participation probably can be traced to the lack of functioning computers city-wide or to the staff's lack of prior knowledge that off-site discussion boards would be implemented in case of emergencies.

In his answer, Query goes on to say that in the future Tulane plans to rely on a backup system provided to members of the Association of South Eastern Research Libraries (ASERL) (of which Tulane is one) by the Southeastern Library Network (SOLINET/Lyrasis) Consortium (Florida State University, 2007). While this is an improvement from having no backup communications system at all, it is not a panacea since one would still need access to a working computer with online connectivity in order to take advantage of the SOLINET system.

In November of 2010, just over five years had passed since Katrina. It seemed an appropriate time to revisit some of the questions posed by Diamond right after the disaster at Tulane's main library. To this end, several of Diamond's questions were presented to Eric Wedig, the librarian from Tulane who was quoted in the October 2005 *American*

Libraries article and who continues to be the librarian responsible for the library's government documents collection, as well as serving as Chief Bibliographer for Social Sciences and Jewish Studies.

Specific questions revisited include the one about how effective the disaster plan was, with a renewed emphasis on the university's plan. Since Query had given credit to the university's plan as a viable alternative to the library's plan, it seemed reasonable to question, five years later, just how well the university's plan did end up working. Wedig's comments strongly imply that although the university's plan was the more effective of the two, it was still not up to the task of confronting such a massive disaster. As Wedig dramatically points out:

> . . . the university's plan was [not] as well conceived as it could have been, but I do not know that an even more comprehensive plan could have dealt with the realities of the environment several days after Katrina. A future disaster similar to or greater than Katrina may prove a death knell to the university. I am not sure we would be able to go through this type of recovery again. (Wedig, 2010)

Another question yielding a slightly more optimistic answer five years after the fact was the one mentioned above concerning communication channels. Wedig explains that the university has made efforts to compile alternative e-mail addresses and telephone numbers for its employees – 'alternative' including contact information for employees' relatives outside of New Orleans. Although this certainly is a step in the right direction, it must be repeated that without functioning equipment on the 'calling' end of the equation, e-mails and telephone calls will not be connected to the necessary infrastructure to reach those being 'called.'

Case study: University of Hawai'i at Manoa's Hamilton Library

As is evident from Tulane's experience detailed above, the patron services provided by an academic library hit by disaster are among the first casualties. However, academic library patron services are in large part dependent upon the collections held by individual libraries. A second model for comparing the effects of disaster on academic libraries close to the disaster to the effects on academic libraries a distance away from the disaster emphasizes the loss of rare and often unique materials. This model focuses on the University of Hawai'i (UH) at Manoa's Hamilton Library – a library whose disaster preceded the disasters in New Orleans by approximately a year and, coincidentally, involved the complete flooding of lower floors that held large collections of government documents, maps, and other local historical materials.

The coincidence ends there. In Manoa, the source of the water was an overflowing creek bed that sent a wall of water onto the campus and into the library. Damage from the creek's flooding the areas surrounding the Hawaiian university was not as extensive as damage from the hurricane's flooding within New Orleans and its suburbs. However, in the long run, the destruction of Manoa's collections was probably worse than the destruction of Tulane's collections.

Another notable difference in the circumstances of Hamilton Library's flooding was its ability to regroup as quickly as possible to provide patrons with whatever library services could be quickly brought back. This ability to regroup was due to the relative lack of damage done to areas outside of the library. Acknowledging that services like those provided by LSU Libraries after the 2010 oil spill would be impossible to provide until much later, if at all, Hamilton's service goals were necessarily limited to the return of some access to the collections not destroyed by the flood and to the librarians who intermediated those collections.

Four days after the flooding, UH's website made the following announcements concerning library services at Hamilton:

> Parts of the library experienced loss of electricity and phone service since Saturday, affecting services including the Voyager Online Catalog System. The system has since been moved to a safe area where it can be remedied. Power has also been restored to Hamilton Library Phase III, which includes the Science Technology Collection. Also restored is the online electronic database system, www.sinclair. hawaii.edu, in which faculty, students and staff can access some online resources. . . . Plans are currently being discussed to have limited circulation services available. (University of Hawai'i at Mānoa, 2004)

In a November 2010 personal interview with University of Hawai'i Librarian Gwen Sinclair, she remembers that

> When the generators were connected, about two months after the flood, we were finally able to open the main entrance and allow patrons into the stacks. At about the same time, technical services

staff were moved into temporary locations, so they were able to resume dealing with the two months' worth of materials that had accumulated in the meantime. (Sinclair, 2010)

To commemorate the one-year anniversary of the Manoa flood, the *Honolulu Advertiser*'s Loren Moreno interviewed University of Hawai'i library staff for an article updating the results of the flooding. Moreno states that:

> A year after floods ravaged the University of Hawai'i-Manoa campus, destroying parts of Hamilton Library, basic services are back up, with students using research material, digital databases and studying till all hours. But the library's one-acre basement – once home to a rich collection of rare maps and documents – sits empty, with no reconstruction date in sight. (Moreno, 2005)

What this article points out is the difference between an academic library's providing 'basic services' and services offered only in major academic research libraries. This difference highlights one of the key elements that separate how a public library functions after a disaster versus how an academic library functions after a disaster – it is all in the dissimilarity of mission. A brief overview of Manoa's mission is stated below:

> With more than 3 million volumes, the Hamilton Library at the University of Hawai'i at Manoa is the leading research library serving the university, the state of Hawai'i and the Pacific region. The library supports the teaching, research and information needs of faculty, students, staff and the community. It helps preserve the local cultural heritage as well as provides physical and intellectual access to the world of knowledge. (University of Hawai'i at Mānoa, 2004)

Other articles written at the time of the flooding, and even later, recognize this particular academic library's mission to include being a source of serious and sometimes unique research materials. On December 13, 2004, an article by the *Advertiser*'s Education Writer, Beverly Creamer, gave examples of some of Hamilton's rare materials lost in the disaster:

> Librarians hope they can save about 20 percent of the library's 166,000 maps, including historic maps going back to the 1600s, and almost all of its 91,000 aerial photos [In an earlier *Advertiser* article (Nov. 2, 2004), Staff Writer Mike Leidemann reports that

among the items lost to the flood were 'the first known aerial photographs of Micronesia.'] . . . Among the losses is a set of books once belonging to Prince Kuhio that was published shortly after the Civil War. Called 'War of the Rebellion,' the several hundred volumes described the various events of the war. . . . Also lost are rare congressional materials dating to the 18th and 19th centuries, including documents about early western explorations. One about the Fremont Expedition in the 1840s described part of the United States' expansion toward the Pacific. . . . Hamilton also possessed a copy of the original volumes of Admiral Perry's report to Congress about his expedition to Japan in the 1850s. They, too, were destroyed. (Creamer, 2004)

In her article, Creamer goes on to paraphrase the previously quoted Gwen Sinclair, Head of Government Documents and Maps at Hamilton, in which Sinclair emphasizes the uniqueness of parts of the collection which were lost:

Many of these rare volumes were gifts from individuals, libraries on the Mainland, or came from collections originally part of the Hawaiian kingdom. After the overthrow of the monarchy, they reverted to the territorial government and were eventually given to the university when it was founded at the turn of the century as the College of Hawai'i. (Creamer, 2004)

So far, the contrast between academic libraries not directly affected by a disaster and those directly affected implies that 'directly affected' is synonymous with losing almost all ability to fulfill one's mission for a very long time. Conspicuously missing is any speculation on how quickly an affected academic library can turn around and get back to its function as a resource – its normal 'comfort zone.' In the following section, this 'turn around' is not only addressed but is also promoted as a goal.

Academic libraries post-disaster: lessons learned and suggestions articulated

Academic libraries have a great deal to offer both their institution and their community in a disaster situation. In order to reach their full potential, academic librarians must learn to take the initiative and get the library involved in response efforts early, preferably making themselves part of the disaster-planning process. One of the things LSU librarians learned from the recent oil spill disaster is that getting oneself involved after the fact is full of obstacles and pitfalls. Those already involved in the response are often overwhelmed both with work that needs to be done and with well-intentioned, but often inapplicable, offers of help. These responders may be difficult to contact and even more difficult to convince that the library has something worthwhile and unique to offer the situation. A library's specialty is reliable dissemination of information, something that is frequently lacking in the first few days of a major crisis. If the library can establish itself early as a portal and clearing house for information relating to the crisis, it will be in a position to contribute considerably to the response effort.

For this to happen, the attitude of 'take care of ourselves first, others later' has to be modified. Even when the library is directly affected by the disaster, there are a number of ways in which library staff can contribute to the community response while simultaneously dealing with their own losses. Creating and publicizing a guide to important contacts and up-to-date news requires little effort in these days of WYSIWYG (what you see is what you get) web editors and free blog software. Even if the institution's webserver is non-functional, information compiled by librarians may be temporarily hosted on free sites such as Blogger or PBworks. One of the first things an academic library should do after assuring the safety of its staff is to make contact with university administrators, reminding them of the information management and communication expertise of library staff and making them aware of what the library needs in order to function to the best of its ability in that capacity. Make contact early with the Department of Research and Development (or the local equivalent) and request to be involved in any research projects or grants stemming from the crisis. Have liaison librarians contact specific faculty who they know will be involved in the response and ask them what information needs they have and how the library can help fill those needs. The library should be the designated place to collect and manage information related to the disaster as well as the designated place for its storage and preservation. An academic library that has proven itself invaluable in a time of crisis has made great strides toward proving itself a worthwhile and necessary contributor to the university's mission.

A final way the academic library can be helpful is to establish links with other academic institutions in its state or within the region affected by the disaster. This network can serve to help sustain educational support services while sharing information pertinent to the recovery effort.

Libraries have such a special capacity for service that their particular attention will be welcomed in organizing outreach activities that might teach people how to find and fill out forms or locate missing relatives and loved ones. Rather than wait until the library is completely back on its feet before reaching out to other parts of the university and to the community, academic libraries should make getting involved with the relief effort one of their highest priorities and reach out as soon as practicable.

References

Block, M., and Kim, A. (2006). All (librarian) hands on deck. *Library Journal.* Retrieved June 4, 2011 from *http://www.libraryjournal.com/article/CA6312522.html.*

Creamer, B. (2004). UH's Hamilton Library loss catastrophic. *The Honolulu Advertiser.* Retrieved June 4, 2011 from *http://the.honoluluadvertiser.com/article/2004/Dec/13/ln/ln03p.html.*

Diamond, T. (2006). The impact of Hurricanes Katrina and Rita on three Louisiana academic libraries: a response from library administrators and staff. *Library Administration and Management, 20*(4), 192–200.

Eberhart, G. (2005). Katrina's terrible toll: librarians rally to provide information for a devastated Gulf Coast population. *American Libraries, 36*(9), 14–25.

Featherstone, R.M., Lyon, B.J., and Ruffin, A.B. (2008). Library roles in disaster response: an oral history project by the National Library of Medicine. [Article]. *Journal of the Medical Library Association, 96*(4), 343–50.

Florida State University. (2007). Project Documents Retrieved December 16, 2010, from *http://hurricanes.ii.fsu.edu/solinet.html.*

Jaeger, P.T., Langa, L.A., McClure, C.R., and Bertot, J.C. (2006). The 2004 and 2005 Gulf Coast hurricanes: evolving roles and lessons learned for public libraries in disaster preparedness and community services. [Article]. *Public Library Quarterly, 25*(3/4), 199–214.

Kelsey, S., and VandenBroek, A. (2010). Web-mediated resource distribution for a library web site. *Codex: the Journal of the Louisiana Chapter of the ACRL, 1*(1), 49–82. Retrieved June 4, 2011 from *http://journal.acrlla.org/index.php/codex/article/viewFile/14/31.*

Louisiana State University. (2010, April 30, 2010). Information about the oil leak. Retrieved June 4, 2011 from *http://news.blogs.lib.lsu.edu/2010/04/30/information-about-the-oil-leak.*

Mississippi State University. (2010). Deepwater BP oil spill. Retrieved December 10, 2010, from *http://guides.library.msstate.edu/oilspill.*

Moreno, L. (2005). 'Anything but' normal. *The Honolulu Advertiser.* Retrieved June 4, 2011 from *http://the.honoluluadvertiser.com/article/2005/Oct/30/ln/FP510300350.html.*

National Science Foundation. (2010). Dissemination and sharing of research results. Retrieved December 20, 2010, from *http://www.nsf.gov/bfa/dias/policy/dmp.jsp.*

Seneca, T. (2010, May 21, 2010). CDL Archiving Deepwater Horizon oil spill websites. Retrieved June 4, 2011 from *http://www.cdlib.org/cdlinfo/2010/05/21/cdl-archiving-deepwater-horizon-oil-spill-websites*.

Sheldon, T.P., and Hendrickson, G.O. (1987). Emergency Management and Academic Library Resources. *Special Libraries*, 78(2), 93–9.

Sinclair, G. (2010). [Personal interview, November 15, 2010].

State University System of Florida. (2010). State of Florida Oil Spill Academic Task Force. Retrieved December 9, 2010, from *http://oilspill.fsu.edu*.

Texas A&M University. (2010). Gulf of Mexico oil spill. Retrieved December 10, 2010, from *http://library.tamu.edu/help/resource-format-guides/gulf-of-mexico-oil-spill*.

University of Hawai'i at Mānoa. (November 3, 2004). Hamilton Library moves forward in aftermath of Manoa floods. Retrieved June 4, 2011 from *http://www.hawaii.edu/news/article.php?aId=937*.

University of South Alabama. (2010). Federal Deepwater Horizon oil spill incident 2010. Retrieved December 10, 2010, from *http://www.southalabama.edu/univlib/govdocs/gd/oilspill2010.html*.

University of South Florida. (2010). GOSIC: Gulf Oil Spill Information Center. Retrieved December 10, 2010, from *http://guides.lib.usf.edu/gulf-oil-spill*.

Van Scotter, J.R., Pawlowski, S.D., and Cu, T. (2010). An examination of the interdependencies among major barriers to coordination in disaster response: report to disaster management leadership and study participants. Baton Rouge, LA: Louisiana State University.

Wedig, E. (2010). [Personal interview, November 17, 2010].

Will, B.H. (2001). The public library as community crisis center. *Library Journal*. Retrieved June 4, 2011 from *http://www.libraryjournal.com/article/CA185136.html*.

Zach, L., and McKnight, M. (2010). Innovative services improvised during disasters: evidence-based education modules to prepare students and practitioners for shifts in community information needs. *Journal of Education for Library and Information Science*, 51(2), 76–85.

Index

9/11, 1, 65, 69–80, 89

academic libraries, 5–6, 158, 175–90
  Howard-Tilton Memorial Library, 6, 183–5
  Louisiana State University, 179–83
  Manoa's Hamilton Library, 6, 185–90
  post-disaster, 188–90
  roles, 158, 177–9
  vs public libraries, 175–7
Ahmed, A.L., 71, 82
Association of South Eastern Research Libraries, 184

Bhopal gas leak (1984), 4, 68–72, 80
  survivor stories, 69–70
BUILDER Hybrid Library Demonstrator, 167

CCTV technologies, 126
censorship, 13
Center for Hazards and Risk Research, 142
Chile earthquake, 3, 51, 54–60
citizen communications, 2–3, 9, 16, 43–61, 122, 131
citizen reporter, 44–45
collaborative technologies, 134
collective memory, 67, 76, 80–1
Combine Resources Institution, 147
communication platform, 2–5, 44–5, 121, 131, 135, 167

community
  radio, 5, 88, 95, 98, 139–51
  response, 4–6, 87–8, 96–8, 139–51, 155–71, 189
  service and support, 134, 145, 156–63, 175–89
Computer Supported Cooperative Work (CSCW), 12
crisis informatics, 4, 6, 65–83
CrisisCommons, 48
'crowdsourcing,' 2
Cumbrian farmers, 87–100

Danish Refugee Council, 104
data visualisation, 132–4
Delicious, 180
Department of Homeland Security, 78
diffusion of innovation theory, 27
digital archaeology, 80
digital heritage, 65–83,
disaster planning, 6, 157–70, 177–89
Disaster Recovery Centers, 161–3,

Earthquakes, 3, 22, 43–60, 95, 104, 140–4, 165
Eckerman, I., 69–71
Emergency Operations Center, 54, 162–3
emergency response network, 162–6
  benefits of partnering, 163–6
    planning phase, 164
    preparing phase, 164–5